# OFFBEAT PARIS

## Hidden Tourist Gems Of Paris
## And the Île De France

## Hugh Oram

*For Bernadette*

Copyright © Hugh Oram  2006

British Library Cataloguing In Publication Data
A Record of this Publication is available
from the British  Library

ISBN 1846851300
978-1-84685-130-8

Published March 2006 by

Exposure Publishing, an imprint of Diggory Press,
Three Rivers, Minions, Liskeard, Cornwall, PL14 5LE, UK
WWW.DIGGORYPRESS.COM

# Contents

**Author's Note:**

Every effort has been made to ensure that details of opening times,entrance tariffs,etc,are up to date,but visitors are advised to check with the establishment concerned before they set out.

# 1st ARRONDISSEMENT

Charvet,
28 place Vendome,
75001 Paris.
Tel. 01 42 60 30 70
Opening hours, Mon-Sat, all year, 9h00-18h00.
Métro: Pyramids.
This long established mens' outfitters is the last word in elegance, not just in the clothes it stocks, but in its interior decor, right down to the elegant carved wooden tables that grace the place. There's no rush here-if for instance, you decide on the best shirt in the world, several fittings will be needed before it's deemed suitable for wearing.

Église St-Eustache,
rue du Jour,
75001 Paris.
Tel: 01 40 26 47 99
Opening hours, daily, all year, 9h30-19h30.
Métro: Chatelet-les-Halles.
This church, which dominates the Les Halles area, is a large, unprepossessing structure built between 1532 and 1640, noted for the paintings, some ancient, others modern, in the side chapels. But its real claim to fame is the 8, 000 pipe organ, one of the best church organs in Paris. Free recitals are given every Sunday at 17h30.

Electron Libres (Art Squat),
59 rue de Rivoli,
75001 Paris.
Web: http: //www. 59rivoli.org/
Opening hours: daily, 13h30-19h30.
Entrance tariff: free
Métro: Chatelet-les-Halles.
This artists' squat on the rue de Rivoli has a good address and lots of zany artistic ideas! The six floors of the building are filled with artists' studios and as you wander around, you can take a close look, sometimes take part. The building had been unoccupied for 10 years until the artists took over in 1999; they

moved in, cleaned up the place, got electricity and water reconnected and have been there ever since. Visitors are encouraged to wander through the maze-like spaces, 2, 000 square metres of it, talk to the artists about their work and philosophies and admire their work in the gallery. How long the squat is going to be allowed to go on, no-one is sure, but while it's there, it's an interesting and unusual artistic experiment. The website has telephone numbers for the individual artists in the place.

Galerie Véro-Dodat,
75001 Paris.
Métro: Palais Royal.
This delightfully upmarket passageway runs between the rue Croix-des-Petits-Champs and the rue Jean-Jacques Rousseau and has painted ceilings and shop decorated with elaborate panels and separated by black marble columns. The strange name of the passageway comes from the two pork butchers who built it in 1824. These days, the passageway has lost a little of its sheen and style, but some fashionable new shops have started to open up here in the past few years.

Galignani bookshop,
224 rue de Rivoli,
75001 Paris.
Tel: 01 42 60 76 07
Opening hours, Mon-Sat, all year, 10h00-19h00. Closed Sun
Métro: Tuileries
This bookshop is claimed to be the oldest English language bookshop in mainland Europe, dating back to 1801. The Galignani family tradition in bookselling goes back much further; it was known in Venice as long ago as 1560. The Paris shop, renowned for its big skylight, has an enormous stock of books and other material about France, in English and French.

Jardin des Halles,
rue Rambuteau, rue Berger,
75001 Paris.
Opening hours: always open.
Entrance tariff: free
Métro: Chatelet-Les-Halles.

Close to Les Halles, once the great markets area of central Paris, until the markets were moved out to Rungis, near Orly airport, in 1969, these elaborate gardens are still popular with visitors to the area. Alleyways bordered with lime trees mark out the extent of the gardens and there's a fine perspective to the church of St-Eustache. In the southern part of the gardens, you'll find arcades and covered porticos of vegetation, while at the western end, close to the Bourse, four glass pyramids form a tropical greenhouse for the swimming pool. The flowers in this area are arranged in stepped layers. Running the length of the rue Rambuteau, between the Forum and the church, is the childrens' garden, where children can explore such concepts as the volcanic world and tropical forests. However, in many respects the gardens have become run down. While they are lively by day, with groups of tourists wandering through, at night, they can be dangerous-deserted and sinister, with drug dealers offering their wares to passers-by. Now, plans for a massive reconstruction of the whole Les Halles area, including the gardens, are being put in place.

Jeu de Paume,
Jardin des Tuileries,
75001 Paris.
Tel: 01 47 03 12 50
Opening hours, Tues, all year, 12h00-21h00, Wed-Fri, all year, 12h00-19h00, Sat, Sun, all year, 10h00-19h00. Closed Mon, public holidays.
Entrance tariff: EUR6 (reductions)
Métro: Concorde.
Directly opposite the Orangeries, the Jeu de Paume originally housed the State's collection of Impressionist paintings before it was relocated to the Musée d'Orsay. Today, this elegant white building is used mainly for exhibitions of contemporary and near-contemporary art, mainly retrospectives of well-known artists. Cinema, bookshop, café.

La Conciergerie,
1 quai de l'Horloge,
75001 Paris.
Tel. 01 53 73 78 50.
Opening hours, Apr-Sept, daily, 9h30-18h30,
Oct-Mar, 10h00-17h00 daily.

Entrance tariff: EUR5. 50 (reductions).
Métro: Cité.
This medieval fortress was used as a prison during the Revolution; the most celebrated prisoners were Marie-Antoinette, Danton and Robespierre. Some of the structures date from the 14th century; the Tour de l'Horloge, built in 1370, was the first public clock in Paris. But the very medieval looking facade to the Conciergerie was only added in the mid-19th century, so it's entirely fake! You can inspect the list of prisoners held here during the Revolution before being sent to the guillotine and also see Marie-Antoinette's crucifix, in the cell where she was held.


La Samaritaine,
19 rue de la Monnaie,
75001 Paris.
Tel. 01 40 41 20 20.
Web: www. lasamitaraine.com
Opening hours, Mo-, Sat, all year, 9h30-19h00 (Thurs, 22h00).
Métro: Pont Neuf.
One of the great department stores in Paris, La Samaritaine is named after the relief of the Good Samaritan on the nearby Point Neuf. The main building, with its elaborate ironwork and peacock mosaics is a rich source of Belle Époque design. The store itself has been much revitalised in recent years and you can also enjoy spectacular views over Paris from its restaurant and rooftop café.

Louvre des Antiquaires,
2 place du Palais-Royal,
75001 Paris.
Tel. 01 42 97 27 00.
Web: www. louvre-antiquaires. com
Opening hours, Tues-Sun, all year, 11h00-19h00. Closed Sun in July, Aug.
Entrance tariff: free.
Métro: Palais Royal.
This very upmarket antiques centre houses around 250 dealers in antiques and the items on show are suitably elevated in their worth. You find such priceless pieces of antiques here as Louis XV furniture and early Sèvres porcelain.

Louvre-Rivoli Métro station,
rue de Rivoli,
75001 Paris.
This is one of the most interesting of all Métro stations, since it has considerable displays of statuary and other pieces related to the nearby Louvre. You can examine lots of casts, illuminated display cases and even more elaborate displays as you stroll along the platform. Even the benches on the platform are much more artistic than the usual Métro benches, made from a clear Perspex-type material.

Musée du Louvre,
entrance: pyramid, Cour Napoléon,
75001 Paris.
Tel: 01 40 20 51 51
Web: www. louvre.fr
Opening hours, daily, all year, 9h00-18h00.
Entrance tariff: EUR6. 50 (reductions).
Métro: Louvre-Rivoli.
Once a palace of the kings of France, for the past two centuries, the Louvre has remained one of the greatest museums in the world. Known everywhere for the Mona Lisa and the Venus de Milo, those are just two of the best-known items from a vast collection, or rather seven collections. The Louvre covers oriental antiquities, Egyptian, Greek, Estruscan and Roman antiquities, besides paintings, sculptures, graphic art and objets d'art from the Middle Ages to 1850. The pyramid, designed by I. M. Pei, a renowned Japanese-American architect, and opened in the late 1980s, is the main entrance point to the museum and is a talking point in its own right. Renovations and extensions are ongoing: the most recently opened new galleries are dedicated to Italian and Spanish paintings and works from ancient Egypt.

Musée de l'Orangerie,
Jardin des Tuileries,
75001 Paris.
Tel: 01 42 97 48 16.
Métro: Concorde.
This delightful museum in the Jardin des Tuileries right in the centre of Paris should be open now after extensive renovations. The plan is that the new style museum will show the Impressionist

collection of Jean Walter and Paul Guillaume, as well as furniture and decorative objects from the École de Paris.

Musée de la Publicité,
107 rue de Rivoli,
75001 Paris.
Tel: 01 44 55 57 50.
Web: www. museedelapub. org
Opening hours, Tues-Fri, all year, 11h00-18h00, Wed until 21h00, Sat, Sun, all year, 10h00-18h00.
Métro: Palais Royal, Louvre-Rivoli.
The museum devoted to publicity is in the Rohan wing of the Louvre, with the entrance from the rue de Rivoli. It's here together with two other museums, the Musée de la Mode et de la Textile and the Musée des Arts Décoratifs. In the publicity museum, advertising from the 19th century to the present day is commemorated, with many of the famous icons of French advertising, from the Michelin Man to the cheesy Laughing Cow. The museum runs frequent exhibitions and it also has extensive multimedia presentations. Visitors can also log into the extensive computerised archives which tell you everything you need to know about the black art of advertising. The publicity museum used to be in the delightfully named rue de Paradis in the 10th. , but the Louvre is a much more upmarket venue altogether.

There's another museum here, devoted to fashions through the ages; it's on the first and second floors of the Rohan wing of the Louvre. It has vast collections of clothes and textiles and these are shown in exhibitions staged here. The third museum is for decorative arts and has a fascinating collection of religious artifacts and bourgeois decorative items from the Middle Ages to the 20th century. One of its set pieces is the creation of a 14th century castle bedroom, while another is a 15th century reception room, to which have now been added a 20th century bedroom, Art Déco apartments in the style of the 1930s and a salon originally designed for the great exposition of Paris in 1900. Seeing the way in which all these totally different locations were designed and decorated is very informative and visually educative. Finally, the Galerie des Bijoux has 1, 200 pieces of jewellery, from the Middle Ages to the present day.

Palais-Royal,
place du Palais-Royal,
75001 Paris.
Web: www.palais-royal.org
Opening hours: gardens only, dawn to dusk, daily, all year
Entrance tariff: free Métro: Palais-Royal.
Originally built for Cardinal Richlieu in the 17th century, when it was known as the Palais Cardinal, the building was much expanded during the following century. The Duc d'Orléans created a substantial expansion by building a three storey arcade to enclose the gardens. The arcade had cafes, shops, theatres and all kinds of entertainment and the rooms above were used as apartments. In the early years of the 20th century, one of the most famous inhabitants of the Palais Royal was the writer Collette, who lived here until her death in 1954. These days, the buildings at the Palais-Royal have been turned into government offices, while many of the shops in the arcade sell prints and antiques. The gardens are essentially unchanged, a haven of peace and tranquillity, with the only modern intrusion the modern art installation of striped columns of varying heights in the centre of the gardens, created by Daniel Buren.

Ritz Hotel,
15 place Vendome,
75001 Paris.
Tel. 01 43 16 30 30.
Métro: Opéra.
The Ritz Hotel is one of the most elegant hotels in Paris and indeed, the world. It's been a home from home for the good and great for over a century and among the distinguished people who've stayed there have been King Edward VII, Ernest Hemingway and Marcel Proust. The couture designer Coco Chanel lived here for 37 years. These days, the hotel is owned by Mohammed Al Fayed, who also owns Harrods in London; it was from this hotel that Lady Di (Diana, Princess of Wales) left on her fateful journey at the end of August, 1997.

The hotel itself is venerable, magnificently decorated and is priced accordingly for guests. If you're in to cooking, then a course at the École Ritz Escoffier would be very enlightening. Escoffier was the famous 19$^{th}$ century chef at the Ritz, who almost invented the French gastronomic tradition. The classes are held in the hotel, close to the kitchens were Escoffier once reigned. If you just want to wander round and take in the sumptuous decor, you can complement your visit by dropping into the hotel's new champagne bar, Le Bar Cambon, which is round the corner at 38 rue Cambon. It has an enviable collection of Champagne and the price of a glass starts at around EUR20.

rue Saint-Denis,
75001 Paris.
Métro: Chatelet-les-Halles.
This long street, which starts close to the Hôtel de Ville, the Paris city hall, stretches right up into the northern heart of Paris. The street itself and its continuation, the rue du Faubourg St-Denis, is one the seediest in Paris, a centre of the city's sex trade. If you've the stomach for it, walking up the street, safer by day than night, you'll go past lots of places advertising live sex shows. In the doorways, you're likely to see many prostitutes touting for business, although a recent crackdown on prostitution has made them much less visible. It's quite an eye opener, walking along this street, an amazing contrast to the ultra-refined Paris of the 7th and 16th arrondissements.

The Tuileries,
place de la Concorde,
75001 Paris.
Opening hours, Jardin du Carrousel, always open.
Tuileries, Apr-Sept, daily, 7h30-21h00 (July, Aug, Mon-Fri, 23h45, Sat, Sun, 0h45), Oct-Mar, daily, 7h30-19h30.
Métro: Concorde.
These great gardens in central Paris stretch from the Louvre to the Place de la Concorde. They are named after the medieval tilemakers who worked here. The gardens are all that survive from the palace and gardens commissioned by Catherine des Médicis in the mid-16th century; the palace was burned down during the Commune in 1871. In the mid-17th century, Le Nôtre, who designed the landscapes at Versailles, designed these gardens, with their terraces, walkways and pools. In 1783, the Montgolfier brothers launched the first successful hot air balloon from the gardens. After the French Revolution, much replanting took place. In the decade after 1991, much renovation took place and the gardens were more closely integrated with the Louvre next door.

The great storms that swept northern France in December, 1999, destroyed most of the older trees. In recent years, some modern sculptures have been placed at strategic intervals throughout the gardens. A total of 18 statues are in the Jardin de Carrousel, by such renowned sculptors as Rodin and the more modern Giacometti. If you stand in the centre of the gardens, you'll be able to see an amazing vista on a clear day-what's called the Grand Axe is a clear line of sight that runs from the Tuileries, through the Champs-Elysées all the way to La Défense. In July and August, the pleasures are slightly more down to earth, when a huge fairground is put in place in the Tuileries.

W H Smith bookshop,
248 rue de Rivoli,
75001 Paris.
Tel: 01 44 77 88 99.
Web: www. whsmith. fr
Opening hours, Mon-Sat, all year, 9h30-18h00, Sun, all year, 11h00-18h00.
Métro: Concorde.
Another well-known source of books, videos and other material about France, in both English and French. It's equally popular for its stocks of US and UK newspapers.

## 2nd ARRONDISSEMENT

Bibliothèque Nationale de France-Richlieu,
58 rue de Richlieu,
75002 Paris.
Tel: 01 53 79 81 26
Web: www. bnf. fr
Opening hours, Mon-Sat, all year, 9h00-18h00. Closed Sun, two weeks in Sept, public holidays.
Entrance fee: EUR5 (reduction).
Métro: Bourse.
This is the old National Library; the new one is in the 13th (qv) and the previous building has been converted into two galleries, the Mansart and Mazarine, which have vast collections of works on paper. They run from medieval manuscripts and old watercolours to photographs and modern prints. On the first floor,

you can inspect the Cabinet des Médailles, which had many old coins and medals, dating back to ancient Greek and Roman times. One of the highlights of this particular section is the chess set that once belonged to Charlemagne, Emperor of the Holy Roman Empire. La Crypte is a new gallery, in the basement, used for contemporary graphic art.

Boulevard des Capuchines,
75002 Paris.
Métro: Drouot, Opéra.
The odd numbers in the boulevard are in the 2nd arrondissement, while the even ones are in the 9th. You can see two buildings of great historical significance for the arts. At No 14, in 1895, the very first films were shown by the Lumière brothers. Those very early films included shots of a train steaming into La Ciotat station on the Côte d'Azur; audiences were really frightened by these shots of a moving train. Some years before, at No 35, at the studio of a photographer called Nadar, another earth-shattering event took place, the first ever showing of Impressionist paintings, which caused absolute uproar among the Parisian art critics.

Bourse (Stock Exchange),
Palais Brongniart,
place de la Bourse,
75002 Paris.
Tel: 01 49 27 55 55
Web: www. bourse-de-paris. fr
Opening hours: guided tours by arr, phone one week in advance.
Entrance tariff: EUR8 (reduction).
Métro: Bourse.
The Paris Stock Exchange is a very historic building, dating back to 1826 and the time of the First Empire; it was subsequently expanded nearly a century later, in 1906. In the old style building, the brokers gathered around the corbeille or crow's nest, which saw frenetic daily dealing. These days, the Stock Exchange is computerised, but the atmosphere is almost as lively as ever, as brokers cut their deals.

Cinéma Rex,
1 boulevard Poissoniere,
75002 Paris.
Tel: 08 92 68 05 96.
Web: http: //www. legrandrex.com
Opening hours, daily, all year, 10h00-23h00.
Métro: Bonne Nouvelle.
This cinema is one of the great places in Paris for film goers and it's so venerable that in 1981, it was declared an Historic Monument, even though the building only opened in 1934. It is one of the biggest cinemas in Europe and today, still seats 2, 800 people. The architecture is equally flamboyant; outside, the facade is Art Déco style. Apart from its enterprising range of films, the Cinéma Rex has another special treat for lovers of the cinema, the "Stars of the Grand Rex" tour, which is a 50 minute interactive show describing exactly what goes on behind the scenes, from lighting to sound recording and special effects. Many of the stars who've been on screen here over the years are also recalled, with reconstructions of scenes from major films. This tour can be taken daily, including public holidays, 10h00-19h00. The tariff is EUR7. 50 (reductions) and the special phone number for the show is 01 45 08 93 58.

Galerie Colbert and Galerie Vivienne,
75002 Paris.
Métro: Bourse.
These two elegant passageways link the rue Vivienne and the rue des Petits-Champs. The Galeria Colbert has an 1830s style brasserie, with prices and menus to match, that is a favourite lunch spot for senior academics and literary figures from the nearby (old) Bibliothèque Nationale. The Galerie Vivienne is even more upmarket, if that's possible, with elegant fashion wear and other shops and an antiquarian bookshop that dates back to the founding days of the passageway in the early 19th century.

Harry's New York Bar,
5 rue Daunou,
75002 Paris.
Tel: 01 42 61 71 14
Web: www. harrys-bar. fr
Métro: Opéra.

This bar has been a favourite with American and other visitors to Paris for nearly 100 years and it has a great collection of photographs of the many famous newspaper people and entertainers who've frequented it over the years. It was very popular in the 1920s with F. Scott Fitzgerald and Ernest Hemingway and it still retains the Roaring Twenties decor. When you go in, you push swing doors that have come straight out of a Wild West saloon, so it's all very authentic! It's remains a popular haunt, still popularised by the phonetic pronunciation of its address, "sank roo doe nou". You never know whom you might spot enjoying a Bloody Mary, the drink allegedly invented by the first owner.

Françoise Meunier Cours de Cuisine,
7 rue Paul-Lelong,
75002 Paris.
Tel. 01 40 26 14 00.
Web: www.fmeunier.com
Métro: Bourse, Louvres-Rivoli, Châtelet-les-Halles.
If you fancy learning how to improve your cooking, this is one of the best cookery schools to come to in Paris, to learn not just French cooking, but many international styles, too, from Asian to Italian. The shortest course last for just three hours, time enough to find out how to prepare some wonderful dishes that can be tried out later.

Kitty O'Shea's bar and restaurant,
10 rue des Capucines,
75002 Paris.
Tel. 01 42 96 02 99.
Métro: Madeleine.
Kitty O'Shea's claims to be oldest Irish bar in France, complete with authentic Irish decor. It's a well-known venue for sports fans, while on Sunday nights, a traditional Irish band called "Dirty Linen" provides entertainment. The pub has now been joined by a dozen other Irish pubs in Paris; no other non-French nationality has so many. England has a mere three pubs to its name, the same as Australia, while you can even find a Dutch, Canadian or Czech pub.

Passage de Choiseul,
75002 Paris.
Métro: Bourse; Opéra.
This historic passageway is off 23, rue St Augustine, which itself is off the Avenue de l'Opéra. This is its best preserved entrance. The passageway has many interesting small artisan shops and while some of these shops and the restaurants and parts of the passageway itself have been cleaned up, overall, it still retains its old Parisian charm. It's still authentic and atmospheric and as you walk through, it's almost as if the past two centuries of Parisian history have never happened.

Passage du Grand-Cerf,
75002 Paris.
Métro: Etienne-Marcel.
This passageway, which runs from the rue Dusoubs to the Rue St-Denis, just at the back of the Tour de Jean Sans Peur, is perhaps the most stylish of all the tiny passageways that still remain in central Paris. It's quite expansive, rising to three storeys, but the wrought iron balconies, the wooden shopfronts and the glass roof have all been well restored in recent years. The passageway today has plenty of shops devoted to arts, crafts and antiques.

Passage des Panoramas,
75002 Paris.
Métro: Bourse.
This is a grid of arcades just to the north of the Bibliothèque Nationale and they are more workaday than the other passageways in the area. One old brasserie, L'Arbre à Cannelle, has very venerable and amazingly carved wood panelling. Other shops sell all kinds of bric-a-brac as well as stamps. The other passageways in this grid of them are the Galerie des Variétés, named after the Théatre des Variétés in the nearby boulevard Montmartre; the Galerie Feydeau; the Galerie Montmartre and the Galerie St-Marc.

Passage des Princes,
75002 Paris.
Métro: Chausée-d'Antin.
A very modestly proportioned passageway, off the top of the rue de Richelieu, this passageway has been well restored, with its glass ceiling and stained glass decorations, but the shops are shiny and new, replacement for the old style shops that had to close because of high rents.

Passage Sainte-Foy,
75002 Paris.
Métro: Strasbourg-St Denis.
If you want the feeling for Paris in the Middle Ages, a passageway off one of the most disreputable streets in the central city area, will provide just what you're looking for. The rue St Denis is lined with prostitutes, who stand in the doorways, and with disreputable looking strip clubs. But if you venture towards the northern end of the street, at Number 263, you'll find the Passage Sainte-Foy. As you go along the passageway, which stretches for about 80 metres, it gets narrower and narrower, until you reach 13 steep steps, which you then climb to get into the rue Sainte Foy, once called the rue du Rempart, or the street of the ramparts. You can still see parts of the great wall that enclosed Paris between the 14th and 17th centuries. These days, the walk along the passageway brings you into the heart of the Sentier district, or the garment making quarter.

Tour Jean Sans Peur
20 rue Etienne-Marcel,
75002 Paris.
Métro: Etienne-Marcel.
Opening hours: during school terms, Wed. Sat, Sun, 13h30-18h00. During school holidays, Tues-Sun, 13h00-18h00. Guided tours, 14h00.
Entrance tariff: EUR8
This extraordinary building is what's left of the townhouse of Jean Sans Peur, Duke of Burgundy in the 15th century. He was given his nickname because of his fearless exploits in Bulgaria. He built this tower as an addition to his townhouse; he was afraid of being assassinated by one of his numerous enemies, which did happen, as he had anticipated, in 1419. Today, you can climb up the

tower. Halfway up, there's a fine vault with many carvings that denote the duke's Burgundian origins.

## 3rd ARRONDISSEMENT

Fondation Coffim,
46, rue de Sevigné,
75003 Paris.
Tel. 01 44 78 60 00.
Opening hours, Mon-Fri, all year, 10h00-18h00, Sat, all year, 14h00-18h00. Closed Sun.
Entrance tariff: free.
Métro: St-Paul.
The gallery, in what was once a print workshop in the heart of the Marais, is the last word in cool and contemporary style. It stages many exhibitions, mostly of figurative paintings. Bookshop.

Musée d'Art et de l'Histoire du Judaisme,
Hotel de St-Aignan,
71 rue du Temple,
75003 Paris.
Tel01 53 01 86 53.
Web: www. mahj. org
Opening hours, Mon-Fri, all year, 11h00-18h00, Sun, all year, 10h00-18h00. Closed Sat, some Jewish holidays.
Entrance tariff: EUR 6. 10 (reductions).
Métro: Rambuteau.
This intriguing museum was opened in 1998 in an historic mansion in the Marais, one of the main Jewish districts of Paris. The displays are designed to show and explain the various ceremonies and rites of Judaism and how styles were adapted to make decorative pieces in many parts of the world. Among the innumerable items are a Hannakak lamp made in Frankfurt, synagogue furniture from Italy and dresses from North Africa. Much archival material relates to the emancipation of the Jews in France after the revolution and to the Dreyfuss case. The museum also has many works of art created by Jewish artists in early 20th century France, but the one historic event that it doesn't commemorate is the Holocaust. One painting is of the building in which the museum is located; of the Jewish people living in this

building at the start of the Second World War, 13 later died in the concentration camps. Otherwise, the Holocaust is a blank in this particular museum.

Musée des Arts et Métiers,
60 rue de Réaumur,
75003 Paris.
Tel: 01 53 01 82 00.
Web: www.arts-et-metiers.net
Opening hours: daily, all year, 10h00-18h00, except Mon. Thurs, until 21h30.
Entrance tariff: EUR5. 50 (reductions).
Métro: Arts et Métiers.
This amazing museum is housed in the buildings of the ancient abbey of Saint-Martin-des-Champs. An incredible total of 80, 000 objects and technical documents detail and explain all manner of inventions, from the 16th century right up to the present day, in all kinds of areas, from the mechanical to telecommunications. The museum also has an outstanding collection of clocks as well as one of the largest collections in Europe of historic technical drawings.

Musée Carnavalet,
23 rue de Sévigné,
75003 Paris.
Tel. 01 44 59 58 58
Web: www. paris-france. org/musees
Opening hours, Tues-Sun, all year, 10h00-18h00. Closed Mon, some public holidays.
Entrance tariff: free. Exhibitions: EUR5. 50 (reductions).
Métro: St-Paul.
This is an enormously ambitious museum, with over 140 rooms in a magnificent mansion in the heart of the Marais telling the story of Paris in considerable detail, from pre-Roman times up to the early 20th century. The mansion itself is very old, dating back to 1548; it was opened as a museum in 1866 when Baron Haussmann, responsible for the wide streets created in that era in central Paris, persuaded the powers-that-be to open the museum and preserve some of the interiors that would otherwise have been destroyed. The collections are arranged in chronological order and are designed to show the history of the people as seen

by the difference classes living in Paris, from working class to royalty. You'll find everything from 17th and 18th century salons and boudoirs reconstructed in their entirety to a recreation of Proust's cork-lined bedroom, lots of memorabilia from the time of the Revolution down to shop and inn signs. The museum even has lots of models of Paris at different stages in its evolution, as well as a highly regarded collection of photographs. Altogether, it's an enormously impressive collection of material about the city, arranged in admirable order and sequence. The overall effect may be overwhelming and you may need to rest for a while in the quiet garden courtyards.

Musée de la Chasse et de la Nature,
Hotel de Guénégaud,
60 rue des Archives,
75003 Paris.
Tel. 01 53 01 92 40
Opening hours, daily, all year, 11h-18h00. Closed Mon.
Entrance tariff: EUR4. 57 (reductions).
Métro: Rambuteau.
This delightful museum shows many preserved animals from Africa, the Americas and Asia, as well as numerous paintings of animals and countless objets d'art relating to the animal world. While the museum is very interesting, so too is the building in which it is located. The work of 17th century architect François Mansart, it is the only house designed by him that is still left intact, the totality of its construction untouched.

Musée Cognacq-Jay,
Hotel Donon,
8 rue Elzévir,
75003 Paris.
Tel. 01 40 27 07 21.
Opening hours, daily, all year, 10h00-17h40, closed Mon, public holidays.
Entrance tariff: free. Charges are made for temporary exhibitions.
Métro: Chatelet-les-Halles, St-Paul.
This museum has interesting origins; it's based on the extensive collections made between 1900 and 1925 by Ernest Cognacq and his wife, Louise Jay, who were the founders of La Samaritaine department store. Their tastes concentrated on the 18th century,

so the museum has many works by the outstanding French Rococo artists of that period. You can see drawings by Watteau and paintings by Canaletto and Fragonard. Dutch and Flemish artists, including Rembrandt and Rubens, are also represented. All these great works of art are hung in panelled rooms that also furniture, porcelain, sculptures and tapestries from the same period. The town house in which the museum is located is even more historic, dating from 1575. Bookshop.

Musée Picasso,
Hotel Salé,
5 rue Thorigny,
75003 Paris.
Tel. 01 42 71 25 21.
Opening hours: daily, all year, 9h30-18h00, except Tues. Thurs, until 20h00. March
& April, until 17h30.
Entrance tariff: EUR5. 79 (reductions).
Métro: Chemin Vert, St-Paul.
This wonderful 17th century mansion has the largest collection of Picasso's work anywhere. The collections are not the most impressive-you'll see better at the Picasso museum in Antibes, the Picasso gallery in Barcelona and the new Picasso museum in Malaga. But besides the paintings, you'll see lots of sketches, designs and drawings done by the great artist and beside a sense of seeing his artistic capabilities growing, you'll also find lots of intimate personal detail of his life and loves. The museum has even preserved one of his laundry lists. It's a very full and rounded museum, so that by the time you've finished the tour, you'll have a good sense of both Picasso the man and Piccaso the artist.

Musée de la Poupée,
Impasse Berthaud,
75003 Paris.
Tel. 01 42 72 73 11.
Opening hours, Tues-Sun, all year, 10h00-18h00.
Entrance tariff: EUR6 (reductions).
Métro: Rambuteau.
This small, privately owned museum has an amazing collection of dolls, made over the past 150 years. Altogether, the museum has more than 500 on view, from 1800 to the present day and they

give children and adults a fascinating glimpse into changing styles in fashion, accessories and even home decor, in the dolls' houses. Some of the domestic items, like miniature irons and sewing machines, are quite fascinating. A free clinic gives advice on restoration. Library, shop.

Musée de la Histoire de France,
Hotel de Soubise,
60 rue des Francs-Bourgeois,
75003 Paris.
Tel: 01 40 27 62 18.
Web: www. archivesnationales. culture. gouv. fr/chan
Opening hours, Mon, Wed-Fri, all year, 10h00-17h45, Sat, Sun, all year, 13h45-17h45. Closed Tues, some public holidays.
Entrance tariff: EUR3. 50 (reductions).
Métro: Rambuteau, Saint-Paul.
The Hotel de Soubise is one of the grandest mansions in the Marais and extensive renovation works on the building should have been completed by now. The mansion is well worth seeing in its own right, including the apartments of the Prince and Princess de Soubise, for whom the place was built in the 1730s. The decor in these apartments is quite sensational, with glorious plasterwork, panelling and paintings; altogether, the mansion has some of the most extravagant and best preserved Rococo interiors anywhere in Paris. Apart from its architectural and decorative delights, the Hotel de Soubise functions as a museum, concentrating on specific political events in French history that have great significance and resonance, such as the French Revolution. But it also has many more mundane exhibits that are equally fascinating, such as displays of picture postcards from the First World War.

Musée de la Serrure (Lock Museum),
Hotel Libéral Bruand,
1 rue de la Perle,
75003 Paris.
Tel: 01 42 77 79 62
Opening hours: Mons, 14h00-17h00, Tues-Fri, 10h00-12h00, 14h00-17h00. Closed, Sats, Suns, Aug, Sept, public holidays.
Entrance tariff: EUR5 (reduction).

Métro: Rambuteau.
This intriguing lock and key museum was devised by a locksmith called Bricard; the museum itself is the cellars of a grandiose mansion built in 1685 by an architect called Libéral Bruand. The collection covers 2, 000 years of locks and keys, from Roman times to the present time and also takes in all kinds of other related items, like window fastenings and gilded door handles originally designed for Versailles. On these, you will see the almost ubiquitous sunburst motif of Louis XIV.

Oldest house in Paris,
51, rue de Montmorency,
75003 Paris.
Métro: Arts et Metiers
La Maison du Haut or Grand Pignon is the oldest house in Paris, built in 1407 by the writer and alchemist Nicolas Flamel (1330-1418). You can see the facade of the house, which is covered in symbolic decoration. On the cornice at ground level, you can see a long inscription, restored in 1900, which urges everyone to say a "Pastrenotre et un Ave Maria"; it's a reminder that when Flamel was alive, many poor people came to him at this house for food and shelter. Also on the facade, you'll see the inscription "Ore et labora" ("pray and work") which was the alchemists' motto.

Passage de Retz,
9 rue Charlot,
75003 Paris.
Tel. 01 48 04 37 99
Opening hours, Tues-Sun, all year, 10h00-19h00.
Entrance tariff: EUR6 (reductions)
Métro: Filles du Calvaire
This wonderful 18th century mansion right in the heart of the Marais was converted into an art gallery with a difference in the early 1990s. The exhibition space is vast, extending to 750 square metres, and wooden floors, a glass roof and a walled garden outside complete the feeling of a very contemporary gallery in a very historic setting. All kinds of artists, architects and designers show their work here and if the displays aren't enough, stop off in the cafe, with a bar that resembles nothing so much as a silver Zeppelin.

## 4th ARRONDISSEMENT

Atelier Brancusi,
piazza Beaubourg,
75004 Paris.
Tel. 01 44 78 12 33.
Web: www.centrepompidou.fr
Opening hours, Mon, Wed-Sun, all year, 14h00-18h00.
Entrance tariff: included with admission price for Centre Pompidou.
Métro: Hôtel de Ville, Rambuteau.
This small building, immediately north of the Centre Pompidou, is the rebuilt studio of well-known sculptor Constantin Brancusi, who died in 1956. He left his studio and everything inside to the State and the studio that can be seen today is a very accurate reconstruction of the place where he used to work. He made all kinds of fluid sculptures in brass and marble; his two motifs were birds and columns. He was a revolutionary influence on late 20th century sculpture and you can see how in all his works on display here, some in very fragile wood and plaster formats. Even more telling are the two studios, numbers three and four, which were his living quarters. This is one of the best places in Paris to see how a great artist of the 20th century did actually live and work.


Bibliothèque Forney,
Hotel de Sens,
1 rue de Figuier,
75004 Paris.
Tel: 01 42 78  14 60.
Opening hours: Tues-Fri, all year, 10h00-20h00.
Closed, Mon, Sun, public holidays.
Entrance charge: EUR3 (reduction).
Métro: St-Paul.
This library is located in the turrets of the oldest mansion in the Marais, so it's worth seeing just for the historical architecture alone. The library has many examples of applied and graphic arts and it also stages temporary exhibitions.

Centre Pompidou,
rue Saint-Martin,
75004 Paris.
Tel: 01 44 78 12 33.
Web: www. centrepompidou. fr
Opening hours, Mon, Wed-Sun, all year, 11h00-21h00 (23h00 for some temporary
exhibitions). Closed Tues and May 1.
Entrance tariff: EUR5. 50 (reductions). Includes entry to the Atelier Brancusi.
Métro: Hôtel-de-Ville, Rambuteau.
The Pompidou Centre opened in 1977 and its radical design caused a sensation; to make the most of the gallery space inside the centre, the architects, Renzo Piano and Richard Rogers, put all the infrastructural elements, including the tubes for utility services and the escalators, on the outside of the building. Then, 20 years later, the centre was closed for extensive refurbishments, which have given it a new lease of life. But nothing comes for free anymore; once, it cost nothing to take a trip on one of the exterior escalators, for fine views of Paris, but these days, the price is included in the admission ticket.

The first three levels of the centre are devoted to a public library that has an impressive collection of journals, CDs and films. The Musée National d'Art Moderne occupies the fourth and fifth floors. With around 40, 000 pieces of contemporary art, it gives a near complete overview of the history of modern art, with everything arranged in chronological order. Among the earliest artists featured on the fifth floor is Henry Matisse, while the Surrealists, who were busy between the First and Second World Wars, are also well represented on this floor. The fourth floor has much more modern work, including Pop Art, with an inevitable Andy Warhol, and examples of the New Realists. Some of their work, by the likes of Joseph Beuys, is decidedly unsettling, but stimulating nevertheless. Altogether, the Centre Pompidou is just as exciting in its new form as it was in its old and when you emerge, you'll continue to be amused and intrigued, this time by the street artists, including fire eaters, in the square in front of the Centre. Immediately to the south of the centre, in the place Igor Stravinsky, is the Stravinsky Fountain, made up of colourful statues that move ceaselessly amid squirting fountains, very modernistic, but very entertaining.

Fortified walls,
rue des Jardins St-Paul,
75004 Paris.
Web: www.philippe-auguste.com
Métro: Pont Marie, St-Paul.
After Roman times, the first builder of fortifications in Paris was King Philippe-Auguste (1165-1223), was built a great wall around the entire medieval city. The largest surviving section can be seen in the rue des Jardins St-Paul, while there's another and smaller section at 3 rue Clovis in the third arrondissement.

Hotel du Sully,
Patrimonie Photographique,
62 rue St-Antoine,
75004 Paris.
Tel: 01 42 74 47 75
Web: www.patrimoine-photo.org
Opening hours, Tues-Sun, all year, 10h00-18h30.
Closed Mon, some public holidays.
Entrance tariff: EUR4 (reductions).
Métro: Bastille, Chemin-Vert, St-Paul.
Go through a gate in the southwest corner of the place des Vosges and you'll come into the marvellous chateau, garden and orangerie of the Hôtel Sully. The main street entrance to the building is in the rue St-Antoine. Apart from the delights of the garden and house, you can see some unusual approaches to photography in the photographic gallery; what's on show here usually has historical or social themes or is else devoted to one specific theme. In recent years, they've had many such themed exhibitions on such topics as crime photography.

Les Bains du Marais (Hammam baths),
31-33 rue des Blancs Manteaux,
75004 Paris.
Tel. 01 44 61 02 02.
Opening hours, daily, all year.
Métro: Rambuteau.
These Moroccan style steam rooms are worth seeing for their luxurious decor; this is a hammam de grande classe. The decor is sublime and the atmosphere very refined. You can also feel an awful lot better by trying the baths for yourself. It's women only on Mon, Tues and Wed and men only on Thurs, Fri and Sat. Mixed bathing is on Wed and Sun, but bathing costumes are obligatory.

Maison de Victor Hugo,
6 place des Vosges,
75004 Paris.
Tel. 01 42 72 10 16.
Opening hours, Tues-Sun, all year, 10h00-18h00. Closed Mon.
Entrance tariff: EUR5. 50 (reductions).
Métro: Bastille.
Wander through the exquisite colonnades of the place des Vosges until you get to the Victor Hugo House at the south-eastern corner. Victor Hugo lived in this dark and gloomy house from 1832 to 1848, before he went into exile in such locations as St Peter Port, Guernsey in the Channel Islands. Today, the house is a museum to this writer, who is one of France's literary favourites. You can see lots of first editions and other memorabilia connected with him and also some of the furniture made by Hugo himself. Very strangely, some of the wood in this furniture was carved by the great writer-using his teeth. Frequent exhibitions on Victor Hugo themes are staged here.

Maison Européene de la Photographie,
5-7 rue de Fourcy,
75004 Paris.
Tel. 01 44 78 75 00
Web: www.mep-fr.org
Opening hours, Wed-Sun, all year, 11h00-20h00. Closed Mon, Tues, some public holidays.
Entrance tariff: EUR5 (reductions).
Métro: St-Paul, Pont-Marie.
The setting of this gallery of photography is striking, a contrast between the restored 18th century Marais mansion and its extension designed in contemporary and minimalist style, is perfect for the photographic exhibitions staged here regularly. These shows, on a wide variety of themes, are in addition to the material in the permanent collection. The library and vidéothèque can also be consulted.

Musée Chopin,
Bibliotheque Polanaise de Paris,
quai d'Orleans,
75004 Paris.
Tel: 01 55 42 83 83.

Métro: Pont Marie.

The great Polish composer and pianist of French descent, Chopin (1810-1849), studied in Warsaw, but then settled in Paris, where he lived with the novelist George Sand between 1838 and 1847. Chopin remained a fervent nationalist and Polish folk tunes inspired much of his work. The Bibliotheque Polanaise de Paris documents many of the Polish traditions in Paris and it includes the salon that he once used, complete with many of his personal souvenirs. Major reconstruction of the museum has been taking place.

Musée de la Magie,
11 rue St-Paul,
75004 Paris.
Tel. 01 42 72 13 26
Web: www. museedelamagie.com
Opening hours, during school term, Wed, Sat, Sun, 14h00-19h00.
During school holidays, daily, same hours.
Entrance tariff: EUR7 (reductions).
Métro: St-Paul.

This museum is very much meant for children, although adults can get lots of fun out of it. It has all kinds of curiosities and magic for children; all sorts of special props and optical illusions are explained and regular conjuring shows are staged. Special interactive games for children are organised.

Musée de la tradition de la Garde Republicaine,
18 boulevard Henri IV,
75004 Paris.
Tel. 01 49 96 13 13.
Opening hours, first Thurs of each month and other times by arr.
Entrance tariff: free.
Métro: Sully-Morland.

The Garde Republicaine provides the pomp, splendour and musical accompaniments on State visits and other major State occasions. It has a long tradition, stretching back just over two centuries, to 1802 and that tradition is honoured here, with displays of documents, equipment and musical instruments as well as models of men and horses in uniform. If you book six months in advance, you can have a place to watch special formations of the Garde in action.

Paris Plage,
75004 Paris.
Métro: Pont-Neuf.
Opening hours, daily, July, Aug.
In the summer of 2002 and 2003, beaches were created along the riverside paths on the Right Bank of the River Seine; Paris Plage, in the best tradition of French seaside locations, became an instant hit and is likely to continue for further summer outings. Usually, two sand and two pebble beaches are created, with hundreds of deckchairs and all the other items needed for a beach, such as striped beach huts, ice cream vendors and live music. The illusion of a real seaside beach is complete, right in the heart of Paris, except that no-one can bathe in the river-it's too dirty.

place des Vosges,
75004 Paris.
Métro: Bastille, Chemin-Vert, St-Paul.
The place des Vosges is one of the most romantic and liveliest places of old Paris. The square was the first planned development in the city and work on it began in 1605. Completion came in 1612 in time for the wedding of Louis XIII and Anne of Austria and today, the square in the middle, an oasis of greenery, a playground for children and for boules players, is named the Louis XIII square. The square has colonnaded arcades on all four sides, with mansions built overhead in brick and stone, all very symmetrical. Lots of shops, cafes and restaurants occupy the arcades and it's a favourite pastime just to sit on one of the terraces here and savour the world sauntering past. You'll have no shortage of entertainment, as the colonnades attract plenty of buskers. In keeping with the architectural majesty of the place des Vosges, many of these buskers play classical music.

rue Quincampoix,
75004 Paris.
Métro: Rambuteau.
Close to the Centre Pompidou, this narrow street is home to a myriad of small commercial art galleries, showing a variety of works, mostly contemporary, in various genres. Entry is free to all the galleries.

Village Saint-Paul,
rue Saint-Paul, rue des Jardins Saint-Paul,
75004 Paris.
Opening hours, Thurs-Mon, all year, 11h00-19h00.
Métro: Pont Marie, Saint-Paul, Sully Morland.
Over 60 antique shops are clustered together around these two streets and you can rummage through enormous treasure troves of items, everything from old photographs and postcards to old furniture and antique jewellery. Dolls from the 19th century are complemented by more modern Art Deco, furniture and lamps made between 1900 and 1930. The village isn't just a modern marketing phrase; this was the parish of the kings of France between 1361 and 1559, so as in the rest of the Marais district, considerable history is attached.

## 5th ARRONDISSEMENT

Ancien abbaye Royale du Val de Grace,
rue St-Jacques (entrance through the church),
75005 Paris.
Tel: 01 40 51 51 92
Opening hours, Tues, Wed, Sat, Sun, all year, 12h00-17h00.
Entrance tariff: free.
Métro: Cluny-La Sorbonne.
This magnificent Benedictine monastery, built in the 17th century, was converted into a hospital in 1793. You can still see much of the old abbey, while the church, symbolising the Nativity, is an outstanding example of Baroque art.

Arènes de Lutèce,
rue Monge, rue de Navarre, rue des Arènes
75005 Paris.
Opening hours, daily, summer, 8h00-22h00, daily, winter, 8h00-17h30.
Entrance tariff: free.
Métro: Jussieu.
This Roman amphitheatre was discovered in 1869 and subsequently partially restored. Today, the gardens are attractively planted and you can also play boules here, or watch, or go skateboarding. The only other Roman remains in Paris are

the three rooms that are still intact, but all that is left of the original Gallo-Roman baths at the Thermes de Cluny, the Musée du Môyen Age, (qv).

Centre Culturel Irlandais,
5 rue des Irlandais,
75005 Paris.
Tel. 01 58 52 10 30.
Métro: Cardinal Lemoine, Place Monge.
Opening hours: daily, all year.
Entrance tariff: free to exhibitions and the médiatheque
Close to the great church of St Sulpice, the Irish College, which dates back to the 18th century, has seen considerable recent renovation that has turned it into a centre dedicated to Irish culture in Paris. From the 16th century, Irish colleges developed in many European locations; none remain active today, except the Irish College in Paris and the college at Louvain in Belgium. The Irish College in Paris began to develop from the early 17th century and by the 18th century, was well established in the rue du Cheval Vert (Green Horse). Before Catholic Emancipation came in Ireland in 1829, many Irish priests trained here. In 1807, Napoléon was persuaded to change the name of the street from the rue du Cheval Vert to its present title. The present buildings used by the college date back well before 1775, when the College was opened in its present location. One of its treasures is the library, with 10, 000 items, half of which date from between the 15th and 18th centuries. The actual buildings of the college are well worth seeing for their architectural splendour, but the college now has many other facilities, including its médiatheque. It now has accommodation for 45 people at a time, students, artists and writers who want to stay here, while the centre has a dedicated cultural programme that shows a wide range of art forms, linking Ireland inextricably into the artistic life of Paris. For many years after the Second World War, the college was a seminary for Polish students and became very run down, but now the restoration is completed and the centre is a glorious commemoration of cultural heritage.

Galeries d'Anatomie comparée et de la Paléontologie,
2 rue Buffon,
75005 Paris.
Tel: 01 40 79 37 70 (boutique).
Web: www. mnhn. fr
Opening hours, Mon-Fri, all year, closed Tues and May 1, 10h00-17h00, Sat, Sun, Apr-Oct, 10h00-18h00.
Entrance tariff: EUR5 (reductions)
Métro: Austerlitz, Censier Daubenton, Jussieu, Monge.
This museum gives the grand tour of the prehistoric world of vertebrates, with an exceptional collection of dinosaurs, fossils and mastodons, as well as shells, giant birds and enormous insects. Many important specimens are on display here and children especially will find the place fascinating.

Grande Galerie de l'Évolution,
rue Buffon,
75005 Paris.
Tel: 01 40 79 30 30.
Web: www. mnhn. fr
Opening hours, daily, all year, 10h00-18h00,
Closed Tues and May 1.
Entrance tariff: EUR7 (reductions)
Métro: Austerlitz, Censier Daubenton, Jussieu
This highly impressive display is another new creation in the area of the Jardin de Plantes. The old zoological galleries, dating from the 19th century, were transformed in the early 1990s and this new display area opened in 1994. The interior alone is worth seeing, with its vast spaces, and soaring iron columns that support the glass roof. The aim of the museum is to tell the story evolution, relating the development of humans to the natural environment in which they live. This is all done with the help of life-sized stuffed animals, special lighting, audio of birdsong and music and touch screen monitors. In the lower level of the museum, all kinds of creatures from the ocean deeps swim around. On a higher level, the African plains are brought to life, with life-sized and enormous animals native to Africa. Children, who will really love this museum, can also enjoy themselves in the interactive centre especially designed for them, on the first floor.

Institut du Monde Arabe,
1 rue des Fossés-St-Bernard,
75005 Paris.
Tel. : 01 40 51 38 38
Web: www. imarabe. com
Opening hours: museum, Tues-Sun, all year, 10h00-18h00 daily.
Entrance tariff, museum: EUR4 (reduction).
Métro: Cardinal Lemoine.
This highly impressive centre was designed between 1980 and 1987 and it very cleverly reflects two twin themes: modern architectural trends and the influence of Islam. The windows have lots of references to the screens in Moorish palaces, while the whole centre is an assiduous mixture of high tech steel and glass, with strong Arab influences throughout. The museum has a very worthwhile collection of art and archaeology from the Middle East. You can also enjoy many other aspects of Arab culture here, including music and dance. If you go up to roof level, you'll see some stunning views across the rooftops of Paris.


Le Jardin de Plantes,
75005 Paris.
Tel: 01 40 79 30 30
Web: www. mnhn. fr
Opening hours, daily, 7h30-20h00 (summer), 7h30-17h30 (winter).
Entrance tariff: free
Métro: Austerlitz, Censier Daubenton, Jussieu, Monge.
These enormous gardens, full of attractions for the visitor, are close to the Gare d'Austerlitz. They were founded as a modest medicinal herb garden in 1626 and over the succeeding centuries, evolved into the main botanical gardens of Paris, with enough to see and do for a whole day's excursion.
  Some of the trees in the gardens are very old, including a Cedar of Lebanon planted in 1734, while there's also a cross-section of an American sequoia tree that dates back more than 2, 000 years. The birth of Christ and other significant historical events are marked on the rings. Other noted trees include an acacia tree, planted in 1636, just 10 years after the gardens were originally opened, and a Grikgo Biloba tree that is about 150 years old. That makes it a mere youngster, but the species has been in existence

since the time of the dinosaurs, 125 million years ago. Another very old tree is the Sophora tree from Japan, which was planted here in 1947.

The Roseraie is a much newer creation, planted as recently as 1990. It shows some 170 well established species and varieties of rose, as well as nearly 200 varieties that have been newly created during the past few years. For rose lovers, this is paradise.

The Alpine Garden has more that 2, 000 species of mountain plants from such diverse locations as the Caucasus, Corsica, the Himalayas, North America and the Pyrenees. It's closed on Sat, Sun and public holidays.

Les Parterres cover three hectares and have more than 1,000 species, varieties and cultivars of ornamental plants, described as a living catalogue of these plants. Also in the Jardin de Plantes, you can see the work of the Botanic School; it's closed on Sat, Sun and public holidays.

Ménagerie, microzoo,
3 quai Saint-Bernard & 57 rue Cuvier,
75005 Paris.
Tel: 01 44 05 72 72
Web: www. mnhn. fr
Opening hours, Mon-Sat, summer, 9h00-18h00, Sun until 18h30, Mon-Sat, winter, 9h00-17h00, Sun until 17h30.
Entrance tariff: EUR4. 57 (reductions)
Métro: Austerlitz, Censier Daubenton, Jussieu, Monge.
This is the oldest zoo in France, dating back to the time of the French Revolution and one of the oldest zoos in the world. It is substantial in size, covering 5. 5 hectares and it has an impressive collection-240 mammals, 500 birds and 130 reptiles.

The microzoo, which is open daily all year, 10h00-12h00, 13h30-17h30, is equally fascinating, but in a completely different way. It shows all the micro organisms that inhabit all environments, from one's home to the forest.

Musée de l'Assistance Publique-Hopitaux de Paris (Hospitals' Museum),
Hotel de Miramion,
47 quai de la Tournelle,
75005 Paris.
Tel: 01 40 27 50 05.

Opening hours: Tues-Sun, daily, 10h-18h.
Closed public holidays and during Aug.
Entrance tariff: EUR4 (reductions)
Métro: Cité, Maubert-Mutualité, Saint-Michel
This museum of the Paris public hospitals was created in 1934 and it's the oldest such museum in France, with one of the best collections, made up of more than 5, 000 pieces. These include everything from paintings and drawings to medical instruments. It covers the history of the Paris hospitals from the Middle Ages to the present. The exhibits are displayed in a total of five rooms. Among the innumerable exhibits is a painting from 1791 showing irons being fitted to convicts, which attracted many sightseers and a painting from 1907 showing the first use of radiation in the treatment of cancer. The social and religious history of hospitals is as well documented as the diseases of the human body, sometimes squeamish, but always fascinating. Exhibitions are organised frequently to appeal to young people.


Musée Curie (Institut du Radium),
11 rue Pierre et Marie Curie,
75005 Paris.
Tel. 01 42 34 67 49.
Web: http: //www.curie.fr/musees
Opening hours, Mon-Fri, all year, 13h30-17h00. Closed Aug, Christmas holidays,
public holidays.
Entrance tariff: free.
Métro: Place Monge.
Here, the renowned Curie family did their scientific work on radioactivity; the family members were awarded a grand total of five Nobel prizes for their work. Marie Curie (1867-1934) was a Polish chemist who came to France and married Pierre Curie (1859-1906), who was a French physicist.
In the museum, you can see the old instruments that were in use until the 1930s, as well as many photographs and archival documents relating to the Curie family. You can also inspect the original office of Marie Curie and her chemistry laboratory, which was decontaminated only as recently as 1981.

Musée des éclairages anciens (lighting museum),
4 rue Flatters,
75005 Paris.
Tel. 01 47 07 63 47
Web: www. members.aol.com/Lumiara
Opening hours, Tues-Fri, all year, 14h-19h00, Sat, all year,
11h00-17h00. Closed Aug.
Entrance tariff: free.
Métro: Port Royal.
If you're interested in the history of lighting, especially street
lighting, then this is the place. The museum depicts the
development of lighting, from 1850 up to 1925, with all kinds of
gas and petrol lamps and an assortment of lamp posts.

Musée du Moyen-Age (Thermes de Cluny),
6 place Paul Painlevé,
75005 Paris.
Tel. 01 53 73 78 16.
Web: http: //www. musee-moyanage. fr
Opening hours, daily, all year, 9h15-17h45, closed Tues, public
holidays.
Entrance tariff: EUR5. 5 (reductions).
Métro: Cluny-La Sorbonne.
This museum is divided into two very distinct parts; the museum
itself is located in a 15th century Gothic mansion that contains a
wide selection of medieval sculptures, including some from Notre-
Dame cathedral. The museum also details extensively what life
was like in the Middle Ages, not just ordinary domestic life, but life
on the pilgrimages. In 2000, a medieval garden was created
beside the museum. Frequently, concerts of medieval music are
staged here. The second part of the museum is entirely different,
the remains of the Gallo-Roman baths dating back to the third
century and complete with frigidarium (cold room).

Musée de la Préfecture de la Police,
1 bis, rue des Carmes,
75005 Paris.
Tel: 01 44 41 52 50
Web: www. prefecturepolice-paris. interieur. gouv. fr
Opening hours, Mon-Fri, all year, 9h00-17h00, Sat, all year,
10h00-17h00. Closed Sun, public holidays.

Entrance tariff: free.
Métro: Maubert-Mutualité.
For anyone fascinated by Simenon's Inspector Maigret legend, this police museum, set in a dingy real life police station, will give some of the facts behind all the fiction. The museum tells the story of the police in Paris since they came into being in the 16th century and you can see much paperwork, including warrants and edicts, as well as a gory assortment of murder weapons. These include a 17th century sword used to decapitate many members of the nobility. Celebrated criminals are depicted, too, as are ancient prisons. Maigret may conjure up a feeling of a Paris and France long vanished, but this museum brings to life the cruel realities of police work. The more mundane work of the gendarmes, such as traffic control, is also highlighted.

Panthéon,
Place du Panthéon,
75005 Paris.
Tel: 01 44 32 18 00.
Opening hours, daily, summer, 10h00-18h30, daily, winter, 10h00-17h30.
Entrance tariff: EUR7 (reductions).
Métro: Cardinal-Lemoine.
The best approach to the Panthéon is along the rue Soufflot, a very broad street that gives the best perspectives of this great Parisian monument. Louis XV (1710-1774), a man of many mistresses, had the place built as an offering to Sainte Geneviève, patron saint of Paris, for her intercessions in curing his various illnesses. During the French Revolution, it was transformed into a mausoleum for the great and the good in French life; among those whose ashes are interred in the enormous barrel-shaped crypt are Hugo, Rousseau, Voltaire and Zola. Marie Curie was interred here in 1995, the first woman in the crypt. André Malraux, cultural minister under General de Gaulle and renowned writer and Resistance leader, was interred here the following year, 1996, while Alexander Dumas found his last resting place here in 2002. One of the great curiosities here is the reconstruction of the pendulum that Foucault, the great French physicist, made in 1851 to prove that the earth does actually spin on its axis. The theory behind the pendulum may be a little esoteric for some tastes, but anyone with a head for heights can climb the steeply twisting stairs to the colonnade, from where there are some truly magnificent views over the city.

Paris Mosque,
Rue Daubenton,
75005 Paris.
Opening hours, daily tours, all year, except Fri and Muslim holidays, 9h00-12h00, 14h00-18h00.
Entrance tariff: EUR2. 29
Métro: Censier-Daubenton.
For anyone with even a passing interest in the world of Islam, the mosque is well worth a visit and is most interesting. Each of the domes is decorated differently and the minaret is nearly 35 metres high. You can have a look at the sunken garden and the patios, complete with polychrome tiles and carved ceilings. You can't go into the prayer room, unless you're taking part in prayers. The hammam is open to everyone, with different days for the two sexes. The tearoom and restaurant are bastions of peacefulness and you can also buy interesting and unusual souvenirs in the shop.

place de l'Estrapade,
75005 Paris.
Métro: Luxembourg.
This small square is close to the Panthéon and best approached from the steep rue des Fossés-Saint-Jacques. The name of the square is derived from the name of a wooden tower from which deserters from the 17th century army were thrown, with no hope of survival.

Quayside entertainment,
Quai de la Tournelle,
75005 Paris.
Métro: Maubert Mutualité
Two boats moored at the quayside offer evening entertainment. The Kiosque Flottant 2/Le Point de Londres, tel. 01 43 54 19 51, has plenty of entertainment nightly, including jazz on Friday and Saturday nights. The Metamorphosis, tel. 01 43 54 08 08, offers magic-literally.

rue Cardinal Lemoine,
75005 Paris.
Métro: Cardinal Lemoine
In this other unprepossessing street, you can see the facades of two of the most famous literary houses from the Paris of the 1920s, when the city was alive with expatriate writers and artists. At Number 71, James Joyce completed his most renowned work, Ulysses, in the early 1920s, while at Number 74, Ernest Hemingway, who lived in Paris after the First World War, lived and wrote-when he wasn't sampling the Parisian bar life.

rue Mouffetard,
75005 Paris.
Métro: Cardinal-Lemoine.
The Rue Mouffetard is one of the oldest streets in Paris, dating back to the early Middle Ages; it was once the main road to Rome, but these days, it's a narrow little street packed with all kinds of shops selling tourist souvenirs, cheap bistros and student haunts. In the Paris of the 1920s and 1930s, this was a favourite hang-out for impoverished artists, but they have now been replaced by rather better off tourists. The northern end of the street starts in the place de la Contrescarpe, which has been a rendezvous for writers since the 16th century. These days, there aren't so many writers hanging around, but one of the cafes in the square is still a good place to enjoy an espresso or a glass of wine and watch all the other tourists wandering past. At the other end of the street, close to the Eglise Saint-Médard, there's a busy and extremely lively street market held every morning from Tuesday until Saturday and then again on Sunday morning. Another market is held at the nearby place Monge on Wed, Fri and Sun mornings. At Number 6 in the nearby rue Pot-de-Fer, the great English writer, George Orwell, creator of Animal Farm and 1984, lived in 1928 and 1929, in conditions of the utmost poverty. While he was living here, he worked doing the washing up in a local hotel, experiences that he described with incredible vividness in his book, *Down and Out in Paris and London*. These days, the street is less poverty stricken, but the bars and restaurants are still made for those with little money.

Saint-Séverin church,
1 rue des pretres St-Séverin,
75005 Paris.
Opening hours, daily, all year, 8h00-18h00. Free guided tours, Sun 15h30.
Entrance tariff: free.
Metro: Cluny-Sorbonne.
The church of Saint-Séverin is one of the most graceful in Paris, built in the early 13th century after the original church on the site was demolished. It's set right in the heart of the Latin Quarter, which is one of the oldest parts of Paris. The church itself is a wonderful testament to the early Gothic style of architecture and its interior is truly inspiring and gracious. Medieval construction techniques, poetry in stone, theology and the spiritual life all amalgamate in the soaring ecclesiastical style of the early Middle Ages.

Serres tropicale et Mexicaine,
57 rue Cuvier,
75005 Paris.
Web: www. mnhn. fr
Opening hours, daily, all year, except Tues and May 1, 13h00-17h00.
Entrance tariff: EUR2. 30 (reductions)
Métro: Austerlitz, Censier, Jussieu, Monge.
Two huge hothouses, within the Jardin de Plantes, provide the hot and humid environment essential for tropical plants as well as tropical birds. The hothouses are filled with several thousand species and varieties of tropical plants and trees. Plants from Mexico include the ubiquitous cactus, while the unique vegetation of the island of Madagascar is also well represented.

Sorbonne,
17 rue de la Sorbonne,
75005 Paris.
Tel. 01 40 46 22 11.
Web: www. sorbonne. fr
Métro: Cluny-La Sorbonne.
For many people, the Sorbonne is indelibly linked with the student insurrection of May, 1968, when the university was occupied by students, who were subsequently evicted by the CRS riot police

and the air of the Left Bank was full of acrid tear gas. The University of the Sorbonne has a very illustrious pedigree, going back to 1253 when it was founded by Robert de Sorbon. Needless to remark, Napoléon reorganised the whole place. After the events of 1968, the French higher education authorities did exactly the same, scattering the university over a variety of far-flung locations to make it more difficult for students to plan political mayhem in the streets. The buildings that you can see today date mostly from the end of the 19th century. You can wander round and see for yourself, but the architectural highpoint is the 17th century chapel, which is only open to the public during concerts or exhibitions.

## 6th ARRONDISSEMENT

Boulevard Montparnasse,
75006 Paris.
Métro: Montparnasse Bienvenue.
In the Paris of the 1920s and the 1930s, the Boulevard Montparnasse was "home" to many of the more exotic and untamed artistic characters who frequented the city in those far-off inter-war years, when Paris had a world reputation for its bohemian artistic life. These days, large sections of Montparnasse have been hideously redeveloped, including the station, which once had the air of an undisturbed country station. The ghastly Tour de Montparnasse characterises the new style Montparnasse, with the equally dreary rue de Rennes, which is completely soulless. However, the ghosts of artists past still hang around, including that of Samuel Beckett (1906-1989), the great Irish dramatist and poet, who lived a hermetic existence for years in the boulevard St-Jacques, close by. His apartment was very close to the Santé prison. Some of the old literary cafes are still here, including the Coupole and the Rotonde, as well as the posher Closerie des Lilas, where the American writer Hemingway often came to write.

Brasserie Lipp,
151 boulevard St-Germain,
75006 Paris.
Tel. 01 45 48 53 91.
Web: www. brasserie-lipp. fr
Opening hours, daily, all year, 11h30-1h00.
Métro: St-Germain-des-Près.
This is one of the most famous restaurants and cafes in Paris, frequented for many years by the rich and famous. Once, noted politicians like François Mitterand and Valèry Giscard d'Estaing, both former Presidents of France, liked to come here for the odd tete-à-tete. These days, the film set has taken over, the actors and the producers. If you're famous and rich, you won't have any trouble getting a table on the fashionable ground floor, but if you're not, expect banishment to the first floor, where you'll miss most of the fun. Neither is the food earth shattering: the Brasserie Lipp thrives on its name and reputation for attracting famous people, the cognoscenti.


Café de Flore,
172 boulevard St-Germain,
75006 Paris.
Tel: 01 45 48 55 26.
Web: http: //www.cafe-de-flore.com/
Opening hours, daily, all year, 7h00-1h30.
Métro: St-Germain-des-Prés.
The great Surrealist artists of the 1920s and 1930s, when Paris was at the height of its artistic ferment, often came here in preference to the nearby Deux Magots. In the 1940s, one of its regular visitors was Picasso. It's still popular with the artistic and intellectual crowd, but despite being a little less "polished" or accessible than the Deux Magots, it still retains its popularity. The cafe retains its traditional, classic Art Déco decor, but these days, it even has its own shop.

Deux Magots,
Boulevard St Germain,
75006 Paris.
Tel. 01 45 48 55 25.
Métro: St-Germain-des-Prés.
Just across the street from the Brasserie Lipp, the Deux Magots is more of a cafe, with a large terrace on the pavement. It also has more of a literary and artistic reputation than its rival across the road and was once favoured by the likes of Jean-Paul Sartre and Ernest Hemingway. These days, most of the patrons you'll see will be fellow tourists in Paris. The walls of the café are lined with mirrors and the waiters wear the traditional garb, black waistcoats and white aprons. The cafe is named after the wooden statues of two Chinese dignitaries that stand near the door.

Dubuffet Fondation,
137 rue des Sèvres,
75006 Paris.
Tel: 01 47 34 12 63
Web: www.dubuffetfondation.com
Opening hours, Mon-Fri, all year, 14h00-18h00.
Entrance tariff: EUR4.
Métro: Vaneau.
The Fondation that preserves the work and memory of Jean Dubuffet has two locations, one at Périgny-sur-Yerres in the Marne valley (qv) and this location in Paris, a small town house that houses the secretariat. The house also has a permanent exhibition of work by Dubuffet, as well as a history centre and Dubuffet's personal archives, from which the foundation developed its various projects on the artist.

Église de St-Germain-des-Prés,
3 rue St-Germain-des-Prés,
75006 Paris.
Opening hours, daily, all year, 8h00-18h00.
Entrance tariff: free.
Métro: St-Germain-des-Prés.
Standing in a commanding square right in the heart of the 6th. , this church is the oldest in Paris, built by King Childebert in the 6th century. It was rebuilt on several subsequent occasions and in the 1990s, extensive renovations were carried out, but you can still

see one of the three original belfries. Outside the church, in a small, adjacent park, you can see the sculpture of Apollinaire created by Picasso as well as the ruins of a chapel dedicated to the Virgin Mary.

Hotel Lutétia,
45 boulevard Raspail,
75006 Paris.
Tel. 01 49 54 46 46.
Web: www. lutetia-paris.com
Métro: Sèvres-Babylone.
It's worth taking a wander round the lobby of this extraordinary hotel, one of the most expensive in Paris and certainly one of the most striking. It was opened in 1910, designed for shoppers thronging to the nearly Bon Marché department store, the oldest of the grands magasins in Paris and the only one on the Left Bank. The style of the hotel is Art Nouveau and early Art Deco, quite stunning, and today, each of the rooms in the hotel has its own individual style. During the Second World War, the hotel gained notoriety because of its popularity with the German High Command in the city. Yet today, the hotel still retains much of the aura it had during the 1930s. Just across from the hotel, in the small Parc Boucicault, named after the family that founded Bon Marché, you can see a statue depicting Mme Boucicault and her friend Clara de Hirsch, wife of a baron renowned for his charitable works, themselves handing out alms to poor women and children of the district.

Hotel des Saints-Pères,
65 rue des Saints-Pères,
75006 Paris.
Tel: 01 45 44 90 83.
Métro: St Germain des Prés.
The building which contains this elegant hotel has a long and elegant history itself, created as an hôtel particulier in 1658 by Gittard, who was one of the architects who worked for the king at the time, Louis XIV. You can enjoy the garden and the small bar, while the best room to stay in is Number 100, which has an impressive 17th century fresco done by painters of the Versailles school.

Jardin de Luxembourg,
75006 Paris.
Métro: Odéon.
These vast gardens, covering 25 hectares, are the biggest open air space on the Left Bank and a favourite place for walking and talking it easy, among both residents and visitors. Paris has over 400 parks and this easily tops the list of favourites. The gardens have all kinds of manmade facilities, from tennis courts and a boules area to a childrens' playground, with ponies, a merry-go-round and puppet shows in summer. You can even hire out miniature boats to sail on the pond, the Grand Bassin. In the south-east corner of the gardens, which are less cultivated, a pear orchard bears much fruit that is sold off during the autumn fair which takes place in the last week of September every year. The gardens as a whole have plenty of benches for people to sit and watch the rest of the world going by, while the Fontaine des Médicis in the north-east corner is a favourite spot for lovers seeking the shade. The park has many other monumental sculptures. One of the most interesting items in the park is a little hard to find: it's a metre rule on the end wall of the colonnade at 36, rue de Vaugirard. It was put there during the French Revolution, so that people could start using the then new metric system of measurement. The big palace has distinct overtones of the great palaces of Florence; it was built by Marie de Médicis, widow of Henry IV (1553-1610), to remind her of her native city.

Le Procope,
13 rue de l'Ancienne Comédie,
75006 Paris.
Tel. 01 43 26 99 20.
Opening hours, daily, all year.
Métro: Odéon.
This claims to be the oldest restaurant in the world, founded in 1686. Voltaire, the great philosopher, came here to work and drink 40 cups of coffee a day. During the Revolutionary times, Danton, Robespierre and Marat came here. Someone else who enjoyed coming here in his young days was Napoleon I. In the 19th century, Balzac and Hugo were among the writers who frequented the place. Today, the place is a rather classy restaurant, on two levels. Much of the elegant mystique has been preserved and these days, it's home to a diverse assortment of diners, including business people, university professors, models, writers, journalists and tourists.

Les Editeurs,
4 carrefour de l'Odéon,
75006 Paris.
Tel. 01 43 26 67 76.
Opening hours, daily, all year.
Métro: Odéon.
As this cafe is right in the heart of the publishing district in Paris, you'll find that Les Editeurs has a great collection of books from all the nearby publishers. The bookshelves in the cafe are stacked with new editions and there's nothing to stop you dipping into them.

Musée de la Monnaie de Paris,
11 quai de Conti,
75006 Paris.
Tel: 01 40 46 55 35.
Web: www.monnaiedeparis.fr
Opening hours, Tues-Fri, all year, 11h00-17h30, Sat, Sun, all year, 12h00-17h30.
Entrance tariff: EUR3 (reductions)
Métro: Odéon, Pont-Neuf.
This mint was built in the 1770s in very elegant style by Jacques Denis-Antonine. Today, it has a high tech presentation of the story of France's money, from pre-Roman times right up to the present day euro. These displays are very informative, with the 2, 000 coins and 450 medals and tokens in glass displays, so that you can see both sides. The audio-visual presentations are very informative, as are the displays of old equipment for making money, such as ancient engraving machines. You'll also find much information about French history. You can also visit the workshop here, on Weds and Fris, at 14h15, but you have to phone in advance to reserve a place.

Musée National Delacroix,
6 place Furstenberg,
75006 Paris.
Tel: 01 44 41 86 50.
Web: www. musee-delacroix. fr
Opening hours, daily, all year, except Tues and Jan 1, May 1, Dec 25, 9h30-17h30.
Entrance tariff: EUR4 (reductions).

Métro: St-Germain-des-Prés.

The place Furstenberg is a very agreeable part of the 6th arrondissement an it was to a house and studio here that the great artist Delacroix moved in 1857 when he was commissioned to paint vast murals for the Église Saint-Sulpice. His major works are in the Louvre and the Musée d'Orsay, but here in this house, you can see a selection of his smaller works, both oil paintings and sketches. The atmosphere of the studio remains much as it was in his day. He stayed here until his death in 1863. The gardens, too, are very pleasant and they, together with the house and studio, have all been recently renovated.

Musee National Hébert,
85 rue du Cherche-Midi,
75006 Paris.
Tel. 01 42 22 23 82.
Opening hours, Mon, Wed-Fri, all year, 12h30-18h00, Sat, Sun, public holidays, all year, 14h00-18h00.
Entrance tariff: EUR3 (reductions).
Métro: St-Placide, Vaneau.
Ernest Hébert (1817-1908), was a secondary artist well-known during his lifetime for his work, which in its earlier phases, included conventional Italian style landscapes and prudish portraits, then gravitated towards the style of the Impressionists. His work gives a good indication of mid and late 19th century artistic tastes, while the run-down house, dating from the mid-18th century, is of interest for its very dilapidation.

Musée Zadkine,
100 bis, rue d'Assas,
75006 Paris.
Tel: 01 55 42 77 20.
Web: http: //paris.fr/musees/Zadkine/
Opening hours: daily, 10hr-18hr, closed Mons and public holidays.
Entrance fee: free.
Métro: Notre Dame des Champs, Vavin.
Zadfkine (1890-1967) was a well-known Russian painter who arrived in Paris in 1910. He moved into the house and studio at the rue d'Assas in 1928 and worked there for the rest of his life, creating many memorables statues, sculptures and other works of art. Examples of his large statuary can be seen in the garden of

the house. One imposing piece here is the Torse de la Ville détruite, created as homage to the Second World War victims of Rotterdam. He was very much a modern artist, influenced by primitive art, seeking a fusion between man and the natural world.

Poilane bakery shop,
8 rue du Cherche-Midi,
75006 Paris.
Tel: 01 45 48 42 59.
Web: www. poilane. com
Opening hours, daily, all year, 7h00-20h00.
Métro: Sèvres-Babylone, St-Sulpice.
This is one of the most famous bakery shops in Paris and the city has many. For years, this bakery was owned and run by Lionel Poilane, a great publicist of the baking craft, who was killed when his helicopter crashed in Normandy towards the end of 2002. Fortunately, the high craft standards that he set live on and you'll find this small, old-fashioned shop full of charm, as well as truly tantalising aromas from the wood-burning ovens.

Raspail Organic Market,
75006 Paris.
Métro: Rennes.
Near Saint-Germain-des-Prés, this is the largest organic market in Paris and it's held every Sunday morning. You'll find a truly amazing selection of food that has been organically grown or reared, everything form algae bread to free range rabbits and poultry, as well as around 30 varieties of organic honey. The selection is augmented by the vast quantities of organic fruit and vegetables from all over the world, not just France.

Riverside bookstalls,
75006 Paris.
Métro: St-Michel.
Lining the river banks in this part of Paris, within close view of Nôtre-Dame cathedral, many bookstalls hug the quayside walls. The bouquinistes, with their wares displayed in green boxes that are hung on the walls, sell an amazing and immense variety of second-hand items, including books, picture postcards, records and all sorts of other memorabilia. However, while the bookstalls look romantic from a distance, the traffic congestion and the

volume of pedestrians on the pavements in this part of Paris can make for an uncomfortable experience.

Shakespeare & Co. ,
37 rue de la Bucherie,
75006 Paris.
Tel: 01 43 26 96 50.
Web: http: //www.shakespeareco.org/
Opening hours, daily, all year, 12h00-24h00.
Métro: Maubert-Mutualité, St-Michel.
On the right bank, just across the river from Nôtre-Dame cathedral, Shakespeare & Co is one of the city's best-known and loved bookshops, revered among literati because of its 1920s literary connections. The original bookshop was opened in 1921 in the nearby rue de l'Odéon by Sylvia Beach, an American exile in Paris and the daughter of a New England Presbyterian Minister. In the 1920s, such writers frequented the shop as André Gide, James Joyce, Ezra Pound and George Bernard Shaw. For some, such as Joyce, Beach was also a publisher. The shop was opened in its present location in 1951 by another American bibliophile, George Whitman, who called it Le Mistral. In 1964, with Beach's permission, he renamed it Shakespeare & Co. It still has an excellent atmosphere, plenty of new and second-hand books for sale and a library upstairs.


Yves Saint-Laurent,
12 place Saint-Sulpice,
75006 Paris.
Tel: 01 43 26 84 40.
Opening hours, Mon-Sat, 9h00-18h00.
Métro: Saint Sulpice, Saint-Germain des Pres.
One of the great fashion icons, the Yves Saint-Laurent boutique is a temple to his design skills, even though he himself has now retired. You can browse through the shop and enjoy the latest in fashions for men and women. Large flat screen TVs show the latest fashion shows.

St-Sulpice,
75006 Paris.
Opening hours, daily, all year, 8h00-18h00.
Entrance tariff: free.
Métro: St-Sulpice.
The gigantic church was built to the south of Saint-Germain around the turn of the 18th century. It's a very classical edifice and all the towers of the church except one were left unfinished. The most interesting aspect of the dark interior are the murals done by Delacroix (qv). The bleakness of the facade is mellowed a little by the chestnut trees and the fountains. in the square in front of the church. On the northern side of the square, you'll find some of the most fashionable fashion shops in Paris, including Agnès B and Christian Lacroix. Rue Mabillon, which is close to the church, it noted for the row of medieval houses set below the level of the street.

Village Voice Bookshop,
6 rue Princesse,
75006 Paris.
Tel: 01 46 33 36 47.
Opening hours, Mon, all year, 14h-20h00, Tues-Sat, all year, 11h00-20h00. Closed Sun.
Métro: Mabillon.
This bookshop is one of the best regarded in Paris by expatriates and visitors to Paris and it's also an excellent meeting place, as literary events are frequently organised here.

Oscar Wilde's hotel,
L'Hotel,
13 rue des Beaux-Arts,
75006 Paris.
Tel: 01 44 41 99 00.
Web: http: //www. l-hotel.com/lhotel. htm
Métro: St-Germain-des-Pres.
Oscar Wilde (1854-1900), the renowned Dublin-born dramatist and poet, died in this hotel on November 30, 1900. In one of his characteristically amusing epigrams, he said that either he or the wallpaper had to go. The wallpaper won out. Wilde was ruined, socially and financially, by his trial in 1895 that had arisen from his homosexual relationship with Lord Alfred Douglas. After two years

in prison, Wilde retreated to exile in France, dying in what was then the Hotel d'Alsace is a state of extreme poverty. In Paris, he had also stayed at the Hotel du Quai Voltaire in the 7th (qv). The two rooms in L'Hotel occupied by Wilde are now largely as they were in 1900, complete with an assortment of Wilde letters and photographs. Another of the famous people to have a connection with this hotel, Mistinguett, the music hall star so revered in France between the first and second world wars, has Room Number 36 in the hotel dedicated to her memory.

## 7th ARRONDISSEMENT

Assemblée Nationale,
33 quai d'Orsay,
75007 Paris.
Tel: 01 40 63 60 00.
Web: www. assemblee-nat. fr
Opening hours, Mon, Fri, Sat, most of year, 8h40-11h40, 14h00-17h00. Guided tours every 20 mins.
Métro: Assemblée Nationale.
The lower house of the French Parliament has met in the former Palais Bourbon since 1827. The guided tour takes in the debating chamber, as well as the library, which is decorated with the magnificent Delacroix mural, History of Civilisation, and the adjacent Hotel de Lassy, which is the official residence of the President of the Assembly. If you wish, you can also sit in on the debates.

Chapelle de la Médaille Miraculeuse,
Couvent des Soeurs de St-Vincent-de-Paul,
140 rue du Bac,
75007 Paris.
Tel: 01 49 54 78 88.
Opening hours, Mon-Sat, all year, 7h45-13h00, 14h00-19h00, Sun, all year, 14h30-19h00.
Entrance tariff: free
Métro: Rue du Bac.
In the chapel lie the embalmed bodies of Catherine Labouré, who performed many miracles in the early 19th century, and her mother superior. The chapel is full of mosaics, murals and statues

and a series of reliefs tell the story of the nun's life. It's one of the most popular pilgrimage places in France, visited by well over two million people a year.

Du Bon Marché,
24 rue de Sèvres,
75007 Paris.
Tel. 01 44 39 80 00.
Web: www. bonmarche. fr
Opening hours, Mon-Sat, all year, 9h30-19h00.
Métro: Sèvres-Babylone.
This is the oldest department store in Paris, but in recent years, it has been given extensive makeovers, so that these days, it's a very glamorous place to shop. The origins are fascinating; Aristide Boucicault came from the Orne and began as a travelling salesman in Normandy, before coming to Paris, where he met his future wife, Marguerite, who was a junior in a creamery shop in the rue de Bac. After the 1848 revolution, Aristide was out of work and went into partnership, setting up shop in the rue de Bac. The enterprise prospered mightily and in 1867, the foundation stone of their great store was laid. Building took until 1887. Today, it's a vast and very trendy fashion emporium and you can also enjoy browsing through the Grande Épicerie foodhall in the adjoining building, which also has an antiques gallery, a bar and a restaurant.

Église de Saint Clotilde,
23, bis rue Las-Cases,
75007 Paris.
Opening hours, daily, all year, 8h00-18h00.
Entrance tariff: free.
Métro: Solférino.
This church, consecrated in 1858, was the first church built in Paris in the 19th century in the ogival style. The stone came from a quarry in Bourgogne. At the consecration ceremony, one of the guests was Baron Georges-Eugène Haussmann, préfet de la Seine, the man responsible for reorganising central Paris. The church has a marvellous interior, while on the exterior, two towers are each topped with a steeple. St Clothilde has one of the best church organs in Paris, made by Aristide Cavaillé-Coll. Recitals are held regularly. Its first and most famous organist was César

Franck (1822-1890), also a notable composer. In more modern times, the blind Jean Langlais was organist between 1945 and 1987.

Eiffel Tower,
Champs de Mars,
75007 Paris.
Tel: 01 44 11 23 45
Web: www.tour-eiffel.fr
Opening hours, June-Aug, daily, 9h00-24h00, Sept-May, daily, 9h30-23h00.
Entrance tariff: EUR9. 90 (reductions).
Métro: Champs-de-Mars Tour Eiffel.
The world-famous landmark can't be missed from anywhere in Paris and even though it's so popular, it's always worth the trip to the top. After it was built for the 1889 Exposition Universelle, it was widely derided. Despite the present day queues, it's well worth taking the lift to the top; on a clear day, you should be able to see all of Paris and most of the Ile de France. On the first floor level, you can enjoy an audio-visual presentation on the tower, its construction and history and there is also one restaurant on this level and another on the second level.

Fondation EDF-Éspace Electra,
6 rue Récamier,
75007 Paris.
Tel: 01 53 63 23 45
Web: www.edf.fr
Opening hours, Tues-Sun, all year, 12h00-19h00.
Closed Mon, public holidays.
Entrance tariff: free
Métro: Sévres Babylone.
What was once an electricity sub-station owned by EDF, the State company responsible for gas and electricitiy, is now a trendy, interestingly designed venue for all kinds of exhibitions. The variety of exhibitions is interesting and varied, on a host of different topics.

Serge Gainsbourg's place,
5 bis rue de Verneuil,
75007 Paris.
Web: www.gainsbarre.com
Métro: Solférino
Serge Gainsbourg (1928-1991) was the enfant terrible of French pop music, notorious for his wild goings-on. He died in his apartment in the rue de Verneuil on March 2, 1991 and the facade of the building promptly became a shrine. He was buried in the Cimetière Montparnasse (qv) and fans threw all manner of things on his grave, from Metro tickets to empty packets of Gitanes cigerettes, in their profound sadness at his death. Outside his apartment, where he had lived with his then partner, Charlotte Rampling, the fans scrawled all kinds of graffiti, lyrics and other messages. The wall has since been cleaned.

Hotel du Quai Voltaire,
19 quai Voltaire,
75007 Paris.
Tel: 01 42 61 50 91
Web: www.quaivoltaire.fr
Métro: Solférino
This modest hotel on the right bank of the River Seine, just down from the Musée d'Orsay and facing the Louvre, was built in the 17th century as an abbey and opened as an hotel in 1856. In the late 19th century, distinguished artists such as Baudelaire, Siberlius, Wagner and Oscar Wilde stayed here. Camille Pissaro took a room on the fourth floor to paint the view of the Pont Royal. You can see the historical plaque on the facade.

Le Pagode cinema,
57 rue de Babylone,
75007 Paris.
Tel: 01 44 78 12 33
Opening hours; 14h00-23h00, daily, all year.
Métro: Saint François-Xavier, Sèvres-Babylone.
This is a cinema with a difference, built as a pagoda in the 1920s and maintained as such ever since. It's perhaps the most unusual cinema in Paris and apart from the films, you'll be well entertained and intrigued by the exuberance of the classic Asian decor.

Musée des Égouts de Paris (sewers museum)
face au 93 quai d'Orsay,
75007 Paris
Open daily, except Thurs, Fri, 11. 00-17. 00 (summer), closed
16. 00 (winter)
Entrance fee: EUR3. 80 (also reductions).
Métro: Pont de l'Alma.
Go down into the depths of Paris to see the sewers system that
runs beneath the city streets; it's quite hygienic. You'll be able to
see traces of the ancient sewerage systems going right back to
Roman times and the remains of the first covered sewer built in
Paris, in 1370.

Musée de l'Armée,
esplanade des Invalides,
75007 Paris.
Tel: 01 44 42 37 67
Web: www. invalides.org
Opening hours, Apr-Sept, daily, 10h00-18h00, Oct-Mar, daily,
10h00-17h00.
Entrance tariff: EUR6 (reductions). Also includes entry to the
Musée des Plans-Reliefs and the Église du Dôme.
Métro: Invalides.
This vast war museum covers several wings and floors and it
begins with displays of ancient armour and weapons, including
the suit of armour worn by François 1, an early medieval king. The
east wing has vast arrays of material, depicting the history of the
French armed forces through the centuries. The south-west wing
has a particularly interesting new section on three floors, covering
the Second World War. Battles, resistance and liberation are all
portrayed and the section has fascinating contemporary
newsreels.
The Musée des Plans-Reliefs, with the same opening hours, is
also in the Hotel des Invalides. It houses an important and
extensive historic collection of models of strategically fortified
towns in France, once used for military planning purposes.
Beneath the enormous gilded dome of the Hotel des Invalides,
you can inspect two churches, one designed for soldiers, the
other originally designed for the king but now containing the
remains of Napoleon. In the Église du Dome, you can see the
sacrophagus containing Napoléon, sunk into the floor and

surrounded within a gallery. On the walls, friezes depict Napoléon and also have some of his pronouncements.

Musée de l'Histoire Naturelle minéralogie et geologie,
Pavilion Valhubert,
57 rue Cuvier,
75007 Paris.
Tel. 01 40 79 56 01.
Web: www.mnhn.fr
Opening hours, daily, all year, 10h00-17h00. Closed Tues. Between Apr 1 and Sept 30, it's open on Sat, Sun, 10h00-18h00.
Entrance tariff: EUR5 (reductions).
Métro: Jussieu.
This museum, closed to the Jardin des Plantes, has one of the most comprehensive collections in the world of minerals. Begun in the 17$^{th}$ century, it has an amazing assortment of crystals, gems and precious minerals, as well as objets d'art. The Salle de Trésor has an exhibition of giant crystals.

Musée Maillol,
59-61 rue de Grenelle,
75007 Paris.
Tel: 01 42 22 59 58
Web: www. museemaillol.com
Opening hours, Mon, Wed-Sun, all year, 11h00-18h00.
Closed Tues.
Entrance tariff: EUR7 (reductions).
Métro: Rue du Bac.
This delightful museum in an 18th century mansion is comparatively recent, having been opened in 1995 by Dina Vierny, who was principal model for many years for Maillol (1861-1944). The museum has a considerable body of his work, including ceramics, drawings and paintings, but that's only for starters. Maillol depicted the female form in many ways and media and his most famous work, the seated Mediterranean, is at the top of the stairs on the first floor. The museum has a whole bevy of other 20th century works, by artists such as Degas, Picasso and Rodin. A whole room is devoted to Matisse drawings. Dina Vierny was also particularly interested in the work of Russian artists and one of the most striking pieces from the former Soviet Union is the Communal Kitchen by Ilya Kabakov. The museum also stages regular exhibitions. It has a bookshop and a cafe.

Musée National de la Legion d'Honneur
2 rue Bellechasse,
75007 Paris.
Tel. 01 40 62 84 25.
Métro: Solférino.
This intriguing museum, which details the story of the Legion d'Honneur, France's highest and best-known decoration, and many other decorations, from inside and outside France since the 18th century, also has much Napoleonic history. However, it is currently closed for renovations but is due to reopen during 2006.


Musée National Rodin,
Hotel Biron,
77 rue de Varenne,
75007 Paris.
Tel: 01 44 18 61 10
Web: www.musee-rodin.fr
Opening hours, Apr-Sept, Tues-Sun, 9h30-17h45 (gardens close one hour later), Oct-Mar, Tues-Sun, 9h30-16h45 (gardens close at 17h00). Closed Mon, Jan
1, May 1, Dec 25.
Entrance tariff: EUR5 (reductions).
Métro: Varenne.
The museum is in the great house where Rodin (1840-1917) lived for the last years of his life. He was renowned for his big set piece sculptures, including The Kiss, which is in the Tate Gallery in London. The museum here in the rue de Varenne has works of his, including portraits and terracotta pieces, as well as works by his pupil, who was also his mistress, Camille Claudel. But it's the garden that most people enjoy the most, not just for the leafy perspectives, but for the great Rodin statues seen in a natural outdoor setting, such as The Burghers of Calais and The Thinker. There are even several nymphs carved in marble that Rodin never finished.

Musée d'Orsay,
1 rue de Solferino,
75007 Paris.
Tel: 01 40 49 48 14
Web: www. musee-orsay. fr
Opening hours, summer, Tues-Sun, 9h00-18h00, winter, Tues-Sat, 10h00-18h00, sun, 9h00-18h00.
Closed Mon, Jan 1, May 1, Dec 25.
Entrance tariff: EUR7 (reductions).
Métro: Solférino.
Opened in 1900 as a railway terminus serving the south-west of France, the Gare d'Orsay remained as a station until 1939. Immediately after the Second World War, it was used as a transit camp for people returning home from the Nazi concentration camps. On various subsequent occasions, it was used for theatrical and film productions and it was here, on May 19, 1958, that General de Gaulle staged his coup d'état. Fortunately, in the mid-1980s, it was saved from demolition and redevelopment; there was strong public anger that the site might be used as a repetition of what happened with Les Halles on the other side of the river. So the old station was turned into a museum of French art for the period between 1848 and 1914 and it has long been one of the most popular visitor attractions in Paris.

The collections are arranged in the cavernous central space and in three storeys on either side. Many paintings and sculptures by the most famous artists of the period are complemented by some of the most famous Impressionist paintings in the world. These include Manet's Déjeuner sur l'Herbe and the Olympia, Monet's Poppies and Renoir's Dancing at the Moulin de la Galette. Pointilliste and Post-Impressionist artists are also well represented. Furniture, architectural models and models and drawings of the Opéra Garnier, completed in 1875, also feature. From the river side of the museum, you can also enjoy spectacular views across the city to the Sacré Coeur. The museum also has an excellently well stocked shop and a restaurant, but you need to go early because of the queues at lunchtime especially.

Musée du quai Branly,
quai Branly,
75007 Paris.
Web: www.quaibranly.fr
Métro: Champs-de-Mars Tour Eiffel.
You can follow construction progress on this latest of the great Parisian museum projects; it's close to the Eiffel Tower. You can also see how the work is getting on by clicking into the website. The museum is due to open in 2006 and is scheduled to contain many galleries of art and other collections, from Africa, the Americas, Asia and Oceania. Close to 250, 000 items will come from the Musée de l'Homme(qv) in the 16th, on the other side of the river, while about 25, 000 will be transferred from the Musée des Arts d'Afrique et de Océanien. More will come here from the Louvre.

Musée Valentin Hauy,
5 rue Duroc,
75007 Paris.
Tel: 01 44 49 27 27
Opening hours, Tues, Wed, all year, 14h30-17h00 and by arr.
Entrance tariff: free.
Métro: Duroc.
Valentin Hauy (1745-1822) did much for the education of blind people and he invented a system to enable blind people to read that was a forerunner of Braille. He also founded a school for the blind in Paris in 1784. You can see material on his life and works in this small museum.

River boats,
Port de Suffren,
75007 Paris.
Métro: Champs-de-Mars Tour Eiffel.
Flotillas of boats make their way up and down the River Seine all through the year. The best starting place is the Port de Suffren quayside, close to the Eiffel Tower, with departures every 20 or 30 minutes, right up to 22h30, daily. Among the operators is Vedettes de Paris, which has the added attraction of music on its boats. Tel. 01 44 18 19 50. The Guinguette Maxim's boat, which is moored at the Port de Suffren, but on the opposite side of the river to the Eiffel Tower, offers a full scale orchestra. Tel. 01 44 18 96 96.

rue du Bac,
75007 Paris.
Métro: rue de Bac.
This elegant street in the heart of the 7th is one of the best places in Paris for art galleries, with some 20 in residence. The best known is the Galerie Maeght, at 42 rue du Bac, which is connected to the Maeght Foundation in St Paul de Vence in Provence, a high temple of contemporary art. The gallery in Paris also sells its own magnificently produced art books. If you get an invitation to a vernissage, or art show preview, you can enjoy plenty of free wine and artistic chatter.

rue de Bellechasse flood mark,
75007 Paris.
Métro: Solférino.
At the top of the rue de Bellchasse, just before you turn into the boulevard St-Germain, you'll see a flood plaque on the wall. This show how high the flood waters reached, on January 28, 1910, during the great flood of Paris, the worst there had been for 300 years. The floods at the end of that month that much of Paris between the right bank and Montmartre was flooded. On the left bank, in what was then the Gare d'Orsay (now the Musée d'Orsay), the water was so deep that locomotives and carriages in the station were completely covered by the water. All the bridges of the Seine were closed and the floods affected many suburban areas close to the river, such as St-Cloud. The mark in the rue de Bellechasse shows just how high the water rose in the 7th. Fortunately, that day, January 28, was the turning point and the waters then began to recede.

rue Cler,
75007 Paris.
Métro: Latour Maubert.
The Rue Cler, close to the Eiffel Tower, is a very traditional Parisian street that has been pedestrianised since 1984. It still has a wonderful selection of small, traditional shops, selling bread, cheese, chocolate, patisserie and wine, besides many of the other food delights needed for home entertainment. You'll find fresh fruit and vegetables brought in from the market at Rungis, as well as fresh fish. The wine shop classifies all its wines by regions. You'll also find a delightful shop called Tarte Julie, with a

very old fashioned shopfront that's quite a work of art, dating from the 1930s. There's also a creperie, with a great variety of savoury and dessert crepes. Other shops sell all kinds of deli and olive oil and you can buy gifts to take with you when going to dinner in someone's house or apartment and finally, an old style hardware shop. This narrow street has an enticing melange of shops, in the old neighbourhood style, so this is like stepping back into the Paris of 50 years ago.

Saxe Breteuil Market,
75007 Paris.
Métro: Ségur.
Right in the shadow of the Eiffel Tower, this lively and informal market is a delightful contrast to all the sedate, official looking parts of the 7th. It's open for business on Thursday and Saturday mornings and you'll find all kinds of delicacies, from Savoie cheeses to bread made from organic wheat and African dishes.

Solférino Bridge
Near Musée d'Orsay,
75007 Paris.
Métro: Solférino.
There's been a bridge over the Seine at this point, linking the quai Anatole France and the quay beside the Tuileries gardens since 1861, when Napoléon III inaugurated a three arch bridge that was open to traffic. It was demolished in 1960 and replaced in 1961 by a modest single span pedestrian only bridge, demolished in 1992. The present bridge is flamboyant in style, a masterpiece of contemporary design and when you're walking across, you'll enjoy the design of the bridge as much as the views up and down the Seine.

The American Library in Paris,
10 rue du Général Camou,
75007 Paris.
Tel: 01 53 59 12 60:
Opening hours, Tues-Sat, all year, 10h00-19h00, except Aug, Tues-Fri, 12h00-18h00, Sat, 10h00-14h00.

Métro: École Militaire.
Described as the largest English language lending library in mainland Europe, the American Library in Paris has impressive collections. It also organises many special events, including for children.

## 8th ARRONDISSEMENT

American Cathedral,
23 avenue George V,
75008 Paris.
Tel. 01 53 23 84 00.
Web: http: //www.us.net/amcathedral-paris/
Opening hours, daily, all year, 8h00-18h00.
Entrance tariff: free.
Métro: George V, Alma Marceau.
The American Cathedral was consecrated in 1886. Designed in the Gothic Revival style, it also has reproductions of well-known religious artifacts, such as the Black Madonna in Poland. The cloisters and garden are worth seeing. The church has an elaborate First World War memorial, commemorating Americans in France who fought, and died, on the Allied side. The cathedral has another claim to fame, too-its 80 metre high spire, which is illuminated and is reputed to be the tallest church spire in Paris.

Arc de Triomphe,
place Charles de Gaulle,
75008 Paris.
Web: http: //www. paris.org/Monuments/Arc/
Opening hours: Apr-Oct, 10h00-23h00 daily, Nov-Mar, 10h00-22h30 daily.
Entrance tariff: EUR7 (reduction)
Métro: Charles de Gaulle Étoile.
The Arc de Triomphe is one of the great monuments in Paris and it's worth going to the top for the views. It was commissioned in 1806 by Napoléon in honour of his military victories, but wasn't completed until 30 years later. In 1920, two years after the First World War had ended, the tomb of the unknown soldier was placed at its base; an eternal flame burns as a reminder of the lives lost in the two world wars. The traffic round the Arc de

Triomphe is helter-skelter to say the least; it seems to bring out the boy racer in many drivers, but fortunately, there's an underground passageway that takes you there in perfect safety. From the top, which is 50 metres above ground level, the views of Paris are excellent, including of the 12 avenues that radiate outwards from the Arc. Extensive renovations are under way, but they don't detract from visits.

Au Nain Bleu,
406-410 rue St-Honoré,
75008 Paris.
Tel: 01 42 60 39 01
Web: www.au-nain-bleu.com
Opening hours, Mon-Sat, all year, 10h00-18h30. Special hours in August and Suns in Dec.
Métro: Concorde, Madeleine.
Founded in 1836, An Nain Bleu is claimed to be both the oldest toy shop in the world and the greatest one in Paris. You can spend happy hours wandering round, with or without your children, exploring this Aladdin's cave, everything from dolls' houses and miniature racing cars to rocking horses, with all kinds of games in between. Children of all ages will find something close to heaven here!

Champs-Elysées,
75008 Paris.
Métro: Champs-Elysées, Franklin D. Roosevelt, George V, Étoile.
Running from the place de la Concorde to the Arc de Triomphe, this wide boulevard has long been seen as the epicentre of Parisian glitz. In recent years, it has become vulgarised and shabby, full of fast food outlets and airline offices, but restoration efforts seem to be paying off and improving the prospects. Some of the buildings are interesting, including No 68, which dates from 1913 and houses the perfume company of Guerlain. No 74 was once Claridge's Hotel, but it retains its glorious belle-époque facade. No 25 still shows all the signs of its original lavish mid-19th century design. You can also explore two kinds of history in the boulevard. At the Renault showrooms, nos 49 to 53, there's a comprehensive display of cars, motor bikes and vans dating back to the earliest days of the company, in the late 19th century. Admission is free. At Le Fouquet's bar and restaurant, where the

film industry's César awards are staged every year, you can peruse the many photographs in the bar of well-known personalities from the French film industry.

Église de Sainte Marie Madeleine,
place de la Madeleine,
75008 Paris.
Opening hours, Mon-Sat, all year, 7h30-19h00, Sun, all year, 9h00-13h00, 15h30-19h00.
Entrance tariff: free.
Métro: Madeleine.
The church, begun in 1764, is one of the best-known in Paris. Designed like a classical temple, it has a wide single nave, surrounded with Ionic columns. The only natural light in the interior comes from three enormous domes. It's a very popular church for society weddings-and funerals. Just outside the church, there's a daily flower market, while also immediately outside the church is an interesting public building, a loo with a difference. These Art Nouveau toilets are reached by a spiral staircase. Inside, the toilets are decorated with outpourings of brass, mirrors and polished wood, while each cubicle has floral frescoes and a stained glass window. No other public lavatories in Paris are decorated on such a grandiose and sumptuous scale!

Église de Saint Philippe du Roule,
154 rue du Faubourg Saint-Honoré,
75008 Paris.
Opening hours, daily, all year, 8h00-18h00.
Entrance tariff: free.
Métro: St Philippe du Roule.
The church, built by Jean-Francois Chalgrin between 1774 and 1784, was designed very much in the classical style, complete with the peristyle of four columns on the facade. The nave has no transept. Anyone familiar with the pro-Cathedral in Dublin will recognise an immediate similarity-the Catholic cathedral in Dublin was built as a virtual replica of St Philippe du Roule. The church in the Faubourg Saint-Honoré is near the Palais de l'Elysée, the official residence of the President of France, so you might see some very grandiose motorcades sweeping in and out.
Fauchon,

26-30 place de la Madeleine,
75008 Paris.
Tel: 01 47 42 90 10
Web: www.fauchon.com
Opening hours, Mon-Sat, all year, 9h30-19h00
Métro: Madeleine.
Fauchon is the most famous food store in Paris and it's a delight
to wander through the different levels of the shop, where you'll
find all kinds of food displayed at suitably exotic prices. The shop
stocks everything from fish and cheese to exotic delicatessen,
chocolates and confectionery. Its marron glaces and pates des
fruits are a true delight. It offers 30 varieties of foie gras and over
100 different spices. The bakery produces the most scrumptious
breads and patisserie, while the shop also sells 90 varieties of
biscuit. The wine section is among the most extensive in Paris
and among its offerings are a 1961 Bollinger champagne and its
oldest item of all, an 1886 cognac. Lots of different brands of
mineral water are stocked, too, from France, Germany, Italy,
Scotland, Switzerland and Wales. It's a wonderful if expensive
experience, shopping here. You can also enjoy Fauchon at more
than a dozen other locations in Paris; one of its latest openings
was a section in the Galeries Lafayette Haussman, but to
experience all the delights of Fauchon, you need to come to the
place de la Madeleine.


Gare St Lazare,
rue St-Lazare,
75008 Paris.
Métro: St-Lazare.
This is one of the mainline rail stations in Paris, with trains to and
from the north-west of France. But it's down in the Métro here that
you can enjoy a real traveller's treat, a trip on the new Météor line.
The Météor line is state of the art, with driverless trains-
everything's done automatically. The carriages are very high tech,
too, and so are the stations. In December, 2003, the extension of
the Météor line was opened, from Madeleine to St-Lazare. You
can take the new train as far as the Bibliothèque François
Mitterand; in due course, this high speed line will be extended.

Grand Palais
Palais de la Découverte (museum of scientific discovery),
Avenue Franklin D. Roosevelt,
75008 Paris.
Tel: 01  56 43 20 20.
Web: www.palais-decouverte.fr
Opening hours: daily, except Mons, 9h30-18h00. Suns and public holidays, 10h00-19h00. Closed: Jan 1, May 1, July 14, Aug 15 and Dec 25.
Entrance tariff: EUR5. 60 (reductions).
Métro: Champs-Elysées Clemenceau, Franklin D. Roosevelt.
Founded in 1937, this museum is dedicated to scientific discoveries of all kinds and you can wander through the galleries and get a better knowledge of many branches of science. You can also see experiments that demonstrate the great laws of science. The whole museum is devised in a unique way: visitors walk around and through touch screen and similar technology, work all the exhibits and demonstrations themselves. Frequent themed exhibitions are staged. The planetarium is a particularly interesting section of the museum. The museum is in the eastern wing of the Grand Palais; the western wing is devoted to the Galeries Nationales, which are used for large scale exhibitions on popular themes.

Hermes,
24 rue Faubourg Saint-Honoré,
75008 Paris.
Tel. 01 40 17 47 17.
Opening hours, Mon-Sat, all year, 9h00-18h00.
Métro: Madeleine.
The Hermes shop in one of the main fashion streets of Paris is the very last world in elegance. Hermes is noted for its incredibly beautiful and expensive scarves, but it also does all kinds of fashion for both men and women and it's worth strolling round the shop to have a look at the very innovative displays. Close by are some of the other big names in the fashion business, including Pierre Cardin, Louis Féraud and Versace. All the big fashion houses have their main shows twice a year, in January and July, and if you can manage to wangle a ticket, it's well worth going to see not only some really way out designs, but a wonderful array of models and an over-excited atmosphere that you could cut with a knife.

Maison de Proust,
102 boulevard Haussmann,
75008 Paris.
Tel: 01 44 90 40 00.
Opening hours, guided tours once a week, Thurs, 14h00-16h00.
Entrance tariff: free.
Métro: St-Augustin.
That marvellous writer, Marcel Proust (1871-1922), author of such dazzling works of historical recollection as A la Recherche du Temps Perdu, lived in this apartment. Most of his time was spent within easy reach of his bedroom, where he did his writing. Today, the apartment is in a building that is part of the Bank SNVB, but once a week, Proust's place can be visited by arr. The guided tours are very informative and the original atmosphere is easily conjured up. A replica of the room, together with its original furnishings, can be seen in the Musée Carnavalet (qv).


Marionettes des Champs-Elysées,
Jardin des Champs-Elysées,
Rond Pont,
75008 Paris.
Tel: 01 40 35 47 20.
Métro: Champs-Elysées-Clemenceau.
This puppet show is an old-time summer favourite, designed to appeal to children of all ages. The shows take place, Wed, Sat, Sun in summertime, at 15h00, 16h00 and 17h00.


Musée Cernuschi,
7, avenue Velasquez,
75008 Paris.
Tel. 01 45 63 50 75.
Métro: Monceau, Villiers.
This extensive and highly impressive collection of Chinese art, assembled in 1871 by a banker called Henri Cernuschi during a lengthy trip to Asia, has been undergoing major renovations.

Musée Jacquemart-André
158 boulevard Haussmann,
75008 Paris.
Tel: 01 42 89 04 91.
Web: www. musee-jacquemart-andre. com
Opening hours, daily, all year, 10h00-18h00.
Entrance tariff: EUR8.
Métro: Miromesnil, St Philippe du Roule.
This museum houses the collection of 19th century art lover Edouard André and his wife, Nélie Jacquemart, who was a renowned society portrait painter. They particularly worshipped Italian art and the museum has a truly stunning collection of 15th and 16th century Italian art, by such masters as Boticelli and Donatello. The ground floor rooms include the Grand Salon and the library, while on the stairway, three recently restored Tiepolo frescoes are on display. Upstairs, the area that was to have been Nélie's studio, before she gave up painting, has been turned into the Italian section, where all the medieval Italian works of art are on display. The house is splendid in its magnificent-even the ceiling in the tearoom is by Tiepolo. While the interior of the house and its art collection are quite incredible in their magnificence, the museum is also well worth seeing for its glimpses into an extraordinary 19th century artistic marriage and the life of the haute bourgeoisie of the time.


Musée Pierre Marly (spectacle museum),
380 rue Saint-Honoré,
75008 Paris.
Tel: 01 40 20 06 98
Opening hours, Tues-Sat, all year, 10h00-12h00, 14h00-18h00.
Entrance tariff: free.
Métro: Concorde.
If you want to see plenty of glasses and lorgnettes, 3, 000 pairs in fact, this is the place to come. The oldest spectacles on display were made in the 13th century and you can also see the glasses worn by many famous personalities, bygone and contemporary. The glasses worn by that great star of the theatre, Sarah Bernhardt, are on display, as are glasses worn by the singer Elton John.

Palais Garnier,
Boulevard des Capucines,
75008 Paris.
Tel: 01 40 01 25 14.
Web: www.bnf.fr
Opening hours, daily, all year, 11h00-16h30, except Sun and days of performance.
Entrance tariff: EUR6 (reductions).
Métro: Opéra.

Once known as the Opéra de Paris, this gloriously over-the-top building is now usually known as the Palais Garnier to distinguish it from the modern opera building at the Bastille. The Palais Garnier sits at the top of the avenue de l'Opéra, which was kept clear of trees so as not to spoil the view. The facade of the building has all kinds of sculptures and other visual special effects and the interior is no less imposing, complete with a ceiling in the auditorium depicting ballet and opera scenes, painted by Chagall. You can have a look round the interior, including the auditorium, on a daily basis, provided that no rehearsals are in progress. This is a great place, not just for opera, but for ballet, too, as is the other opera house, at the Bastille (qv). You can also visit the museum, which is packed with model sets, 19th century paintings and current exhibitions with operatic themes. The library has impressive material on operatic themes. Shop.


Petit Palais,
avenue Winston Churchill,
75008 Paris.
Tel. 01 42 65 12 73.
Web: http: //www. paris.org/Musees/PPalais
Opening hours: all year, Tues-Sun, 10h00-18h00.
Entrance tariff: free to permanent collection.
Métro: Champs-Élysées-Clemenceau.

Major renovations were done at the Petit Palais from 2001 onwards, but are now completed and it's now known as the Musée des Beaux Arts. The palace, together with its Grand Palais counterpart, was built for the 1900 great exposition. Now that it's fully operational again, it has reverted to its former role, a location for major exhibitions with a substantial collection of works of art, including paintings, sculptures and tapestries from the

Renaissance period right up to the 1920s. While much of the collection, even works by the likes of Manet and Renoir, can seem insipid, the museum does have some really oustanding pieces, such as Boudin's Gust of Wind at Le Havre. The collection also includes Art Nouveau jewellery, 18th century furniture and plaster models made for the Madeleine church in the early 19th century.

Pont d'Alma underpass,
75008 Paris.
Métro: Alma Marceau.
This was the underpass where Lady Di (Diana, Princess of Wales) was killed in a car crash on August 31, 1997. At the entrance to the underpass, near the Pont d'Alma bridge, you'll see an impromptu "shrine" covered in graffiti messages and flowers, recalling that great tragedy when she and her companion Dodi Al Fayed, were killed in a high speed car crash that remains surrounded in controversy and intrigue.


Russian Orthodox cathedral of Alexandre Nevsky,
12 rue Daru,
75008 Paris.
Opening hours, daily, all year, 8h00-18h00.
Entrance tariff: free.
Métro: Ternes.
Paris has long had a substantial community of exiles from Russia and since 1860, they've had their own cathedral in Paris, designed in neo-Byzantine style, which rivals St Basil's in Red Square, Moscow, for architectural magnificence. The cathedral in Paris is at the back of the Salle Pleyel, a main auditorium for classical musical concerts. If you approach the cathedral down the narrow rue Pierre le Grand, you'll get the best views of its gilded onion domes. Inside, the cathedral is decorated with frescoes, gilding and icons, but in Russian Orthodox tradition, it has no stained glass, no statues of Christ, the Virgin Mary or the saints, no pews and no organ. Daily services are held here. For refreshments, visit the Café à la ville de Petrogad, opposite, for a vodka; in 1921, when Picasso married Olga Khoklova, a member of Diaghilev's Ballets Russes, the celebrations started here. This Russian restaurant has welcomed many exiles over the years, from Diaghilev to Stravinsky.

Salle Pleyel,
252 rue du Faubourg St-Honoré,
75008 Paris.
Tel. 01 45 61 53 00.
Métro: Ternes.
The Salle Pleyel is one of the most distinguished classical music making venues in Paris, with regular performances by the Orchestre de Paris and many visiting international orchestras. Tickets for concerts range in price from around EUR10 up to about EUR60. It has been closed for major renovations, but is due to reopen in late 2006.

Scots Kirk,
rue Francois Ier,
75008 Paris.
Tel. 01 48 78 47 94.
Web: www.scotskirkparis.com
Opening hours, daily, all year, 9h00-18h00.
Entrance tariff: free.
Métro: Franklin D. Roosevelt.
The Scots Kirk, in the same arrondissement as the American Cathedral in the avenue George V, is a long established part of the expatriate way of life in Paris and it's a very welcoming place, too, for tourists. This is the only Church of Scotland church in France and the congregation dates back to 1858. The new church was dedicated in 2002.

Théatre des Champs-Elysées,
15 avenue du Montaigne,
75008 Paris.
Tel. 01 49 52 50 50.
Web: www. theatrechampselysee. fr
Performances Mon-Sat, weekly. Closed Sun and from mid-July to end Aug.
Entrance tariff: EUR10-EUR55.
Métro: Alma Marceau.
This is one of the great classical theatres of Paris, close to the place de l'Alma, across the river from the Eiffel Tower. Many famous 20th century performers, from Isadora Duncan to Nijinsky, have taken to the stage here and it's still an excellent place to see big name performances. It's also an excellent if you're a ballet enthusiast.

Louis Vuitton,
101 avenue des Champs-Elysees,
75008 Paris.
Tel. 01 53 57 24 00.
Opening hours, Mon-Sat, all year, 9h00-18h00.
Métro: George V.
The Vuitton shop is well worth walking around for its vast array of luggage, as well as clothes, shoes and accessories for men and women. It's a wonderful complement to the Vuitton museum in Asnières (qv).

## 9th ARRONDISSEMENT

Galeries Lafayette,
40 boulevard Haussmann,
75009 Paris.
Tel. 01 42 82 34 56.
Web: www.galerieslafayette.com
Opening hours, Mon-Sat, all year, 9h30-19h30, Thurs until 21h00.
Métro: Chaussée d'Antin.
This is one of the largest and most extravagant department stores in Paris and in recent years, it has been much revamped. There's plenty of fashion and regular fashion shows are staged every week (details from 01 42 82 30 25), while the store also has the second biggest wine stock in Paris. Restaurant.

Hotel Drouot,
9 rue Drouot,
75009 Paris.
Tel: 01 48 00 20 20.
Web: www.loeildesencheres.com/english/indexe.htm
(this website lists all the Drouot auctions and other major antiques auctions in Paris).
Opening hours, Mon-Sat, all year, 10h00-18h00.
Métro: Richelieu, Drouot.
If you fancy going to an auction, then there's no better place than the Hotel Drouot, where all periods of art, as well as furniture and even fine wines are sold off in the plethora of small sales rooms. A prodigious number of sales are held on a weekly basis, so many in fact that they are all listed in the weekly Gazette de

L'Hotel Drouot, which is sold on Paris newstands. The more upmarket sales take place at Drouot-Montaigne, 15 avenue Montaigne in the 8th (tel. 01 48 00 20 80) and sales are also held at Drouot Nord, 64 rue Doudeauville in the 18th (tel. 01 48 00 20 90).

Le Limonaire,
18 cité Bergère,
75009 Paris.
Tel. 01 45 23 33 33
Web: www. limonaire. free. fr
Opening hours, Tues-Sun, all year, 18h00-1h00.
Métro: Grands Boulevards.
This is a wine bistro with a difference, down at the end of an atmospheric passageway. Lots of traditional music is performed here, including accordion music and they also show silent films, complete with piano accompaniment.

L'Olympia,
28 boulevard des Capucines,
75009 Paris.
Tel. 01 55 27 10 00.
Web: www. olympiahall. com
Métro: Opéra.
Many great entertainers have performed here, from Sinatra to the Beatles and from France, the really big names, including Johnny Hallyday and Edith Piaf. It's still a very popular venue and it's worth checking who's performing.

Max Linder Panorama cinema,
24 boulevard Poissoniere
75009 Paris.
Tel. 08 36 68 50 52.
Opening hours, daily, 14h00-23h00 (and later).
Métro: Grands Boulevards.
This is the place for serious cinema going. The Art Déco cinema is real state of the art, with black seats and walls to prevent any light reflection and a vast 18 metre wide screen. It often has all night showings and screenings of rare vintage films.

Musée de la Franc-Maçonnerie,
16 rue de Cadet,
75009 Paris.
Tel. 01 45 23 20 92.
Opening hours, Tues-Sat, all year, 14h00-18h00. Closed Mon, Sun, some public holidays, July, Aug.
Entrance tariff: EUR2 (reductions).
Métro: Cadet.
This intriguing little museum tells the story of freemasonry in Paris and France, from the Middle Ages right up to the present day. Biographical details on well-known French Masons are included, such as General Lafayette. The museum, which also has a bookshop on the subject, is at the back of the Grand Orient de France, the French Masonic Great Lodge.


Musée Grevin,
10 boulevard Montmartre,
75009 Paris.
Tel. 01 47 70 85 05.
Web: www.grevin.com
Opening hours, Mon-Fri, all year, 10h00-17h30, Sat, Sun and public holidays, all
year, 10h00-18h00.
Entrance tariff: EUR16 (reductions).
Métro: Grands Boulevards.
This waxworks museum is very venerable, dating back to 1882. It has close to 300 life-size models of some of the best-known people in the world, right up to Elton John and Madonna. You can be photographed beside them. In addition, the museum tells the history of France through the wax figures of 50 famous personalities from different epochs of French history. In the theatre at the museum, you can see the story of Paris told, from the 1900 Exposition Universelle onwards, while in the Palais de Mirages, new technologies of imagery and lighting plunge spectators into a fantastic universe, a metamorphosis between illusion and reality.

Musée du Parfum-Fragonard,
9 rue Scribe,
75009 Paris.
Tel. 01 47 42 04 56.
Web: www.fragonard.com
Opening hours, daily, all year, 9h00, 18h00. Nov-Mar, closed Sun.
Closed public holidays.
Entrance tariff: free.
Métro: Opéra.
In a fine 19th century mansion close to the original Paris Opera, this museum depicts the history of 5, 000 years of perfume making. It includes many details of the ingredients that go into perfume making and the methods of production, including at the Fragonard factory in Grasse near Nice in Provence.

Paris Story,
11 bis rue Scribe,
75009 Paris.
Tel: 01 42 66 62 06.
Web: www.paris-story.com
Opening hours, Apr-Oct, daily, 9h00-20h00. Nov-Mar, daily, 9h00-20h00.
Entrance tariff: EUR: 8 (reductions).
Métro: Opéra.
This multimedia show is brief, 45 minutes, but it gives a good insight into the history of Paris, from its Roman origins as Lutetia, 2000 years ago, right up to the present day. The cinema-based show is a spectacular presentation, with music and sound effects to match, and it gives a fascinating and lightening speed zip through the history of Paris the city and its famous people.

Pigalle,
75009 Paris.
Métro: Pigalle.
This is the sleaziest part of Paris, with plenty of live sex entertainment on offer along the boulevard de Clichy and surrounding streets. Apart from the Rue St Denis, which starts in the Ist arrondissement (qv), no other part of Paris has such a plethora of these sex shows. However, in Pigalle, as elsewhere, street walkers are not so much in evidence these days since the government clamp-down on prostitution.

Printemps,
64 boulevard Haussmann,
75009 Paris.
Tel. 01 42 82 50 00.
Web: www.printemps.com
Opening hours, Mon-Sat, all year, 9h30-19h00 (22h00 on Thurs).
Métro: Havre-Caumartin.
Just along the boulevard Haussmann from the Galeries Lafayette is this other enormous department store, with six floors of exquisite fashions for men and women. The store is also excellent for home decorations, furnishings and kitchen utensils. If you take the lift to the nine floor, you can relax in the terrace restaurant, beneath its striking Art Nouveau cupola.

## 10th ARRONDISSEMENT

Canal Saint-Martin,
75010 Paris.
Métro: Boncourt, République
The canal starts at the River Seine, at Pont Morland, and goes underground before emerging overground close to the place de la République. Even though the area beside the canal has become very gentrified, it's still an interesting part of Paris, with excellent walks along the canal bank. The most attractive section of the canal is just south of the Bastille, in the 4th, with cobbled quays and plenty of greenery. It's this area where the most refurbishment and redevelopment has been done in recent years.
  The most renowned building in the northern section, which runs from near the place de la République up as far as La Villette and the Cité de Science, is the Hôtel du Nord. The 1938 Marcel Carné film of the same name, one of the most famous French films of all time, was filmed in this immediate area, with the hotel used extensively. The canal lock and the bridge over the canal were re-created in the studio, but the hotel itself was for real and is today an historic monument.
  You can also take a daily boat trip along the canal, from the Bastille to La Villette, a journey that takes three hours. Details from Canauxrama, tel. 01 42 39 15 00 and www. canauxrama. com

Fondation Icar,
159 quai de Valmy,
75010 Paris.
Tel. 01 53 26 36 61.
Web: www.icarfondation.org
Opening hours, Wed-Sun, all year, except Aug, Sept, sone public holidays, 13h00-19h00.
Entrance tariff: free
Métro: Chateau Landon, Colonel Fabien.
This gallery was once a factory, beside the Canal St-Martin, and it has been converted into a striking looking gallery that's American-funded. Its infrequent exhibitions of American conceptual art, as well as its music performances and lectures, are always stimulating.

Passage Brady,
46 rue du Faubourg St-Denis-43 Faubourg St-Martin,
75010 Paris.
Métro: Chateau d'Eau, Strasbourg St-Denis
This small passageway is one of the seedier parts of north Paris, but it's interesting because of its strong Indian shop connections. It's best to visit during daytime.

Pinacothèque de Paris,
30 bis rue de Paradis,
75010 Paris.
Tel. 01 53 34 06 70.
Web: http: www.pinacotheque.com
Opening hours, daily, all year, including public holidays, 10h00-19h00, Mon, Fri, until 22h30.
Entrance tariff: EUR12 (reductions).
Métro: Bonne Nouvelle.
Standing where the Musee Baccarat was once housed, before it moved to the 16th in 2003, the Pinacotheque is a new and expansive art gallery that aims to present large scale exhibitions with a difference. One recent exhibition was of the collection of Jacqueline Picasso.

# 11th ARRONDISSEMENT

Bibliothèque Meden,
Maison de la Culture Yiddish,
18 passage Saint-Pierre-Amelot,
75011 Paris.
Tel. 01 47 00 14 00
Web: www.yiddishweb.com
Opening hours, 10h00-22h00 daily, except Sat.
Entrance tariff: EUR5 upwards for individual events.
Métro: St Sébastien Froissart.
Yiddish is an old language used by Jews in eastern and central Europe; many of them came to France. The Bibliothèque works to conserve the Yiddish patrimony, including its culture and language. The centre has a well-archived Mediatheque, as well as a bookshop and cafes. Courses are run in cookery and many other aspects of Yiddish culture and frequent musical and literary performances are staged.

Bistro with a vineyard,
42 rue Leon Frot,
75011 Paris.
Tel. 01 43 70 59 27
Métro: Charonne
The Mélac bistro is unique in Paris for having its very own vineyard. The vines are planted in the cellar and grow up through the floor into the bistro itself; in season, the bistro is full of real grapes, producing about 20 bottles of wine a year. The bistro, which has been in the Mélac family for over 60 years, is run by Jacques Mélan, who with his enormous moustache, bears a passing resemblance to Cyrano de Bergerac. Just across the street, at Number 43, Pierre Charrial, who transcribes music for mechanical organs, has his back garden full of vines. You can visit his workshop and have a look at his vines.

Cirque d'Hiver (Winter Circus),
110 rue Amelot,
75011 Paris.
Tel: 01 47 00 12 25
Web: www.cirquedhiver.com
Métro: Filles du Calvaire

This truly magnificent indoor building for circus performances was designed in the style of Napoléon III; it still has its original floor put in for circus performances and the ancient stables, as well as its imperial restaurant. The decor of the hall alone is worth seeing, but in addition, real extravaganza performances are staged twice a year, putting on animal shows, cabaret and international performance artistes in a style so beloved in France. These shows are as unmissable as the venue itself.

Musée du Fumeur,
7 rue Pache,
75011 Paris.
Tel. 01 46 59 05 51
Web: www. museedufumeur.net
Opening hours, Tues-Sat, all year, 10h30-19h30, Sun, all year, 12h30-19h30.
Entrance tariff: free
Métro: Voltaire
At a time when smoking has become so unfashionable, illegal even in many places, this museum is an unashamed exposition of smoking, which still largely retains its popularity in France, despite legislative attempts to discourage people from lighting up. It has examples of tobacco leaves and many other plants from all over the world, all used for smoking and it has many objects used for smoking, such as 18th century clay pipes. Opium smoking also counts and the museum has the old pipes once used by Chinese dignitaries to smoke opium.

Musée de Piaf,
5 rue Crespin du Gast,
75011 Paris.
Tel: 01 43 55 52 72
Web: www. pantheon.cis.yale.edu
Opening hours, Mon-thurs, all year, 13h00-18h00, by arr.
Entrance tariff: free
Métro: Ménilmontant
This small museum in an apartment is dedicated to the memory of Edith Piaf (1915-1963), the diminutive cabaret artiste and music hall singer, often known as the "sparrow". The museum can only be seen by prior arrangement, but it has lots of Piaf memorabilia, including photographs and posters as well as some of her personal possessions.

Richard-Lenoir Market,
rue Richard-Lenoir,
75011 Paris.
Métro: Bastille.
This Sunday morning market, close to the Bastille, is very popular for promenading before lunch. You'll find plenty to entertain you, from a good selection of street entertainers to political activists. On the food front, you'll find a truly eclectic mixture, everything from ready-to-cook snails to hand-made cheeses and African snacks. This market area is very lively on Sunday mornings, but this part of the 11th. , stretching into the 3rd. , is also very lively on Saturday nights. The 11th is also one of the few neighbourhoods in Paris, which tend to be working class areas, where you'll find food shops and small supermarkets open until late at night. In most parts of the more bourgeois and genteel 7th and 16th arrondissements, you'll be hard pressed to find any shops open after 18h00.

Rue de Lappe,
75011 Paris.
Métro: Bastille.
A traditional Parisian music hall, the Balajo, survives here, a relict of the 1930s and gai Paris, when Edith Piaf, Jean Gabin and Rita Hayworth performed here. These days, the street also has lots of bars, so that at the weekends, it's one of the most popular and busiest places in Paris.

## 12th ARRONDISSEMENT

Chai de Bercy,
41 rue Paul Belmondo,
75012 Paris.
Opening hours, daily, all year, 10h00-17h00 (18h00 in summer).
Entrance tariff: free.
Métro: Cour Saint-Emilion.
If you're into wine making, you'll be interested in one of the newer and less known vineyards of Paris, here in the 12th, where the vines cover all of 600 square metres. They were planted in 1996 and produce about 250 litres of wine a year.

Cimitière Picpus,
35 rue de Picpus,
17012 Paris.
Tel. 01 43 44 18 54.
Opening hours, Tues-Sun, all year, 14h00-18h00.
Entrance tariff: free.
Métro: Nation.
This rather small and often overlooked cemetery in the 12th is worth seeing for its Revolutionary connections. During the worst time of the French Revolution, just over 1, 300 of the people who were guillotined in the place de la Nation, between June 14 and July 27, 1794, were buried here, in the Cimitiere Picpus. Also buried here is the French naval officer Lafayette, who played such a prominent part in the American Revolution.

Gare de Lyon,
20 boulevard Diderot,
75012 Paris.
Métro: Gare de Lyon.
The Gare de Lyon, built between 1895 and 1902, is a very busy mainline station serving the south and south-east of France with TGV trains; international departures for Switzerland, Italy and Greece also leave from here. At ground floor level in the station, you can observe a series of nudes painted in the early 20th century, allegorical representations of the march of technology-electricity, mechanics, navigation and steam. But the real attraction for visitors to the station, apart from catching their train, is Le Train Bleu restaurant, an extraordinary place approached up a flight of stairs from the main station concourse. The Belle Époque interior is as it was when the restaurant opened in 1901, with 40 paintings on walls and ceilings illustrating the cities served by what was then the PLM railway company. Lighting, too, is extravagant and the restaurant even has a golden cockerel presiding over proceedings. The banquette type seats and free standing chairs at the tables may not be the most comfortable, but the food is good (and expensive), with the wine list likewise. Unbelievably, the restaurant was destined for demolition by SNCF at the beginning of the 1970s, in what would have been an unprecedented act of cultural vandalism in the city, but after an appropriate Parisian uproar, the Train Bleu restaurant was saved for posterity.

Marché d'Aligre,
rue d'Aligre,
75012 Paris.
Métro: Gare de Lyon.
This outdoor market is open every morning of the week, except Mondays. It's close to the big St Antoine hospital. Not only is it one of the cheapest markets in Paris, but it's one of the most voluble, so even if you don't buy any of the fruit, vegetables, meat and cut-price clothes that it's famous for, you can enjoy the sheer spirit of the occasion.


Musée des Arts Africains et Océaniens,
293 avenue Daumesnil,
75012 Paris.
Tel: 01 43 46 51 61.
Opening hours, Mon, Wed-Fri, all year, 10h00-17h30.
Sat, Sun, until 18h00.
Entrance tariff: EUR5 (reductions).
Métro: Porte Dorée.
This museum, on the edge of the Bois de Vincennes in eastern Paris, is one of the least visited in the city, but it's arguably one of the most interesting. It all dates back to the great colonial exposition in Paris in 1931 and it includes an Art Deco bas relief glorifying France's colonial past, as well as two display rooms done out in the Art Deco style. Many of the objects are interesting, from masks to statues and utensils, but there's a strong sense of colonial collectors at work. Few of the African artifacts are dated. Down in the basement, there's what's called, with some hyperbole, an aquarium, but in reality, it's a small pond with a few alligators surrounded by tanks of fish. However, time is nearly up for this particular museum in its present location; it's due to be relocated to the brand new museum of art and civilisation being built at quai Branly, close to the Eiffel Tower. All the various ethographic collections in Paris are due to be transferred to this new location and will also include some collections from the Musée de l'Homme in the 16th (qv). The museum is due to open in 2006.

Musée du Cinéma,
51 rue de Bercy,
75012 Paris.
Tel: 01 56 26 01 01.
Web: www.cinemathequefrancaise.com
Métro: Bercy.
The former cinema museum is due to be reformed in spectacular fashion in the former American Center in the rue de Bercy, with an opening date scheduled for 2006. The museum had been founded in 1972 and was based in the 16th; it closed in 1997. Even though the new cinema museum itself is way off completion, the cinématheque is still organising screenings, at the Salle du Palais Chaillot in the 16th and at the Salles des Grands Boulevards in the 10th. Programme details are available from 01 56 26 01 01.

Musée des Art Forains,
53 avenue des Terroirs,
75012 Paris.
Tel: 01 43 40 16 22.
Opening hours, daily, all year, by arr, groups only.
Entrance tariff: EUR11. 80 per person.
Métro: Cour St-Emilion.
This museum, the collection of Jean-Paul Pavand, celebrates the fairground way of life in France and Europe, with reconstructions of traditional fairgrounds. Its displays include 14 merry-go-rounds, complete with bobbing horses, and 16 fairground stalls. The collection covers the period from 1850 to the present day and is described as one of the largest collections of fairground material in the world.

Opéra Bastille,
120 rue de Lyon,
75012 Paris.
Tel: 01 44 61 59 63.
Web: www. opera-de-paris. fr
Métro: Bastille.
The new opera, opened in 1989, generated much controversy during its design competition and building and continues to do so to this day. However, in its favour, it is a very modern theatre with all the technical facilities that present day technology can bring and the standard of its orchestra is first class. The programmes

are a mix of the traditional and the obscure. You can have a look round the foyer and the auditorium as well, if you're going to a performance, but you can't see backstage and it's too new to have a museum, unlike the Palais Garnier. However, like the Palais Garnier, it does also stage regular ballet performances in addition to opera.

Palais Omnisports de Paris-Bercy,
8 boulevard de Bercy,
75012 Paris.
Tel: 08 03 03 00 31.
Web: www. bercy. fr
Métro: Bercy.
The giant arena at Bercy is a well-known venue for all kinds of events, including entertainment. However, if you want more comfort and better acoustics, go to the more expensive upper levels.

Viaduc des Arts (Arts Viaduct),
9-129 avenue Daumesnil,
75012 Paris.
Web: http: //www.antiquites.com/viaduc/liste.htm
Opening hours: daily, 10hr-18hrs.
Métro: Gare de Lyon, Bastille.
In the heart of the 12th arrondissement, close to the Gare de Lyon and the Bastille, the old viaduct once carried the railway line that linked the Bastille district with the Bois de Vincennes in the east of Paris. The trains have long gone, but these days, the spaces underneath the viaduct have been turned into workshops and showrooms for around 60 artisans of art and creative artists. You'll find all kinds of craft work and artistic endeavours carried on here, including antique lace restoration; cabinet making; contemporary furniture making; hand painting of china; trompe l'oeil paintings and tapestry renovation. The 12th is one of the liveliest arrondissements of Paris, enhanced by all the artistic and craft work done underneath the old viaduct. What was the old railway track along the top of the viaduct has been transformed into a pedestrian walkway planted with roses and shrubs. Walking along here gives you excellent views of the neighbourhood.

# 13th ARRONDISSEMENT

Bibliothèque Nationale de France,
quai François-Mauriac,
75013 Paris.
Tel: 01 53 79 53 79.
Web: www.bnf.fr
Métro: Bibliothèque, Quai de la Gare.
Opening hours: Tues-Sat, all year, 10h00-20h00, Sun, all year, 12h00-19h00. Closed for two weeks in Aug and two weeks in Sept/Oct.
This national library was the last of the great projects that were the brainchild of former President François Mitterand; others include the glass Pyramid at the Louvre. The library was also the most expensive of these projects and its design seems curiously dated and impractical. The more than 10 million books are stored in four glass towers, but when the library was built, the architect, Dominique Perrault, forgot to add sunblinds to protect the books. The vast reading room, down in the basement, can accommodate 3, 000 readers and anyone can have access to the vast collection of books, newspapers and magazines. Regular concerts and exhibitions are staged here and you can also enjoy the garden in the centre of the library, between the four L-shaped towers. The trees for this garden were brought at great expense from Fontainebleau. In many ways, the library was considered a folie de grandeur when it opened, but now that its many teething problems have been sorted out, it's an interesting modernistic venue for bibliophiles. The opening of the library should also help the 13th in its ambition to become the new Left Bank area of Paris, but there's way to go, because much of the district is made up of railway lines, from the Gare d'Austerlitz; very run-down streets and extensive building sites. The planned extension of the new high tech Météor line on the Metro system beyond the new library, will also help. But already, the shiny new galleries of contemporary art in the rue Louise Weiss are assisting this process of reinvention.

Manufacture des Gobelins (Gobelins carpet and rug factory),
42 avenue des Golelins,
75013 Paris.
Tel: 01 44 54 19 33.
Opening hours: Tues, Wed, Thurs, guided tours at 14h15 and 14h45
Entrance tariff: EUR8 (reductions).
Métro: Gobelins.
This grandiose factory was created in 1664, as ornate as any manufacturing place in France, to make tapestries, carpets and rugs in a style that became renowned worldwide for design and elegance. You can see how they continue to be made, using age old methods, on the highly polished surfaces. Visitors can also take in the chapel and the Beauvais tapestry workshops.


rue Nationale,
75013 Paris.
Métro: Porte d'Ivry.
Much of the old slum quarters around the rue Nationale was replaced by tower blocks in the 1950s and 1960s, all distinctly unappealing architecturally. However brutish these new landscapes appear, a couple of quartiers in this particular part of Paris have remained untouched and retain their old, shabby charm. The Buttes-aux-Cailles quartier, with its small streets and artists' studios, is still attractive. The street itself, the rue Buttes-aux-Cailles, was given new cobblestones and lamp-posts a few years ago, which brighten the place up. The street has plenty of bars and restaurants that stay open until well into the night, so the after dark ambiance is excellent. The area between the rue de Tolbiac, the avenue de Choisy and the boulevard Masséna, is a quartier called Chinatown, with plenty of Cambodian, Chinese, Thai, Vietnamese and other Asian restaurants and shops to match.

## 14th ARRONDISSEMENT

Cimitière du Montparnasse,
3 boulevard Edgar-Quinet,
75014 Paris.
Tel. 01 44 10 86 50
Opening hours, daily, all year, 8h00-18h00.
Entrance tariff: free.
Métro: Edgar-Quinet, Raspail.
Many of the most prominent names in 20th century artistic and cultural life in Paris are buried here, including Jean-Paul Sartre (1905-1980) and Simone de Beauvoir (1908-1986). They share a tomb. Samuel Beckett (1906-1989) is buried next to his wife Suzanne. Marguerite Duras (1914-1996) is here. Well-known composers, such as César Franck (1822-1890) and Saint-Saens (1835-1921), are here. So too is Captain Alfred Dreyfus (1859-1935), subject of much national and international scandal around the end of the 19th century and eventually cleared. André Citroen (1879-1935), the car man, is here. Among the show business people buried here are Jean Seberg (1938-1979), the American actor and Serge Gainsbourg (qv), that icon of the 1960s. Jacques Demy (1931-1990), who directed the film Les Parapluies de Cherbourg, is buried here. Among the most recent celebrities to be buried here is Jean-Pierre Rampal (1922-2000), one of the greatest flautists of his generation. The plan of the cemetery is easy to follow. You can also see a 17th century windmill, the sole survivor of 30 in this part of Paris. When the cemetery was built in 1824, the windmill was enclosed within its walls. The windmill is empty but can only be seen from the outside.

Cité Universitaire,
boulevard Jourdan,
75014 Paris.
Web: www.ciup.fr
Train: RER B4 line to Cité Universitaire.
To give the place its full title, it's the Cité Internationale Universitaire de Paris, which was designed and built in the 1930s. A total of 30 pavilions were built for the students to live in and each is supposed to represent the characteristics of the country in question. The Cambodia pavilion, for instance, has some strange looking statues at its entrance. The Dutch pavilion does look very

stolid and Dutch, while Le Corbusier, the great Swiss architect, designed the Swiss pavilion, which isn't particularly Swiss-looking but is certainly modernist in its design. The overall effect of the "village" is very cosmopolitan, which is enhanced by the fact that several thousand students from over 100 different countries live here while they're studying in Paris.

Fondation Henri Cartier Bresson,
2 Impasse Lebouis,
75014 Paris.
Tel. 01 56 80 27 00.
Web: www.henricartierbresson.org
Opening hours, Tues-Fri, all year, 13h00-18h30. Sat, all year, 11h00-18h45.
Entrance tariff: EUR4 (reductions).
Métro: Gaité.
Henri Cartier Bresson, one of the world's greatest photographs, whose work spans much of the 20th century, is recalled at this centre, which has an impressive collection of his photographic archives. Many of the photographs are displayed in frequent exhibitions here.

Les Catacombes,
1 place Denfert Rochereau,
75014 Paris.
Web: http: //www. catacombes. free. fr/
(this website has details of the Catacombes and all the other quarries in Paris and its suburbs).
Opening hours: Tues, all year, 11h00-16h00, Wed-Sun, all year, 9h00-16h00. Closed public holidays.
Entrance tariff: EUR5 (reduction).
Métro: Denfert Rochereau.
These subterranean passages go on for many kilometres. They were first dug in Roman times, nearly 2, 000 years ago, but weren't expanded until the late 18th century, when the traditional cemeteries in Paris had reached bursting point. Many corpses were transferred to the catacombs and it's said that the remains of six million people down here include many who were killed during the period of Revolutionary Terror at the very end of the 18th century. It's quite intriguing and not too terrifying to wander along some of the ancient passageways and see lots of bones and tablets with poetic inscriptions.

Marché aux Puces de Vanves,
avenue Georges Lafenestre and avenue Marc-Sangrier,
75014 Paris.
Métro: Porte de Vanves.
Opening hours, Sat, Sun, all year, 7h30-19h00.
The smallest flea market in Paris, this is also considered the most friendly. If you're looking for items like old dolls, costume jewellery, photographs or magazines, this is just the place to browse.

Musée Lénine (Lenin Museum),
4 rue Marie-Rose,
75014 Paris.
Tel: 01 42 79 99 58.
Opening hours: Mon-Fri, all year, 9h30-17h00 by appointment only.
Entrance tariff: free.
Métro: Alésia.
This is one of the smallest museums in Paris, the tiny apartment where Lenin, the Russian revolutionary leader, his wife Kroupskaia and her mother, lived and Lenin worked on his revolutionary theories, from July 1909 until June, 1912. The apartment has been reconstructed as it was in Lenin's time and the work is authentic.

Observatoire de Paris,
61 avenue de l'Observatoire,
75014 Paris.
Tel. 01 40 51 23 01.
Web: http: //www. obspm.fr
Opening hours, first Sat every month, from 14h30, group visits, Tues, Wed, 14h00.
Entrance tariff: EUR4. 5
Metro: Denfert Rochereau, Port Royal.
The observatory was built in 1667 and from then, until 1884, all French made maps had the zero meridian running through this complex in south Paris. In 1884, the zero longitude was changed to run through a small village in Normandy, which is due south of Greenwich near London. In the observatory itself, you can inspect the collection of speaking clocks, including the first one created, in 1933. On the first floor, the gallery has a superb collection of

scientific instruments used by the Observatory over the years, while on the second floor, in the Cassini room, you can see the north-south meridian marked out. The original meridian line is also marked by a plaque in the pavement in the boulevard Arago, just beyond the gardens. The observatory has another site at Meudon, in the Ile de France, which has a large assembly of working telescopes (tel. 01 45 07 76 27) and a radioastronomy section at Nançay (tel. 01 40 51 23 01 for details).

Parc Montsouris,
boulevard Jourdan,
75014 Paris.
Train: RER B4 line to Cité Universitaire.
This is one of the most enticing parks in Paris, with lawns that slope down to the large artificial lake. The park is well wooded and it's also well planted with flowers, so it's very attractive for a pleasant stroll. One noted historical person who used to frequent the park was Lenin, when he lived nearby during his time in Paris. It has some curious oddities, too, including a meteorological office, a kiosk run by the French Astronomy Association, down by the south-west entrance, and near the boulevard Jourdan, a marker for the old meridian line. After all, the Paris Observatory is close by.

rue de l'Alésia,
75014 Paris.
Métro: Alésia, Plaisance.
The 14th arrondissement is a lively suburb in southern Paris, noted still for its artistic communities. The rue de l'Alésia is the main thoroughfare, crossing from east to west, has a host of interesting shops, particularly ones selling couturier labels at discounted prices. A small food market is held every Thursday and Sunday between the Plaisance Metro station and the rue Didot. Some of the streets in this district are ideal for a casual stroll. The Cité Bauer goes from the rue Boyer-Barret to the rue Didot and it has many delightful houses and gardens. The rue des Thermopyles still has lots of quaint courtyards and at the corner of the rue du Moulin Vert and the rue Hippolyte-Maindron, you can still see what was the house where Giacometti, the artist, once lived. Another artist, this time Georges Brassens, the song writer, is commemorated by a bronze relief on the tiny house where he

once lived and worked. It's at the end of the tiny Impasse Floriment, behind a filling station on the rue de l'Alésia.

If you head south from this street, in the direction of the Porte de Vanves and the Boulevard Brune, which has lots of public authority housing totally lacking in any kind of design style, you'll come to another great market area. On Saturdays and Sundays, one of the most expansive and least expensive of all the flea markets in Paris is held along the avenue Marc-Sangnier and the avenue Georges-Lafenestre, stretching as far as the place de la Porte-de-Vanves.

## 15th ARRONDISSEMENT

Allées des Cygnes,
75015 Paris.
Métro: Avenue du Président Kennedy/Maison de Radio-France.
This elongated island in the River Seine is downstream from the Eiffel Tower, opposite the round studios of Radio France in the 16th. It's best approached from either the direction of the Radio France building, across the Pont de Grenelle. Go down steps to the island and walk along the single, narrow, tree lined road that runs the length of the island. You'll get good views of the river traffic and of the 15th and 16th arrondissements on either side of the river.

Jardin de l'Atlantique,
75015 Paris.
Opening hours: dawn to dusk, daily, all year.
Museum of the Second World War,
Tel: 01 40 64 39 44.
Web: www. paris-france.org/musees/Memorial/accueil
Opening hours, Tues-Sun, 10h00-18h00. Closed Mon, public holidays.
Entrance tariff: EUR4 (reductions).
Métro: Montparnasse-Bienvenue, Gaité.
The entrance to this new garden, opened in 1995, is hard to find. You can get into it either from the Gare de Montparnasse itself or from the nearby place des Cinq-Martyrs-du-Lycée-Buffon. The whole garden is suspended over the tracks of the railway station; it's a very restful place, set in the midst of many office and

apartment blocks. Despite its location, it's very pleasant, with lots of paths and plantings, including bamboo trees. Through small gaps, you can see the trains down below. The garden also has a museum dedicated to the Second World War, the role of the Résistance and the liberation of Paris in 1944. The museum commemorates Maréchal Leclerc, the commander of the Free French Forces and the left wing Resistance hero, Jean Moulin. The museum has lots of documentary material, as well as film archives and a panoramic slide show.

Le Cordon Bleu,
8 rue Léon Delhomme,
75015 Paris.
Tel. 01 53 68 22 50.
Web: www.cordonbleu.edu
Métro: Vaugirard.
The term "Cordon Bleu" has been synonymous with culinary excellence since the 16th century; King Henry III of France created the knightly Order of the Holy Spirit (l'Ordre du Saint Esprit). The feasts that went with their ceremonies become the stuff of legend and the members of the Order became known as Cordon Bleu because of the broad blue ribbon they wore. Le Cordon Bleu has been recognised as the world leader in the superior instruction of French cuisine and pastry since it was created in Paris in 1895. One of the many courses you can do are the gourmet sessions highlighting different French culinary themes, from breadbaking to market tours; these sessions last from one day to one month.

Maison de la Culture Japon,
101 bis, quai Branly,
75015 Paris.
Tel. 01 44 37 95 01.
Web: www.mcjp.asso.fr
Opening hours, Tues-Sat, all year, 12h00-19h00 (Thurs, 20h00).
Closed Sun, Mon, Dec 25, Jan 3.
Entrance tariff: EUR5 (reductions).
Métro: Champs-de-Mars Tour Eiffel.
The Japanese cultural institute has frequent exhibitions of contemporary and 20th century art, including paintings and sculptures. It also organises lectures and seminaires, while in the

special hall provided, you can take part in the Japanese tea ceremony.

Marché aux livres,
rue Brancion,
75015 Paris.
Opening hours, Sat, Sun, all year, 9h00-18h00.
Métro: Porte de Vanves.
This book market is organised throughout every weekend, in what used to be the sheds of an old horse market. It takes place next to the Parc Georges Brassens. Book lovers may well find a venerable volume, antiquarian specimens, bargain books and books sold by weight, they are all here. You'll also find plenty of more general bargains at the nearby Marché aux Puces, at the junction of the rue Marc-Saugnier and avenue Georges Lafenestre, which is also open on Saturdays and Sundays.

Musée Bourdelle,
rue Antoine Bourdelle,
75015 Paris.
Tel: 01 49 54 73 73.
Opening hours: Tues-Sun, all year, 10h00-17h40.
Entrance tariff: EUR3. 35
Métro: Montparnasse-Bienvenue.
Just opposite the Montparnasse Museum, you can inspect another place of artistic pilgrimage. Antoine Bourdelle was a distinguished early 20th century sculptor, much influenced by ancient Greece. You can see a selection of his sculptures in the garden, while his studio has been kept much as it was in his day, complete with casts and the other tools of his trade.

Musée du Montparnasse,
21 avenue du Maine,
75015 Paris.
Tel: 01 42 22 91 96.
Opening hours: Wed-Sun, all year, 13h00-19h00.
Entrance tariff: EUR3. 80 (reductions),
Métro: Montparnasse-Bienvenue.
During the first three decades of the 20th century, Montparnasse was an artistic hub of Paris, thronged with lesser and greater artists and writers. Today, sadly, with all the recent

redevelopment, much of that atmopshere has been swept away, but you can still sniff a little of that intoxicating atmosphere in the museum. It's in the former workshops of Russian artist Marie Vassilieff, which were saved from demolition and opened as a museum in 1998. Approached up an ivy clad alleyway, the artistic feeling lingers and you can just imagine the bon mots that were exchanged here, where she ran an artistic canteen. Diners included Braque, Chagall, Modigliani and Picasso. Today, the museum also has frequent exhibitions of works by artists past and present with Montparnasse connections.

Musée Pasteur,
25 rue du Dr Roux,
75015 Paris.
Tel: 01 45 68 82 83.
Web: http: //www.pasteur.fr/pasteur/musees/
Opening hours: Mon-Fri, all year, 14h00-17h30. Closed Aug, public holidays.
Entrance tariff: EUR3 (pass available from the office in the Institute Pasteur).
Métro: Pasteur, Volontaires.
You can take a guided tour through the typically 19th century middle class apartment home of Louis Pasteur, the great scientist, with its sombre Art Deco style decor and rather astonishing plumbing. It's an enormous place and it was here that he spent the last seven years of his life, until he died in 1895. You can also inspect his laboratory and see the nearby mausoleum designed in a neo-Byzantine style, where he is buried.

Musée de la Poste (Postal Museum),
34 boulevard de Vaugirard,
75015 Paris.
Tel: 01 42 79 24 24.
Web: www. laposte.fr/musee
Opening hours: daily, 10h00-18h00, except Suns and public holidays.
Entrance fee: EUR4. 50 (reductions).
Métro: Montparnasse-Bienvenue.
The postal museum is engrossing even for the non-specialist visitor, with a total of 15 sections telling the story of the French postal service since its exception. One of the sections explains

how horse drawn postal carriages were used first, hen the arrival of the telegraphic system. Other fascinating aspects include the development of aerial postal services; as early as the 1920s, the French were using aircraft to carry the post in many parts of the world. Contemporary systems of transporting mail include the TGV. Stamps may be universal, as the museum explains, but in France, the postage stamp has a very special place in the psychology of the nation, reflecting the image of the country. The museum has historical collections of archives and documents. Two intriguing international exhibits are the 1880s post boxes from England and Ireland. They are both exactly the same, except that the English one is painted red and the Irish one, green. Regular and fascinating series of stamps are issued frequently in France and these can be bought in the shop at the museum.

Parc Georges-Brassens,
75015 Paris.
Métro: Porte de Vanves.
This park was built in the 1980s on the site of a former abattoir and has all kinds of interesting features for children, including puppet shows and a merry-go-round. For adults, the park includes a small terraced vineyard, beehives and a mountain stream; an Alpine landscape has been created in the southern suburbs of Paris. A garden of scented herbs and shrubs was created for blind people. In the streets adjoining the park, the rue Brancions and the rue des Morillons, lots of new restaurants and bistros have opened, making the area an agreeable place for an afternoon or evening out. On the western side of the park, in the passage Dantzig, you can see a polygonal shaped building called La Ruche, that was designed by Eiffel for use as the wine pavilion in the 1900 World Exposition in Paris. After the fair was over, the building was dismantled and re-erected on its present site, as living and working quarters for poor artists. In 1970, the buildings were on the schedule for demolition, but following a campaign led by the artist Marc Chagall, were saved and today, the studios are still used by mainly foreign artists living and working in Paris.

Tour Maine-Montparnasse,
33 avenue du Maine,
75015 Paris.
Tel: 01 45 38 52 56.
Opening hours: daily, all year, 9h30-23h30 (closes 22h30 in winter)
Entrance tariff: EUR7. 55 (reduction).
Métro: Montparnasse-Bienvenue.
The best place to see this tower is from inside; from the rest of Paris, it's a hideous skyscraper that rises 56 storeys with no redeeming design features. However, the lift to the top is very quick and once you're there, the views from the rooftop terraces are just as good as those from the Eiffel Tower, which is slightly higher. Sometimes, classical musical performances are staged on the terraces; the backdrop is outstanding.


Vélodrome d'hiver site,
Boulevard de Grenelle,
75015 Paris.
Métro: Bir Hakheim.
The Vélodrome cycling stadium, long since demolished, earned a notorious place in French history in July, 1942, when just over 13, 000 Jewish people were rounded up and kept here in atrocious conditions for a week before being deported to inevitable death in the Nazi concentration camps. The deportation plans were inefficiently executed; the plan had been to round up 30, 000 people. The episode was one of the most notorious events during the occupation of France in the Second World War. The actual site of the stadium is now occupied by a block of apartments, but in the place des Martyrs Juif du Vélodrome d'Hiver, you can see the memorials and in the nearby park, a striking sculpture by Walter Spitzer.

# 16th ARRONDISSEMENT

Artesian well,
square Lamartine,
75016 Paris.
Métro: Avenue Henri-Martin.
On the square Lamartine, which is between the avenue Victor Hugo and the avenue Henri-Martin, you'll often find people queuing to get water from a well. It was dug in 1855 to augment the water supply for the river and lakes in the nearby Bois de Boulogne. Its therapeutic properties have been long known in the district and even today, people bottle the water, which they claim is very effective for stomach pains and other ailments, besides being a sleeping draught.

Atelier-Musée Henri Bouchard,
25 rue de l'Yvette,
75016 Paris.
Tel. 01 46 47 63 46.
Web: www. musee.bouchard.com
Opening hours, Wed, Sat, all year, 14h00-19h00. Closed last two weeks of March, June, Sept, Dec.
Entrance tariff: EUR4 (reductions).
Métro: Jasmin.
This marvellous studio, dating from the 1920s, has been preserved exactly as it was, complete with casts, moulds and sketchbooks. It belonged to a sculptor with a prodigious output, Henri Bouchard, who moved in here in 1924. Today, the studio is cared for lovingly, by members of his family. You can see exactly how the great sculptor worked and how he created a vast array of monuments, everything from the gigantic (in every sense) Apollo at the Palais de Chaillot to his slim, modern reliefs for the church of St-Jean-de-Chaillot.

Auteuil,
Métro: Église d'Auteuil.
This interesting quarter is the most southerly part of the 16th arrondissement, between the River Seine and the Parc des Princes. Several buildings close to the Metro station were built in the late 19th century in Art Nouveau style. Rue d'Auteuil was the old main street and it leads up to the place J Lorrain (beside the

Michel Ange Auteuil Métro station). Here, in this place, a substantial market is held every Saturday. In the Rue Poussin, which leads off this place, you can see the exterior of the Villa Montmorency, a 19th century development where the elaborate houses had English-style gardens and where the small streets are still leafy. It's a very exclusive area and former residents included the writer André gide and the Goncourt brothers, after whom is named the Prix Goncourt, the most prestigious of French literary awards.

Baccarat Musée de Cristal,
11 place des Etats-Unis,
75116 Paris.
Tel. 01 40 22 11 00.
Web: www. baccarat. fr
Opening hours, Mon-Sat, all year, 10h00-18h00.
Entrance tariff to museum: EUR3 (reductions).
Métro: Iéna.

Baccarat is one of the most legendary names in crystal glass making in France; it was founded in 1764, at the behest of King Louis XV. Ever since, it has catered for the wealthiest clients, including members of Royal families; the last Tsar of Russia, Nicholas II, always drank out of a Baccarat glass. When he had finished his drink, he threw the glass over his shoulder, so that no-one else could drink from the same glass. Over more than a century and a half, the company also created many extravagant pieces for universal expositions in Paris and elsewhere. Among the pieces you can see for yourself are the brandy decanters commissioned by Prince Rainier of Monaco when he married Grace Kelly and the crystal used on board the yacht of Aristotle Onassis. For its work, the company received numerous gold medals and Grand Prix awards. Until 2003, the company had its museum and showrooms in the Rue de Paradis in the 10th, but it's moved to much more spacious and elegant surroundings in the 16th. The museum is packed with countless examples of the company's work over the years, showing how designs and technologies evolved, while the decor of the showrooms is equally stunning. Among the items here is a 13 metre long crystal table that displays the home decoration range. Restaurant.

Bois de Boulogne,
75016 Paris.
Métro: Porte d'Auteuil, Porte Dauphine.
This large park on the western side of the 16th arrondissement is agreeable and safe enough by day, with its trees, lakes, walkways, cycling paths and picnic places. The best area of the park for walking is the south-western portion, which is the least landscaped. The Parc de Bagatelle in the northern section of the Bois has attractive displays of flowers in season, including tulips in April and roses in June. You can also enjoy horse racing at the Longchamp and Auteuil courses here. However, at night time, it's a different story, for the Bois de Boulogne has long been one of the main areas for the sex trade in Paris, even after the recent crackdown on prostitution. Prostitutes of both sexes as well as hermaphrodites, still ply their trade here and the Bois is still crime-ridden after dark, so it's best avoided after 18h00.

Cimitière de Passy,
2 rue du Commandant-Schloesig,
75016 Paris.
Tel. 01 47 27 51 42.
Web: www. findagrave.com
Opening hours, Mon-Fri, all year, 8h00-17h45, Sat, opens 8h30, Sun, opens 9h00.
Entrance tariff: free.
Métro: Trocadéro.
This has been one of the most fashionable places to be buried in Paris. Many well-known generals and political figures are buried here and so too are some of the great figures of the French artistic scene since the 1870s, including Debussy, the composer and Manet, the painter.

Cité Marine, Aquarium de Trocadero,
avenue Albert de Mun,
75116 Paris.
Tel: 01 47 23 62 95.
Web: www. musee-marine. fr
Métro: Trocadéro.
The aquarium beside the Palais de Chaillot has been closed for a long time, since 1985 in fact, but ambitious plans are under way to reopen the aquarium in a totally new and high tech format that will

display numerous underwater species in very effective and informative ways. The tropical sands and coral reefs will be well recreated an an aquadome will allow visitors who want to dive in to take the plunge literally. The project is being overseen by the City of Paris and this ravishing new style aquarium is reopening after a gap of 20 years.


Exploradome,
Bois de Boulogne,
75116 Paris.
Tel: 01 53 64 90 50.
Web: www.exploradome.com
Opening hours, daily, all year, 10h00-18h00.
Closed public holidays.
Entrance tariff: EUR4. 50 (reductions).
Métro: Porte d'Auteuil, Porte Dauphine.
This interactive, multimedia facility has much material on the weather and is designed for children aged between six and 14, a place where they can do experiments with clouds and tornadoes and create optical illusions. Visitors can create all kinds of multimedia applications. Temporary exhibitions.


Fondation Mona Bismarck,
34 avenue de New-York,
75016 Paris.
Tel. 01 47 23 38 88.
Opening hours, Tues-Sat, all year, 10h30-18h30.
Closed Sun, Mon, public holidays, Aug.
Entrance tariff: free.
Métro: Alma-Marceau.
The Foundation often has temporary exhibitions from collections abroad that are sometimes erudite, but always interesting. In recent years, they've done exhibitions on such diverse themes as ancient Italian ceramics to North American Indian art.

Hédiard food shop,
70 avenue Paul-Doumer,
75016 Paris.
Tel. 45 04 51 92.
Opening hours, Mon-Sat, all year, 9h00-18h00.
Métro: La Muette.
For anyone with a sweet tooth, this is the place to explore.
Francois Hédiard opened his first shop in the place de la
Madeleine in the 8th in 1854 and there are now more than 250 of
them around the world, including this superb example in the 16th.,
one of several in Paris. It stocks an enormous selection of
prepared foods and wines, but for chocolate lovers, this is close to
heaven. You'll also find over 20 varieties of fruit jellies on sale. It
rivals the renowned La Mère de Famille sweet shop at 35, rue de
Faubourg-Montmartre in the 9th. , which was founded in 1761 and
is now an Historic Monument.

Jardin du Ranelagh,
avenue Muette,
75016 Paris.
Métro: La Muette, Ranelagh.
This agreeable park, heavily wooded, is in the western part of the
16th. It's attractive strolling territory, before you get to the Bois de
Boulogne and one of its features is a statue of the 17th century
writer La Fontaine, author of Aesop's Fables, complete with eagle
and fox.

Karamanlis plaque,
21 boulevard de Montmorency,
75016 Paris.
Métro: Jasmin.
Greek politician the late Constantine Karamanlis lived here in
Paris for 11 years, as a political exile, before returning home with
the fall of the military regime in Greece. While he was in exile, he
often took long walks in the Bois de Boulogne. In July, 1974, he
returned home in the aircraft of the then French President Valéry
Giscard d'Estaing and Athens that night was a sea of people
holding lighted candles. The plaque, which was put up in October,
2003, commemorates the fact that the man who was to become a
President of the Hellenic Republic, lived here.

Les Serres d'Auteuil,
3 avenue de la Porte d'Auteuil,
75016 Paris.
Tel: 01 40 71 75 23.
Opening hours, daily, 10h00-18h00.
Entrance tariff: EUR0. 80.
Métro: Porte d'Auteuil.
These enormous and breath-taking glass houses were built in the late 19th century, opened in 1895 to provide plants for parks and public spaces across Paris. Depending on the season, there are marvellous displays of exotic flowers such as begonias and orchids, while there's also a suitably steamy tropical section, complete with a pool full of Japanese carp.

Maison de Balzac,
47 rue Raynouard,
75016 Paris.
Tel: 01 55 74 41 80.
Web: www. paris. fr/musees/balzac/default/html
Opening hours, Tues-Sun, all year, 10h00-18h00.
Closed Mon, public holidays.
Entrance tariff: house is free.
Temporary exhibitions: EUR3.35 (reductions).
Métro: Les Sablons.
In the mid-19th century, this part of Paris was still semi-rural and the house where Balzac took refuge is very much in the style of a country villa, surrounded by trees and greenery, a picturesque country retreat, almost but not quite in the city. For the great writer Balzac, it was somewhere where he could escape the wrath of the debt collectors and at the back of the house, you can see the doorway through which he often escaped into the lane when the bailiffs came knocking at the front door. Today, the house is filled with Balzac memorabilia, including first editions, corrected proof sheets and lots of paintings of friends and mistresses, including his Polish mistress, Mme Hanska. You can also see an enormous family tree of the characters that adorn his novels; the chart is so large that it covers the space of several walls. Perhaps the most homely and the most appealing part of the house is Balzac's study, where you can see his desk and chair and the all-important coffee pot with his monogramme. Balzac was in the habit of writing through the night, so this was essential equipment. Quite often, exhibitions on literary themes are held in the house.

Musée Bouchard,
25 rue de l'Yvette,
75016 Paris.
Tel: 01 46 47 63 46.
Web: www. musee-bouchard.com
Opening hours, Wed, Sat, all year, 14h00-19h00. Closed on public holidays and on the 16th to the 31st of the following months-Mar, June, Sept, Dec.
Entrance tariff: EUR4 (reductions).
Métro: Jasmin.
The studio of renowned sculptor Henri Bouchard (1975-1960) has been preserved very authentically, just as when he was working here. Many examples of his work, in bronze, marble and stone, are on display, as well as explanations of the techniques of his sculpture work. Larger pieces, such as the great figure of Apollo from the Palais de Chaillot, are displayed in the garden.

Musée de la Contrefaçon,
16 rue de la Faisanderie,
75116 Paris.
Tel. 01 56 26 14 00.
Opening hours, daily, all year, 14h00-17h30, closed Mon and public holidays.
Entrance tariff: EUR2. 50 (reductions).
Métro: Porte Dauphine.
This museum goes back a long way, to 1951, when it was founded by the Union des Fabricants, the first association in France to battle against counterfeit goods. Then, counterfeiting was small scale; today, it's done on a vast scale and there's hardly a big internationally known brand that hasn't been copied so that it can be sold for far less than the authentic item. The museum is really intriguing and you can have great fun trying to decide what is for real and what is actually a fake. These days, all manner of things are produced as counterfeit items, everything from clothes and household goods to pens and cigars. Sports and games are counterfeited and even Champagne hasn't escaped. In the museum, you can trace the history of forged goods right back to Roman times, with a Gallo-Roman amphora that's nearly 2, 000 years old and is a fake. The museum is so up to date that the ways in which computer age products, such as software and games, are forged, are also displayed. The way in which forgeries

are sold and the means of payment are also explored. It's a fascinating story and one that becomes more compelling by the year.

Musée Dapper,
35 bis, rue Paul Valéry,
75016 Paris.
Tel. 01 45 00 01 50.
Opening hours, Wed-Sun, all year, 11h00-19h00. Closed Mon, Tues, some public holidays.
Entrance tariff: EUR5 (reductions).
Métro: Victor-Hugo.
This museum is rather different to many of the Paris museums; it's small, specialised and devoted to sub-Saharan art. The Foundation Dapper, which runs the museum, is comparatively recent, having been founded in 1983 and the museum itself got a substantial and attractive make-over even more recently, reopening in 2000. Among its features are an exhibition, where regular exhibitions are staged; a glass bridge; a bookshop and a cafe.

Musée d'Art Dentaire (Dental Museum),
22 rue Emile Ménier,
75016 Paris.
Tel: 01 45 53 40 05.
Opening hours: Weds, 14h30-17h30 by appointment.
Entrance tariff: free.
Métro: Porte Dauphine.
For anyone who wants a little twinge of anticipation, the sort that comes from a visit to the dentist, this little museum of dental history will be perfect. It has collections of paintings from the 17th century Dutch School, showing medieval dentists at work, with absolutely no anaesthetics; dental instruments from the 17th to the 19th century and ancient books on the art of dentistry, published between the 16th and 19th centuries. Compared to present day dentistry, this old style dentistry is primitive in the extreme. You can also see some pretty rudimentary toothbrushes, made between the time of Charles X, who was king of France between 1824 and 1830 and the end of the 19th century. After completing the tour of this fascinating museum, you'll thanks heavens for modern oral hygiene and won't be too bothered about going to the dentist again.

Musée de l'Homme,
Palais de Chaillot,
17 place du Trocadéro,
75116 Paris.
Tel: 01 44 05 72 72.
Web: www. mnha. fr
Opening hours, daily, all year, 9h45-17h15. Closed Tues.
Entrance tariff: EUR5 (reductions).
Métro: Trocadéro.

This ambitious museum shows the evolution of man in terms of anthropology and ethnology from prehistoric times to the present day, a span of over 3. 5 million years. The range of items are amazing, from a polar bear that has been carefully stuffed, to the reconstruction of a Mayan temple from Mexico. Tribal costumes add many colourful flourishes. Many themes are elaborated upon, from disease to racial differentiation. The collections will be transferred to the museum of the quai Branly (qv) now under construction on the opposite side of the River Seine and due to open during 2006. Then, the Musée de l'Homme will close. Café, cinema, library.

Musée de la Marine,
Palais de Chaillot,
place du Trocadéro,
75016 Paris.
Tel: 01 53 65 69 69
Web: www. musee-marine.fr
Opening hours, Mon, Wed-Sun, all year, 10h00-18h00. Closed Tues, some public holidays.
Entrance tariff: EUR6 (reduction).
Métro: Trocadéro.

This fascinating museum of the sea has lots of material on French naval history, from a series of paintings of French ports done in the mid-18th century to a model of a nuclear submarine. You can also see the imperial barge built for Napoléon in 1810, as well as a vast array of other exhibits. These range from old maps to antique instruments, maritime paintings to diving equipment. You can also see how the world's biggest liner, the Queen Mary 2, which had its maiden voyage in early 2004, was built in the St Nazaire shipyards in Brittany. Extensive renovation has been taking place at the museum but none of the sections of this almost endless museum have been closed to the public as a result.

Musée de Radio-France (Television and Radio Museum),
116 avenue du Président Kennedy;
Paris Cedex 16, 75015.
Tel: 01 56 40 21 80.
Web: www.radio-france.fr
Opening hours: Mon-Fri, five a day, between 10h00 and 11h00; 14h30 and 16h300. Closed for public holidays. The tours have to be booked a month in advance.
Admission tariff: EUR5 (reductions).
Métro: Mirabeau, Ranelagh.

The great circular complex that houses the main studios of Radio-France also has an interesting museum devoted to the development of radio in France since the 1920s and television since the late 1940s. A sound tour outlines the history and you can also see many of the pieces of equipment, such as microphones and cameras, as well as biographical material on well-known personalities connected with French broadcasting. Pioneers of radio in France are commemorated and you can see the documentary evidence of the first radio message sent between the Eiffel Tower and the Panthéon at the start of the 20th century. You can also see documentary evidence of the coded broadcasts that the Free French made from London during the Second World War. Past collides with the present; from the museum, you can look down into the studios to see programmes being presented. Sometimes, live recordings will be taking place in the France Musique auditorium and you can sit in on these.

Musée du Stylo et l'Ecriture,
3 rue Guy de Maupassant,
75106 Paris.
Tel. 01 47 20 87 05.
Opening hours, Sun, all year, 14h00-18h00 and daily, by arr.
Entrance tariff: EUR2 (reductions).
Métro: léna, Alma Marceau.

If you're intrigued by pens and the art of writing, which is fast disappearing in this online age, you'll enjoy musing on the collection of pens here. The museum claims to have the largest collection in the world of pens, dating back to the first in 1750 as well as many samples from the 19th and 20th centuries. It also displays many examples of the art of calligraphy.

Musée du Vin (wine museum),
rue des Eaux,
75016 Paris.
Tel: 01 45 25 63 26.
Web: www. museeduvinparis.com
Opening hours: daily, all year, 10h00-18h00, closed Mon and Dec 24-Jan 1.
Entrance fee: EUR8 (includes one glass of wine).
Métro: Passy.

The wine museum of the 16th is in an interesting historical setting, ancient vaults that were first developed in the Middle Ages and which were later used as cellars by the Minimes Brothers of the Passy monastery. In this most appropriate setting, the wine museum explains how Champagne is made and tells the story of the Paris vineyards-only one is left, in Montmartre-details the making of cognac and tells the story of Turkheim, one of the main wine villages in Alsace. It even has a space for the Grand Marnier story. Old vineyard tools and memorabilia add to the atmosphere and the museum also has a cooper's workshop. The museum has a substantial collection of grand cru wines, the best of the best from Bordeaux and other wine regions.

Musée National des Arts Asiatiques,
6 place d'léna,
75016 Paris.
Tel. 01 56 52 53 00.
Web: www. museeguimet.fr
Opening hours, daily, all year, 10h00-18h00, except Wed.
Entrance tariff: EUR4 (reductions).
Métro: Boissière, léna.

The extraordinary collections here of Asian art owe their origins to an industrialist from Lyons called Émile Guimet, who was fascinated by Asian art and religion. He assembled this remarkable collection of 45, 000 objets d'art, paintings and sculptures. They include classic Chinese art, Japanese and Korean art. In the auditorium, frequent Asian performances are staged, including drama and music. In the Galeries du Panthéon, which is just along the street at Number 19, the annexe to the museum reveals many Buddhist treasures from China and Japan and includes a Japanese garden. You can also take part in a Japanese tea ceremony. For anyone interested in Asian art and culture, this is the place to visit in Paris.

Musée Nationale des Arts et Traditions Populaires,
6 avenue du Mahatma-Gandhi,
75016 Paris.
Tel: 01 44 17 60 00.
Opening hours, Mon, Wed-Sun, all year, 9h30-17h00.
Closed Tues, some public holidays.
Entrance tariff: EUR4 (reductions).
Métro: Les Sablons.
There's nothing over-artistic or high-flown about this museum, which is a down-to-earth reconstruction of the folk ways, culture and crafts of pre-industrialised France. Ironically, the building itself is modern, dating from the 1960s. You'll find sections devoted to rural crafts, such as boat building and weaving. Traditional workplaces, such as the forge and the pottery, are brought to life, as are the old ways of farming, when horses pulled ploughs. The displays are all very informative and interesting. You can also see many old household items, such as ancient stoves and scrubbing boards. One particularly lively section is devoted to old-time beliefs, and includes such items as a crystal ball. Old medicines, based on herbal remedies, are also portrayed and you can see what kinds of entertainment people enjoyed up to the mid-19th century. The museum also has a library and a sound archive, which can be visited by prior arr. There's also a shop. Altogether, the museum is a very vivid recreation of the old rural ways of life, right in the middle of one of the most middle class and prosperous areas of Paris. However, the museum is due to be relocated to Marseille in 2008.

Paris Basket Racing,
Stade Pierre Coubertin,
82 avenue Georges Lafont,
75016 Paris.
Tel. 01 45 27 79 12.
Métro: Porte de Saint-Cloud.
Basketball is a very popular sport in France and it's played regularly at this stadium, home to the Paris Basket Racing team, which is in the French first division. You'll find basketball with a French accent rather different to the American style.

Roland-Garros tennis museum,
2 avenue Gordon Bennett,
Porte des Mousquetaires,
75016 Paris.
Tel: 01 47 43 48 48.
Web: www. fft. fr
Opening hours, Tues-Sun, all year, 10h00-18h00. Closed public holidays.
Entrance tariff: free.
Métro: Porte d'Auteuil.
For anyone fascinated with tennis, this museum, opened in 2003, is full of interesting expositions and displays. Multimedia displays show the whole history of tennis over the past 500 years, while you can also look at the lives and careers of mythical tennis figures, such as Suzanne Lenglen. Many historic objects help to tell the story and you can also see many presentations of photographs and paintings. Archive films of outstanding tennis matches date back to 1897 and the archives go right up to the present day. You can also explore the development of the Roland-Garros stadium.
Shop, restaurant.


Shakespeare Garden,
75016 Paris.
Opening hours: daily, all year, 14h30-16h00.
Métro: Porte d'Auteuil.
The Shakespeare Garden was created in 1953 by Robert Joffret, the then head of conservator of gardens and parks in Paris. He created the garden in an old quarry and the stones from the quarry were used for the pathways. On the stage underneath the cypresses, Shakespeare's plays are performed regularly in summer. For information on the plays, phone: 01 40 19 95 33.
 Adjacent to this garden, you'll find the Auteuil cactus garden, where many varieties of cacti are grown, both outdoors and in the glasshouse. Opening of the cactus garden is on demand, during weekday afternoons and on Sundays.

Villa Roche,
8 square du Docteur-Blanche,
75016 Paris.
Opening hours, Mon-Fri, Sept-July, 10h00-12h30, 13h30-18h30.
Closed Aug.
Entrance tariff: EUR2. 30
Métro: Jasmin.
This cul de sac, off the rue du Docteur-Blanche, has the first private houses built by the Swiss architect Le Corbusier, in the early 1920s. One of these houses, the Villa Roche, is owned by the Fondation Le Corbusier and is open to the public. The architectural style is strictly Cubist and minimalist, while the spacious interior is hung with Cubist paintings. When this group of houses was built, they caused a sensation and even today, you can still sense that innovatory feeling.

## 17th ARRONDISSEMENT

Institut Vatel,
107 rue Nollet,
75017 Paris.
Tel. 01 42 26 26 60.
Web: www. vatel. fr
Métro: La Fourche.
This is another well-known establishment in Paris that teaches culinary skills; they do a wide range of diploma and degree courses. You can dine-lunch or dinner-at the institute's restaurant and sample the students' course work. The restaurant is open to the public from Mondays to Fridays. Appropriately, the nearest Metro station is La Fourche (the fork).

James Joyce pub and restaurant,
71 boulevard Gouvion St Cyr,
75017 Paris.
Tel. 01 44 09 70 32.
Métro: Neuilly Porte Maillot.
This Irish bar and restaurant, connected to Kitty O'Shea's in the 2nd arrondissement, was founded in 1993. Since then, it's become popular with people looking for some Irish history and literature; 12 stained glass windows tell the story of James Joyce's Ulysses,

while other windows commemorate other distinguished 20th century Irish writers. The restaurant is well-known for its traditional Irish and French cuisine.

Le Cinéma des Cinéastes,
7 avenue de Clichy,
75017 Paris.
Tel. 01 53 42 40 20.
Opening hours, daily, all year, 14h00-23h00.
Métro: Place Clichy.
This cinema is beloved of real enthusiasts of the genre; the decor of the cinema resembles the movie studios of the 1920s and 1930s. Included in the programmes are many gems from world cinema, while the cinema also has festivals on particular themes.


## 18th ARRONDISSEMENT

Amélie's Montmartre,
75018 Paris.
Métro: Abbesses.
The Amélie film was a tremendous hit with cinema audiences in France and elsewhere when it was released in 2001, with its full title of Le Fabuleux Destine d'Amélie Poulain. One of the starring locations in the film was the cafe where the character of Amélie worked and it was the real life Café des Deux Moulins, taken over for the film production. It's a very popular spot for visitors and it's just as it appeared on screen.

Au Lapin Agile,
22 rue des Saules,
75018 Paris.
Tel. 01 46 06 85 87.
Opening hours, daily, all year, 21h00-2h00, closed Mon.
Entrance tariff: EUR24.
Métro: Lamarck Caulaincourt.
A great spot for traditional cabaret, this was a great meeting place for artists, writers and poets in Montmartre, up to 1914 and the start of the First World War. Today, many younger singers perform here, reinventing the old songs as the place lives up to its reputation of "Chansons, Humour et Poésie". The name of the

pub dates back to 1875 when a painter and caricaturist called André Gill painted a sign showing a rabbit jumping out of a saucepan.

Cimitière de Montmartre,
20 avenue Rachel,
75018 Paris.
Tel: 01 53 42 36 30.
Web: http: //www. paris.org/Expos/PereLachaise/
Opening hours: daily.
Métro: Blanche.
It's a wonderful cemetery, built below street level in an old quarry, that's more like a park, full of flowers and benches. It also gives an good insight into the history of the Montmartre quarter and gives a good feeling for artistic Paris that every visitor long for. The best starting point is the map near the entrance, which details all the famous people buried here. Among them are Hector Berlioz, composer (1803-1869); Marie Antoine Careme, the king of chefs and king of chefs (1783-1840); Leo Delibes, composer (1836-1863); Nijinski, the legendary Russian dancer (1888-1950); Jacques Offenbach, creator of the can-can (1819-1880); Patrick Pons, French motorcycle champion, killed in a race at Silverstone (1952-1980); Emile Zola, novelist (1840-1902), together with his wife Alexandre.

Clos Montmartre (Montmartre vineyard),
12 rue Cortot,
75018 Paris.
Métro: Lamarck Caulaincourt.
Round at the back of Sacré Cour, you'll find the largest vineyard in Paris. Contrary to popular opinion, it's not the only one, since there are several other small ones in Paris, including a minute vineyard in the Parc Georges-Brassens in the 15th. Back in 1933, 2,000 vines were planted in the Montmartre vineyard, representing the varieties most frequently grown in France. They've managed to thrive ever since and you can buy the reasonably tasting wine from the vineyard at a number of shops in the locality, including the shop in the adjacent Musée de Montmartre (qv). Every October, a festival is staged in Montmartre to celebrate the wine harvest in the vineyard and it's a lively affair, with parades, music, plenty of dégustations (tastings) and a traditional style market.

Éspace Montmartre,
11 rue Poulbot,
75018 Paris.
Tel: 01 42 64 40 10.
Web: www.dali-espacemontmartre.com
Opening hours: daily, 10am-6pm.
Entrance fee: EUR7 (reductions).
Métro: Abbesses.
This museum has plenty of Salvador Dali material, including original drawings, lithographs and sculptures-it's the largest collection in France of the works of this renowned Spanish surrealist, who lived from 1904-1989 and who joined the French surrealists in Paris when he was 25. Some of the pieces here are true Dali classics, such as the melting watch and the long legged elephant sculpture.

Halle Saint-Pierre,
2 rue Ronsard,
75018 Paris.
Tel. 01 42 58 72 89.
Web: http: //www.hallesaintpierre.org/
Métro: Anvers.
Opening hours, daily, all year, 10h00-18h00.
Entrance tariff: EUR6. 50 (reductions).
This old covered market, built at the foot of the Butte Montmartre in 1868, with Sacré-Coeur as a backdrop, is now a striking place for showing contemporary culture, with frequent temporary art exhibitions. Art naif is very much on the menu, as it is in the museum that's part of the complex.
Bookshop, cafe/restaurant.

Jardin Sauvage Saint Vincent (wild garden for children),
Rue St Vincent,
75018 Paris.
Tel: 01 43 28 47 63.
Opening hours: Sat, all year, 14h00-18h00 and also in the school year, between Apr and Oct, open on Mon, 16h00-18h00.
Métro: Lamarck Caulaincourt.
This delightful wild open space, extending to 1, 500 square metres, has been left uncultivated and it's especially designed for children, so that they can wander round and have a look at all the plants that are growing free and wild. Eco-educators are there to explain the role played by birds, insects and the wind.

Musée de l'Erotisme (museum of erotica),
72 boulevard de Clichy,
75018 Paris.
Tel: 01 42 58 28 73.
Opening hours: daily, all year, 10h00-02h00.
Entrance tariff: EUR7 (reductions). .
Métro: Blanche
Right in the heart of the seedy sex entertainment district of Paris, the museum of erotica has everything that anyone with an interest in that direction would wish to see, four floors of exhibits, everything from "fun sex" to contemporary art with sexual themes. Most Parisians wouldn't be bothered visiting, but for visitors in search of the "ooh, la, la", this might be just the place to titillate the senses.

Musée de Montmartre,
12 rue Cortot,
75108 Paris.
Tel: 01 46 06 61 11.
Web: www. museedemontmartre. com
Opening hours: daily, except Mons, 10hr-12. 30; 13. 30hr-6pm.
Entrance fee: EUR5. 50 (reductions).
Métro: Lamarck Caulaincourt.
It's a rather slight museum that is designed to display artistic Montmartre in the 19th century, with Toulouse-Lautrec posters; a mock-up old style zinc bar and paintings of the Butte in the 19th century, when the area was still semi-rural. You can also buy wine here that comes from the adjacent Montmartre vineyard.

Musée Placard d'Erik Satie,
6 rue Cortot,
75018 Paris.
Tel. 01 42 78 15 18.
Opening hours, by arr.
Entrance tariff: free.
Métro: Lamarck Caulaincourt.
Erik Satie (1866-1925) was a noted composer of the early 20th century and some of his spiky but very original works retain their popularity. He was noted for his eccentricity and sense of humour and what is billed, jokingly, as the smallest museum in the world, is a tribute to this composer with a difference.

Sacré-Coeur,
Montmartre,
75018 Paris.
Web: www. sacre-coeur-montmartre. com
Opening hours, daily, all year, 8h00-19h00.
Dome, daily, 9h00-18h00.
Entrance tariff: free (basilica). Crypt and dome, EUR5.
Métro: Abbesses.
The white domes of the church can be seen from most parts of Paris and are as evocative of the city as the Eiffel Tower. It was designed in a mixture of Romanesque and Byzantine styles and construction began in the 1870s, an atonement by the Catholic church for the excesses of the Paris Commune, which lasted for 72 days in 1871, after the fall of Paris in the Franco-Prussian war. The church itself is best approached by climbing the series of monumental staircases that rise from the square Willette; or you can approach it by the futuristic looking funicular railway. The basilica was named after the local artist, who proclaimed on the day that the church was inaugurated: "long live the devil! ". Once you get inside the church, you can also explore the crypt, but the best part is the climb up to the top of the dome, which is open daily. The entrance cost of EUR5 covers both the dome and entrance to the crypt. From the top of the dome, you'll have a view of Paris that's only rivalled by the Eiffel Tower.

## 19th ARRONDISSEMENT

Cité des Sciences et de l'Industrie (City of Science and Industry),
30 avenue Corentin Cariou,
75019 Paris.
Tel: 01 40 05 80 00.
Web: www.cite-sciences.fr
Opening hours: all year, Tues-Sat, 10h00-18h00,
Sun, 10h00-19h00.
Entrance tariff: starts at EUR7. 50
Métro: Porte de la Villette.
The city of science is a vast place, that will easily take up a whole day and you'll still want to come back for more, there's so much to see. The whole development is in the Parc de Villette, which was

once the main meat market for Paris. In the park, a number of separate developments can be explored.

*Cité des Enfants*

This section of the park is designed for children up to 12 years of age and an incredible number of attractions are organised for them. They can make buildings and put together their own TV news bulletins.

**Explora**

This is the main permanent exhibition area, including all manner of topics, from energy and light to robotics and space. There are all kinds of interactive displays, many of them computer driven. You can do all kinds of things, like driving robots through a maze. The best way of guiding yourself through the exhibition is by using the English language audioguide. Apart from Explora, you'll find the actual design of the science museum completely overwhelming, with its futuristic walkways, lifts and escalators.

*L'Argonaute (submarine)*

Entrance fee: EUR3

The submarine rests on dry land in the Parc de la Villette Park. The submarine dates from the 1950s and its weaponry was removed in 1982. Visitors can tour through the submarine, using self-guiding headphones, seeing everything from the crew station to the tubes from where torpedoes were launched. The submarine also has an exhibition on the history of submarine development and the way in which submarine techniques have been enhanced.

*Musée de la Musique*

This museum is within the whole Cité de la Musique and it has vast displays of musical intruments, 4, 500 in all, showing the development of music from Renaissance times right up to the present day. The design of the buildings here is equally intriguing, with musical themes turned into architectural shapes. There's also a concert hall here and a cafe de la musique.

*Park*

In the park itself, there are many themed gardens, designed mostly for children. Among them are the Dragon Slide and the Folie des Arts Plastiques.

*Planetarium and cinemas*

The planetarium can be visited for an extra charge (EUR2.50). You can see more than 10, 000 stars simulated. and the park also has two cinemas. The Louis Lumière cinema shows 3D films, while the Salle Jean-Bertin shows French language documentaries. You can also see 180 degree films in the Géode, a big bubble of steel. In the Cinaze cinema, 70 mm films that show films shot at 30 frames a minute, the seats move, so enjoy the films in a sober state!

*Techno Cité*

This is designed for both teenagers and adults and its purpose is to show the application of technology to industry and you can do all sorts of things, like design a racing bike or make a computerised game.

Conservatoire National Supérieur de Musique et de Danse de Paris,
209 avenue Jean Jaurès,
75019 Paris.
Tel: 01 40 40 46 46.
Web: www.cite-musique.fr
Métro: Porte-de-Pantin.

The many music students at the Conservatoire take part in master classes and also put on performances for visitors, all of which provide excellent free entertainment.

Lycée Hotellerie,
12 rue Jean-Quarre,
75019 Paris.
Tel: 01 44 84 19 00.
Métro: Place des Fetes.

This college for teaching students going into the hotel industry has two restaurants, the Beauregard and the Courtille, that serve the catering work of those students for lunch. Some interesting and tasty dishes are promised.

Parc des Buttes-Chaumont,
rue Botzaris,
75019 Paris.
Opening hours, always open.
Métro: Buttes-Chaumont.

This park, which is open day and night, was designed by Gustav Haussmann, the man responsible for the new streets in central Paris in the 1860s. He created this park that era and the site had been a quarry, a rubbish dump and a place for public executions. Today, the park has all sorts of vertical cliff faces, as well as paths that wander in and out, past waterfalls, a place with magnificent landscapes and terraces. The park even has a man-made cave, complete with an artificial stalactite. The central feature of the park is an enormous lake, reached by two footbridges. On the island, the principal attraction is the reproduction Corinthian temple. The park itself is also an excellent place from which to see Paris-the views over the city are just incredible. To the east of the park, you'll find a very attractive residential area, several small and very hilly streets, packed with small houses and gardens; up and down these streets makes for an unusual and invigorating walk-and climbs.

MK2 sur Seine,
14 quai de la Seine,
75019 Paris.
Tel. 08 36 68 14 07.
Web: www.mk2.com
Opening hours, daily, all year, 10h00-23h00.
Entrance tariff: from EUR8. 20 (reductions).
Métro: Jaurès, Stalingrad.
This is real state of the art entertainment, in an ultra modern cinema, shiny and smart, where the walls and the seats are all black, to prevent any stray light marring performances for perfectionists. The programming, too, is very imaginative and sometimes includes some rare films made in the earliest days of cinema.

Musée du Taxi,
44 rue Armand Carrel,
75019 Paris.
Tel: 01 44 52 23 80.
Opening hours, Mon-Thurs, all year, 9h00-12h00, 14h00-17h00.
Entrance tariff: EUR5.
Métro: Jaurès, Laumière.
The museum depicts the history of the taxis of Paris, from the mid-17th century to the present day. From 20th century taxis, the museum has a collection of equipment, such as radios and lighted signs. Many photographs tell the story of Parisian taxi drivers and their cars. The museum had been closed for renovation, but should be open again now.

## 20th ARRONDISSEMENT

Parc de Belleville,
Rue des Couronnes,
75020 Paris.
Métro: Couronnes
This park is one of the newest in Paris, having only been opened in 1988, but it's already a firm favourite with many people who live in the locality. The fountains in the park are very modernistic in style, ideal for children to play games. If you visit during the spring, you'll be overwhelmed by the lush smells of the collections of shrubs here. The park is laid out in terraced style with lots of waterfalls. Another of its delights is that from here, you have exceptional views across Paris, as far as the Eiffel Tower on the opposite side of the city.

Père Lachaise cemetery,
75020 Paris.
Opening hours, daily, all year, 7h30-18h00.
Entrance tariff: free.
Web: http: //www.paris.org/Expos/PereLachaise/
Métro: Père Lachaise, Philippe Auguste, Alexandre Dumas, Gambetta.
The Père Lachaise cemetery is by far the largest in Paris and it's one of the most celebrated anywhere in the world. At the beginning of the 19th century, several new cemeteries, including Montmartre, Montparnasse and Père Lachaise, replaced the ancient cemeteries dating back to the Middle Ages. Père Lachaise is a veritable pantheon of the great and the good of France and strolling along the great walkways, you'll see many famous names from French history, past and recent, who've been buried here. At weekends in summer, many families come to see their loved ones and have a picnic at the same time, so the vast cemetery, rather than being so forbidding, has almost an atmosphere of family gaiety. In the south of the cemetery, you'll find a somber historical note, the Mur des Fédérés, against which were shot the 147 leaders of the Paris Commune, on May 28, 1871.

The list of the famous people here is lengthy indeed. Just a few of the most noted are Pierre Abélard (1079-1142), philosopher and lover of Héloise; Honoré de Balzac (1799-1850), writer; Gilbert Bécaud (1927-2001), singer; Sarah Bernhardt (1844-

1923), actor; Maria Callas (1923-1977), opera singer; Frédéric Chopin (1810-1849), composer; Edith Piaf (1915-1963), singer; Marcel Proust (1871-1922), writer and Simone Signoret (1921-1985), actor. Two of the most famous graves here are those of Jim Morrison (1943-1971), the American singer, and Oscar Wilde (1854-1900), the writer and playwright. Sadly, Wilde's modernistic white marble tomb, like other prominent tombs in the cemetery, has been badly defaced by graffiti.

rue de Belleville,
75020 Paris.
Métro: Belleville
The main street in one of the most colourful districts of northern Paris, the rue de Belleville has lots of Chinese, Thai and Vietnamese shops and restaurants. The rue Ramponeau, which is just off the boulevard de Belleville, has many kosher shops, which are run by Sephardic Jews from Tunisia. A market is run in the boulevard de Belleville every Tuesday and Friday morning and it has all sorts of treats and delights from Africa and Asia, everything from fabrics to spices. It also has a fine cosmopolitan atmosphere.

rue de Ménilmontant,
75020 Paris.
Metro: Ménilmontant
From this immediate area, you'll enjoy excellent views over Paris. If you go up to the rue de l'Ermitage and the rue Boyer, you will have tremendous views over the Pompidou Centre and the Beaubourg quarter.

rue des Pyrénées,
75020 Paris.
Métro: Pyrénées
This small area is like Montmartre without all the tourists. Some of the old streets around the rue des Pyrénées still survive as reminders of what working class Paris was like in the 19th century, especially some of the small cu de sacs and alleyways to the immediate east of the street.

rue St-Blaise,
75020 Paris.
Métro: Porte de Bagolet
The main street of what was once one of the "villages" of northern Paris, Charonne, is a reasonably interesting location for a stroll. The rue St-Blaise was once one of the most attractive small shopping streets in northern Paris, but it has been prettified so much that much of its charm is now ersatz. However, the 13th century Église St-Germain-de-Charonne, a Romaneseque church in the place St-Blaise, hasn't changed at all with the centuries.

## ÎLE DE FRANCE

AINCOURT,
20 km north of Paris.
Train: RER D1 line to Sarcelles.
Road: N16 from Paris.

Jardin Japonais du centre hospitallier de Vexin,
Parc d'Aincourt,
95510 Aincourt.
Tel. 01 34 79 44 30.
Opening hours, May-Sept, Thurs, Sat, Sun, 14h00-18h00.
Entrance tariff: free.
At this centre, you can see typical Japanese landscapes, laid out in traditional style, with ponds, bridges and rock gardens. Many Japanese plants adorn the neatly cultivated landscape.

ASNIÈRES,
10 km north-west of Paris.
Métro: Porte de Clichy,

Cimitière des Chiens.
Web: http: //cheny. net/grenier/0056/
Opening hours: Mar 16-Oct 15, daily, except Mon, 10h00-19h00, Oct 16-Mar 15, daily, except Mon, 10h00-17h00.
Entrance tariff: free.
Out of all the cemetries in the Paris region, this is the most unusual, since it's reserved for animals only. More than 100, 000 domestic pets are buried here and often, the inscriptions on the

graves are unusual to say the least. It's not just dogs and cats that have their last resting place here; a gazelle, a lion and a monkey are also buried here. The actual location of the cemetery is quite interesting, the Ile de Ravageurs in the Seine, but it's easily accessible.

Le Mémorial de la Déportation du Camp de Drancy,
15 rue Arthur Fontaine,
93700 Asnières.
Tel: 01 48 95 35 05.
Métro: Mairie de Clichy.
The internment camp at Drancy, a notorious place during the Second World War, was made into an historic monument in 2001. The place was originally built as a housing estate in the 1930s, but in August, 1941, just over 4, 200 Jews, many of whom had escaped to France from elsewhere in Europe, were rounded up and interned here, even though the camp was still unfinished at that stage. During the course of the war, around 70, 000 people were held here, with most eventually shipped to Auschwitz and certain death. What's left of the Drancy camp today is a chilling place, that brings to life all too vividly the horrifying fate that was suffered by most of the Jewish people held here.

Musée Vuitton,
18 rue Louis Vuitton,
92600 Asnières.
Tel. 01 41 32 32 70.
Web: http: //vuitton.com
Opening hours, by arr.
Entrance tariff: free.
Métro: Mairie de Asnières.
Yes, this is all about luggage. Louis Vuitton is world renowned for its brand of luxury luggage, a symbol of elegance. The original Louis Vuitton was born in the Jura in 1819 and when he was 14, set out to walk to Paris, a trip that took him two years. He then learned his trade his trade with a packing case maker. The firm of Vuitton was founded in 1854 and the workshops were moved to Asnières in 1859. In this privately owned museum, the collections of Louis Vuitton are put in their historical context, including luggage for the great days of the railways and the liners and the early days of flying. The part played by luggage in the great

colonial explorations of the late 19th century is explored and so too is the Vuitton presence in many world expositions. Its influence on decorative design is also highlighted. While many of the items date from the 19th and 20th centuries, the sumptuous collection of luggage has items as old as the 16th century.

AUVERS-SUR-OISE,
35 km north-west of Paris.
Train: Gare St-Lazare, Paris to Auvers-sur-Oise.
Road: A15 from Paris.

Auberge Ravoux (Maison de Van Gogh),
52 rue Général de Gaulle,
95430 Auvers-sur-Oise.
Tel: 01 30 36 60 60.
Opening hours: daily, all year, 10h00-18h00, except Mon.
Entrance tariff: EUR5 (individual), EUR10 (family).
The charm of this quiet village seduced Van Gogh and other well-known late 19th century painters and in the heart of the village, you can see the room in the inn where Van Gogh lodged. The atmosphere in the present day bar is convivial and you can try a legal absinthe, using a special absinthe glass, so that you can recreate the ritual surrounding this once famous and often abused drink.

Le Musée de l'Absinthe,
44, rue Callé,
95430 Auvers-sur-Oise.
Tel: 01 30 36 83 26.
Web: www. absinthe.com/lafee.absinthemuseum.htm
Opening hours: Sat, Sun, public holidays, all year, 11h00-18h00.
Also, Wed-Fri, June-Sept, 11h00-18h00.
Entrance tariff: EUR4 (reductions).
Absinthe played a prominent role in artistic and cultural life in 19th century France. Enjoying absinthe from a long stemware glass was quite a ritual in itself; the absinthe was clear, but water was added to turn it milky and sugar gave sweetness. France had a growing alcoholism problem towards the end of the 19th century as industrially manufactured alcohol became cheaper and absinthe was finally made illegal in 1915 because it was considered to harmful to health with its 114 proof. But a

tremendous legend has grown up around absinthe, especially as it was such as integral part of the artistic and cultural life of Paris. The absinthe museum brings to life the era of French life when the drink was so popular; a late 19th century bar has been recreated in the museum and it also has a collection of the special glasses used to drink the stuff.

Musée Daubigny,
Rue des Samsonne,
95430 Auvers-sur-Oise.
Tel: 01 30 36 80 20.
Opening hours: daily, all year, 14h00-18h00, except Mon, Tues.
Entrance tariff: EUR4 (reductions).
This museum has drawings, engravings and paintings done in the 19th and 20th centuries of the locality. Also in Auvers, you can walk through the Van Gogh park and see the statue of the artist created by Zadkine. Auvers also has underground quarries dating back to the 10th century. During Heritage Days in September, you can visit the main quarry, named after Saint Martin.

BARBIZON,
57 km south of Paris.
Train: RER D line to Melun, then taxi.
Road: A6 from Paris to Fontainebleau.

Barbizon is a most delightful village, largely unspoiled, close to Fontainebleau and the forest of the same name. It's a delight for wandering around, absorbing the artistic atmosphere. In the latter part of the 19th century, many painters and some writers settled here. The painters created what became known as the "Barbizon School". That artistic atmosphere lives on today, in the well-kept flower clad streets. It's about an hour's drive from Paris; access by public transport is less easy, but it's such a delightful place that it's well deserving of a visit.

L'Auberge Ganne-Musée de l'École de Barbizon,
92 Grande Rue,
77630 Barbizon.
Tel. 01 60 66 22 27.
Opening hours, daily, except Tues, all year, 10h00-12h30, 14h00-17h30.

Entrance tariff: EUR3 (reductions). This was the famous inn and boarding house in Barbizon run by the Ganne family, renowned for its country cooking and accommodation. Many of the painters and writers who stayed in the village in the latter part of the 19th century found cosy lodgings for themselves here, where they were well looked after by the Ganne family. Today, much of the atmosphere of the old boarding house has been preserved, even though it's been turned into an art museum depicting the Barbizon School.

Maison Atelier de Jean-François Millet,
Grande Rue,
77630 Barbizon.
Tel. 01 60 66 21 55.
Opening hours, daily, except Tues, all year, 10h00-12h30, 14h00-17h00.
Entrance tariff: free.
Jean-François Millet (1814-1875) was one of the most renowned French painters of the mid-19th century. He came from peasant stock and his works reflected his upbringing in a deeply rural environment. Millet settled in Barbizon in 1849, producing many works that were sometimes melancholis, often sentimental. He was one of the mainstays of the Barbizon School of painting. His two best-known works were The Gleaners in 1857 and The Angelus in 1859. In Barbizon, you can visit the house and studio where he lived and worked and it has been left much as it was in his day.

BAZOCHES-SUR-GUYONNE,
30 km south-west of Paris.
Train: Gare de Montparnasse, Paris to Montfort-Méré.
Road: N12 from Versailles.

Maison de Jean Monnet,
Houjarray,
78490 Bazoches-sur-Oise.
Tel: 01 34 86 12 43.
Web: www. jean-monnet. net
Opening hours, Mon-Fri, all year, 10h00-17h00, Sat, all year, 14h00-17h00.
Entrance tariff: free.

This old house with its thatched roof was where Jean Monnet, one of the founding fathers of the European Community, lived from 1945 until 1979 and worked on his plans for Europe. You can see his sitting room, dining room, office and the bedroom where he died in 1979. You can also see many of his personal possessions and also historic and private documents. The house is today the property of the European Parliament and the first floor is devoted to information on Europe.

BEAUMONT-SUR-OISE,
25 km north of Paris.
Train: Gare du Nord, Paris to Persan Beaumont.
Road: N1 from Paris.

This small town has a very ancient history, but its development did not begin in earnest until the 13th century, when it became part of the royal domaine. It's situated attractively, between the River Oise and the Foret Carnelle, which covers nearly 1, 000 hectares. From the high points in the forest, there are elevated views of much of the Ile de France north of Paris. The town's fortified chateau, built in the 10th century, is now extensive ruins. Also worth seeing in the town is the Église Saint-Laurent, with a nave dating from the 13th century and the choir from the end of the previous century.

BEAUVAIS,
80 km north of Paris.
Train: Gare du Nord, Paris to Beauvais.
Road: A16 from Paris.

Cathédrale,
place de la Cathédrale,
60000 Beauvais.
Opening hours, Apr-Oct, daily, 9h00-12h12, 14h00-18h15, Nov-Mar, daily, closes at 17h30.
Entrance tariff: free.
The cathedral right in the centre of Beauvais miraculously escaped the destruction wrought on Beauvais during the Second World War. Work began in 1225, but the nave was never built. The choir dates from the 13th century and has the highest church vaults in the world.

Galerie de la Tapisserie,
rue St-Pierre,
60000 Beauvais.
Tel. 03 44 15 39 10.
Opening hours, daily, all year, 9h30-12h30, 14h00-18h00.
Entrance tariff: EUR4 (reductions).
The gallery shows a wonderful collection of tapestries made in Beauvais over three centuries. There's also a good selection of antique furniture.

Horloge astronomique,
Cathedral,
60000 Beauvais.
Entrance tariff: EUR4 (reductions).
This astronomical clock was built by Auguste Verité, who completed his handiwork in 1868. The clock is immensely detailed, with a total of 52 faces. Altogether, it contains over 90, 000 moving parts. On the hour, the 68 automats, figures from the celestial city, move around the top of the clock, performing a scene from the last judgement. Regular "Son et Lumière" performances take place daily throughout the year.

Manufacture Nationale de la Tapisserie,
24 rue Henri Brispot,
60000 Beauvais.
Te, . 03 44 14 41 90.
Opening hours, Tues, Wed, Thurs, all year, 14h00-16h00.
Entrance tariff: EUR3. 20 (reductions).
For more than three centuries, tapestry making and Beauvais were inextricably linked. The tapestry factory was founded here in 1664 and became State owned during the Napoleonic era. In 1989, the tapestry factory was revived and visitors can inspect the whole design and weaving process.

Musée de l'Aviation,
60000 Beauvais.
Tel. 03 44 89 26 51.
Web: www. musee-aviation-warluis. com
Opening hours, Sat, Thurs, all year, 14h00-18h00.
Entrance tariff: EUR5. 50 (reductions).
This aircraft museum, just south of Beauvais, off the A16 autoroute, has several historic aircraft, around 1, 000 pieces of aviation equipment and nearly 2, 000 photographs and documents.

Musée Départmental de l'Oise,
1 rue de la musée,
60000 Beauvais.
Tel. 03 44 11 43 83.
Opening hours, daily, all year, 10h00-18h00, closed Tues and some public holidays.
Entrance tariff: EUR2 (reductions).
The Departmental museum is in the old Bishop's Palace, right beside the cathedral; you approach the museum through a 14th century gatehouse. The ground floor of the museum has a considerable collection of medieval sculptures and antiques, while another of its distinctive features is an Art Nouveau dining room. The museum also has many ceramics and a spectacular $16^{th}$ century charpentre (framework).

Musée des Dirigeables,
31-33 rue de Paris,
Quartier Sud Voisinlieu,
60000 Beauvais.
Tel. 03 44 02 69 31.
Opening hours, Feb-Nov, daily, 10h00-17h30, closed Aug 4-17. Also by arr.
Entrance tariff: EUR3 (reductions).
The other aviation museum in Beauvais is also just outside the city, on the southern side, but it is linked to a specific tragedy that happened at Allonne, a small village close to Beauvais. On Oct 5, 1930, the airship R-101, on its way from England to India, crashed. The museum has many relics and much documentation on the subject; the memorial to the disaster is 3 km from the museum.

BELLOY,
15 km north of Paris.
Train: Gare du Nord, Paris to Belloy.
Road: N16 from Paris.
This delightful little village isn't too far beyond Roissy, yet it remains unspoiled. The village can trace its history back to 725. During the 19$^{th}$ century, the area surrounding the village was very productive for cereals and other agricultural products. It also had an important distillery, which closed down in 1951. The coming of the railway in the 19th century helped to open up the village, while in much more recent times, the construction of Charles de Gaulle airport at Roissy had implications for the extension of the village. In the event, the inhabitants decided in favour of extending the village around its periphery and the charming and unspoiled centre was left untoched.

BIÈVRES,
12 km south-west of Paris.
Train: Gare Montparnasse to Anthony.
Road: D906 from Paris.

Musée française de la photographie,
78 rue de Paris,
91570 Bièvres.
Tel. 01 69 35 16 50.
This photographic museum has much material on the two great pioneers of photography in France, Nicéphore Niépce and Louis-Jacques Mandé Daguerre, including some of their early equipment and very rare early photographs. The museum has a considerable array of other cameras, ancient and modern. The museum has been substantially renovated.

BLANDY,
60 km south-east of Paris.
Train: Gare de Lyon, Paris to Melun, then taxi.
Road: A5 E54 from Paris.

Chateau Blandy,
77000 Blandy.
Opening hours, Apr-Nov, daily, 10h00-13h00, 14h00-18h00. At weekends and on public holidays, 19h00. Closed Wed. Nov-Mar, Sat, Sun, public holidays, 10h00-13h00, 14h00-17h30.

Entrance tariff: EUR4 (reductions).
This great fortified castle was built in the 14th century, on the orders of Charles V, expanded in the 16th and 17th centuries and then partly demolished, with some it turned into a farm in the 18th century. In recent years, it has been substantially restored, including its four towers, 35 metre high donjon and archives.

BLÉRANCOURT,
30 km north-east of Paris.
Only accessible by road (A1, A26).

Musée national de la co-opération franco-américaine,
Tel: 03 23 39 60 16.
Opening hours: open daily, 10h-12h30 and 14h-17h30, except Tues. Closed on Jan 1, May 1, Dec 25. Gardens open daily, all year, 8h-19h.
Entrance tariff: EUR4 (reductions).
This marvellous chateau with its parklands and gardens, remains a potent symbol of France-American co-operation over the decades, despite recent difficulties over the 2003 war in Iraq. The chateau was built between 1612 and 1619 and it was used as the headquarters for CARD, an American humanitarian organisation, between 1917 and 1924. Since 1931, it has housed the national museum of Franco-American co-operation. Anne Morgan, a wealthy American heiress, began the CARD fund, which helped in the reconstruction of Picardy after the First World War and she went on to found the museum, which highlights the many links of friendship between France and the US since the 18th century. The chateau also has many works of art created by American artists living in Paris. In the 1920s, a veritable deluge of American artists descended on Paris. Going back to the First World War, the museum also depicts the American humitarian effort and exhibits include an American Field Service ambulance. Outside, you can explore the gardens of the New World, planted with species from the American continent. There are also gardens for the spring, summer and autumn, with an arboretum for the Indian summer months of September and October. The chateau and its grounds are a little off the beaten track, but well worth visiting, for the chateau itself, the museum and the splendid gardens.

BONNEUIL EN VALOIS,
60 km north-east of Paris.
Train: Gare du Nord, Paris to Bonneuil.
Road: N2 from Paris.

Abbaye Royale Note-Dame du Lieu Restauré,
60123 Bonneuil en Valois.
Tel: 03 44 88 55 31.
Openinghours, Sat, Sun, Apr-Oct, 10h00-12h00, 14h00-18h00,
Nov-Mar, Sun, 10h00-12h00, 14h00-18h00. Closed Jan 1, Dec
24, Dec 25.
Entrance tariff: EUR2. 30 (reductions).
This great abbey, still well preserved, was built in the 12<sup>th</sup> century.
Substantial alterations were made in the following two centuries,
then in the 15th and 16th centuries, it was partially rebuilt. The
abbey is well worth seeing for one of the finest rose windows in
France, while the abbey's archaeological museum also tells the
history of the abbey itself.

BOREST,
50 km north of Paris.
Train: Gare du Nord, Paris to Senlis.
Road: A1 from Paris to Senlis, then N33

Jardin de Saint-Vincent,
1 rue Elizabeth Roussel,
60300 Borest.
Tel. 03 44 54 21 52.
Opening hours, June-Sept, Fri-Mon, 12h30-18h30 or by arr.
Entrance tariff: EUR5 (reductions).
This most attractive park extends for three hectares and belongs
to an early 19th century house that's situated on the edges of the
Forest of Ermenonville. Features of the garden include an ancient
wind pump, centuries old trees, La Nonette river and a kitchen
garden.

BOULOGNE-BILLANCOURT,
8 km south-west of Paris.
Métro: Boulogne-Pont de Saint-Cloud.

Biblioètheque Marmottan,
7 place Denfert-Rochereau,
92100 Boulogne-Billancourt.
Tel: 01 41 10 24 70.
Opening hours, Wed, Thurs, Fri, all year, 14h00-18h00, Sat, all year, 9h30-12h00, 14h00-17h00.
Entrance tariff: EUR3
Paul Marmottan was a great collector and historian of the Napoleonic era and he set up this library in Boulogne in the early part of the 20th century. Eventually, it was bequeathed to the Institute of France's Academy of Fine Arts, which runs the house, the museum and the gallery here as the Fondation Marmottan. The museum has an impressive collection of paintings, prints, Empire style furniture and publications from 1811 onwards, from all over Imperial Europe. The house, too, gives an impressive insight into the decorative splendours of the Imperial Age.

Éspace Albert Kahn,
14 rue du Port,
92100 Boulogne-Billancourt.
Tel: 01 46 04 52 80.
Opening hours, Tues-Sun, all year, 11h00-18h00.
Entrance tariff: EUR (reductions).
Albert Kahn was a wealthy banker who moved to Boulogne-Billancourt in 1893. He was an active member of the intelligensia of his time and many big names then in the world of the arts and politics, such as Auguste Rodin, the sculptor, came to the soirées in this fabulously decorated house. Today, the house is carefully preserved as a museum and its archives include the photographic and film journalism that he commissioned and which now gives an immensely interesting insight into the times in which he lived. The 3. 9 hectares of the adjoining gardens are very diverse, including an English garden, a formal French garden and a Japanese garden, as well as a rose garden and a fruit garden. One of the key attractions is the tea ceremony conducted by a Japanese tea master. The gardens were badly damaged during the tempests of December, 1999, which caused so much destruction across France, but much subsequent restoration work was done.

Fondation Pinault
The former Renault car factory, which closed down in 1992, is in the process of being converted into the Fondation Pinault, a contemporart art museum. It promises to be very expansive and enormously impressive, but you'll have to wait until its scheduled opening in 2006.

Musée des Années 30,
Espace Landowski,
28 avenue André-Morizet,
92100 Boulogne-Billancourt.
Tel. 01 55 18 46 42.
Web: www. boulognebillancourt. com
Métro: Marcel Sembat.
Opening hours: Tues-Sun, all year, 11h00-18h00. Closed Mons, Aug 15-31, public holidays. Guided visits (in French), Sun, 14h30.
Entrance tariff: EUR4. 10 (reduction)
This museum is dedicated, as its name suggests, to the art of the 1930s, with some 800 paintings and 1, 500 sculptures and other works. Some of the work on show is rather mediocre, but the museum does have outstanding modernist sculptures by the Martel brothers, as well as fine still lifes and drawings by Juan Gris. For many visitors, the highlight is the collection of architectural designs by such renowned modern architects as Le Corbusier.

Renault museum,
27 rue des Abondances,
92100 Boulogne-Billancourt.
Tel: 01 46 05 21 58.
Opening hours, Tues, Thurs, all year, except Aug, 14h00-18h00.
Entrance tariff: free.
Métro: Boulogne, Port de Saint-Cloud.
The Renault museum tells the story of the founders of the French car company, Louis and Marcel Renault, the history of the company and the people who worked for it, as well as detailing its technological achievements and its numerous competition successes. The cars on show date back to the earliest days of the Renault empire and include examples of such classics as the pre-Second World War 2CV, so beloved of Inspector Maigret. One of the very earliest cars on view is the Voiturette, made in 1898, with

its gleaming hardwood running boards, yellow painted wheels and enormous headlamps.

BRAY-SUR-SEINE,
85 km southeast of Paris.
Train: Gare de Lyon to Bray-sur-Seine.
Road: A5 E54 from Paris.
The delightful riverside village of Bray is on the River Seine, close to the medieval town of Provins. You can enjoy excellent walks along the riverside promenades, as well as visiting "old" Bray with its market hall, built in 1841, old houses and church. Bray has a lively open air market held in the Market Hall on Friday mornings.

BRETEUIL,
100 km north of Paris.
Road: A16 from Paris. No train.

Musée Archéologique,
5 rue de l'Église,
60120 Breteuil.
Tel. 03 44 07 15 12.
Opening hours, July, Aug, Thurs-Sun, 14h00-18h00, Sept-June, Sun, 14h00-18h00.
Entrance tariff: EUR1. 50 (reductions).
This archaeological museum is dedicated to current excavations being carried out in this region. The items on display cover from prehistoric times up to the Middle Ages.

BRIEUL-LE-SEC,
80 km north of Paris.
Train: Gare du Nord, Paris to Clermont.
Road: N16 from Paris.

Garden and park,
68 rue du Carrouel,
60120 Breuil-le-Sec.
Tel. 03 44 50 10 05.
Opening hours, July, Aug, 15h00-19h00.
Entrance tariff: EUR5 (reductions).
This a lovely spot, 20 km north of Creil. The magnificently designed park has a large lake with an island, numerous trees

and a flowering kitchen garden that covers 6, 000 square metres. It has lots of vegetables, fruit trees, rose bushes and flowers, plenty for any gardening enthusiast.

CERNY-LA-FERTÉ,
50 km south of Paris.
Train: Gare Montparnasse to Cerny.
Road: E15 A6/A77 from Paris.

Aerodrome Jean-Baptiste Salis,
91590 Cerby-le-Ferte.
Tel. 01 64 57 55 85.
Opening hours, Sat, Sun, public holidays, all year, 134h00-18h00.
Entrance tariff: EUR5 (reductions).
This airfield has a vast collection of old aircraft, over 50 in all, including a Blériot X1, a Boeing B-17 and a Fokker Dr. 1. Most of the planes date from the First World War and the 1920s. Sometimes, flying displays are organised.

CERNAY-LA-VILLE,
47 km south-west of Paris.
Road: A13/A12/N10. No train.

Abbey of Les Vaux de Cernay,
78720 Cernay-la-Ville.
Tel: 01 34 85 23 00.
Opening hours, Sat, public holidays, all year, 14h00-19h00, Sun, all year, 11h00-18h00 (19h00 in summer).
Entrance tariff: EUR4 (reductions).
The ruins of this former 13th century Cistercian abbey is well worth a visit. You'll find the Monks' Hall and the ruins of the abbey church and you can have an admirable stroll through the 65 hectares of grounds, in the lush greenery of the Chevreuse valley. Among the features of the park are an ancient dovecote and the Saint-Thibault fountain. Eventually, you'll arrive at the lake, where you can enjoy a cruise on one of the small pleasure boats there.

CHAALIS,
55 km north-east of Paris.
Train: Gare du Nord, Paris to Ermenonville.
Road: N2 from Paris to Ermenonville.

Abbaye Royale de Chaalis,
Tel. 03 44 55 04 02.
Web: www.ac-amiens.fr/chaalis
Opening hours, Mar 1-Nov 11, daily, 11h00-18h00. Nov 12-Feb 28, Sun, 11h00-17h00. Park open daily, 10h00-18h00. Closed Dec 25.
Entrance tariff: EUR6. 50 (park and museum).
The ruins of this abbey are in the Forest of Ermenonville, 2 km north of the town of the same name. The abbey itself dates back to the 12th century and you can also see the ruined 13th century church, the rose garden and the formal French garden. The park, with its 300 year old trees and ponds, was designed by Cardinal d'Este, who designed the Tivoli Gardens near Rome. The 3, 500 square metre rose garden was restored recently to its former glory. The site has a museum telling the story of this royal abbey, one of the most interesting in the region. Also, in the nearby forest, you can see the memorial dedicated to the victims of the 1974 air crash, which happened near here.

CHAILLY-EN-BIÈRE,
55 km south of Paris.
Train: Gare de Lyon to Fontainbleu.
Road: A6 E15 from Paris.

Médiamusée,
17 rue de la Fromagerie,
77930 Chailly-en-Bière.
Tel. 01 60 69 22 16.
Opening hours, Wed-Sun, 14h00-18h00.
Closed mid-Jan-mid-Mar.
Entrance tariff: EUR4. 50 (reductions) or EUR6. 75 (reductions) for the two museums.
This museum has an interesting array of equipment showing how images and sound have been projected over the years, from ancient phonographs and magic lanterns to modern CDs and video cameras.

Le Musée du Père Noel
Address, opening hours and entrance tariff as above.
This is the other museum at the same address; this one is dedicated to Father Christmas, his history and origins, going right

back to Viking times and Saint Nicolas. You can also see all kinds of ancient games and presents related to the theme.

CHAMANT,
55 km north of Paris.
Train: Gare du Nord, Paris to Senlis.
Road: A1 from Paris.
Euro Balloon SNC.
Tel. 03 44 32 18 14.
The only way to see the French countryside-by balloon. This company organises hot air balloon trips on a daily basis, weather permitting.

CHAMBOURCY,
25 km west of Paris.
Train: Gare St-Lazare, Paris to Poissy, then taxi.
Road: A14 from Paris.

Désert de Retz,
Allée Frédéric Passy,
98240 Chambourcy.
You won't be able to see much of this extraordinary folly, as it's closed at the moment, apart from glimpses from the road. Built in the 18th century, it had such delights as a Temple of Pan, an open air theatre and an ice house. Today, although some of the buildings have been demolished in recent decades and many remain, the whole atmosphere is of ruin and desolation.

CHAMPIGNY-SUR-MARNE,
20 km south-east of Paris.
Train: RER A2 line.
Road: N4 from Paris.

Guinguette de l'Ile du Martin Pecheur,
94500 Champigny-sur-Marne.
Tel. 01 49 83 03 02.
Opening hours, Mar-Dec, daily.
This establishment is one of the better known places along the River Marne for guinguette entertainment, old style tavern singing and dancing. It has a terrace and gardens overlooking the river. The island itself was one of the famed weekend resort locations for Parisians towards the end of the 19th century.

Musée de la Résistance Nationale,
Parc Vercors,
88 avenue Marx Dormoy,
94500 Champigny-sur-Marne.
Tel: 01 48 81 00 80.
Web: www. musee-resistance. com
Opening hours: Tues-Fri, all year, 9h00-12h30, 14h00-17h30. Sat, Sun, all year, 14h00-18h00. Closed Mon, weekends in Aug, Sept.
Entrance tariff: EUR3. 81 (reduction).
Train: RER A to Champigny-sur-Marne, then bus.
The five floors of the 19th century villa tell the story of the Résistance in France during the Second World War. The museum has all kinds of artefacts, from a wall display of numerous machine guns and pistols to the devices used for distrupting the railways. There are hundreds of photographs and masses of newspaper cuttings. You can also view some short archive films. All the material is in French.

CHAMPLIEU,
70 km north-east of Paris.
Train: Gare du Nord to Compiègne.
Road: N2/D332 from Paris.

Gallo-Roman site,
60129 Champlieu.
Opening hours, daily, all year, no restrictions.
Entrance tariff: free.
At Champlieu, on the southern edge of the great Forest of Compiègne, you can wander round an important Gallo-Roman site, where once stood a major settlement, complete with temple, theatre, baths and a fortified camp.

CHANTILLY,
40 km north of Paris.
Train: Gare du Nord to Chantilly.
Road: N16 from Paris.

Cat Seven,
3 rue des Otages,
60500 Chantilly.
Tel. 03 44 62 19 06.

Web: www.cat-seven.com
If you ever fancied driving a racing car at full tilt, this is the place the indulge yourself. The cars used are Caterham Super Seven 1. 8 litre models that were raced frequently in the 1960s. You can hire one for a day, half a day or whatever length of time you want, enough for you to get behind the wheel and zoom off for some speedtrack fun.

Chateau de Chantilly,
60500 Chantilly,
Tel: 03 44 62 62 62.
Web: www. chateaudechantilly. com
Opening hours, Mar-Oct, daily, 10h00-18h00, closed
Tues. Nov-Feb, Mon, Wed-Fri, 10h30-12h45, 14h00-17h00.
Entrance tariff: EUR7 (reductions).
The chateau is the main highlight of this noted horse racing town; the chateau itself dates from the late 19th century and replaces one destroyed in the Revolution. The main attraction in the chateau are the galleries full of paintings. Also particularly interesting is the library, where the greatest treasure is the Les Très Riches Heures du Duc de Berry, the most renowned of the medieval Books of Hours. The original is far too delicate to put on display but you can see some very authentic looking facsimiles. In the grounds of the chateau, you can enjoy wandering around the pathways and pools. You can also take a 25 minute boat trip, complete with commentary, around the chateau. Daily, between March and October, weather permitting, you can also take a short trip in a hot air balloon. You can also enjoy a taste of the local Chantilly cream, which is whipped and full of sugar, quite delicious; it's on sale in the grounds.

Hippodrome de Chantilly,
60500 Chantilly.
Tel. 03 44 62 41 00.
Chantilly racecourse is the most famous in France, together with Longchamps. During mornings, you can take a tour round the racecourse, by arr. Tel. 44 57 51 51.

Musée Vivant du Cheval,
60631 Chantilly.
Tel. 03 44 57 13 13.
Opening hours, Apr-Oct, Mon, Wed-Sun, 10h30-17h30. Closed Tues. July, Aug, also Tues, 14h00-17h00. Nov-Mar, Mon, Wed, Fri, 14h00-17h00, Sat, Sun, 10h30-17h30.
Entrance tariff: EUR8 (reductions).
More than 40 breeds of horses and ponies are stabled in the main hall of the museum; the building, which is five minutes' walk from the main chateau, was constructed in the 18th century by the then owner of the chateau, who believed that he would be reincarnated as a horse. Frequent demonstrations are organised in the ring, while the museum also has lots of life sized models of horses. You can also inspect all manner of equipment and tackle, from bridles and saddles to veterinary equipment, while the museum also has a reconstruction of a blacksmith's forge. Children will find the collection of childrens' horse toys appealing.

CHARLES DE GAULLE AIRPORT,
95711 Roissy.
Train: RER B3 line; TGV.
Road: E15 E19 from Paris.
Tel. 01 48 62 22 80/01 48 62 12 12.
Web: www.adp.fr
This is the main airport for the Paris region, opened in 1974 as a brand new airport. The appeal of its concrete modernism has worn thin over the years, but the airport has continued to expand at a relentless pace. It now has three terminals; the most recent addition is Hall E in Terminal 2, which offers wireless broadband Internet access for travellers. This new hall also has 20 brand new duty free shops, but these are only useful if you're travelling outside the EU. The various terminals have a reasonable selection of bars, restaurants and shops.

CHARTRES,
90 km south-west of Paris.
Train: Gare Montparnasse, Paris to Chartres.
Road: A11 E50 from Paris.

Cathedrale Notre-Dame,
28000 Chartres.
Opening hours, daily, all year, 8h30-19h30.
Entrance tariff: free (cathedral), EUR2. 50 (reductions) for crypt,
EUR4 (reductions) for tower.
The cathedral at Chartres is the pinnacle of Gothic architecture,
one of the most impressive in France. Now on the UNESCO
World Heritage list, the cathedral was built between 1134 and
1260; a fire in 1194 destroyed much of what had been built, but
rebuilding was completed in just over 30 years. Inside the
cathedral, you can marvel at the intricacies of the stone work in
the three portals and the wonderful 172 stained glass windows.
The Saint-Piat chapel has the Virgin Mary's veil. The crypt, which
can be visited, is the largest in France. You can also climb the
north tower and steeple, over 100 metres high, for wonderful
views over the town.

Centre International du Vitrail,
5 rue du Cardinal Pie,
28000 Chartres.
Tel. 02 37 21 65 72.
Web: www.centre-vitrail.org
Opening hours, Mon-Fri, all year, 9h30-12h30, 13h30-18h00. Sat,
Sun, public holidays, all year, 10h00-12h30, 14h30-18h00.
Entrance tariff: EUR4 (reductions).
Located just 50 metres from the cathedral, this centre was
founded in 1980 in a medieval store house. It's a fascinating
centre, showing how old style and contemporary stained glass
was and is made, through courses, lectures and workshops. All
the different stages of a very complex process are explained in an
easy-to-follow fashion.

Conservatoire de l'Agriculture Compa,
Point de Mainvilliers,
28000 Chartres.
Tel. 02 37 84 15 00.
Web: www. lecompa.com
Opening hours, Tues-Fri, all year, 9h00-12h30, 13h30-18h00. Sat,
Sun, public holidays, 10h00-12h30, 13h30-19h00. Closed Mon.
Entrance tariff: EUR3. 80 (reductions).
This is the largest museum in France given over to agriculture,

presenting old style and contemporary rural life and practices. The museum has around 1, 200 pieces of farm equipment; the oldest tractor is a 1910 Sawyer-Massey, made in the US, while there's lots of equipment from the 19th century. An interactive presentation, a multimedia area and frequent temporary exhibitions are also included in the museum.

Maison Picassiette,
22 rue du Repos,
28000 Chartres.
Tel. 02 37 34 10 78.
Opening hours, Apr-Oct, 10h00-12h00, 14h00-18h00, closed Tues, Sun mornings.
Entrance tariff: EUR4 (reductions).
The house was completely decorated, inside and out, by its owner, Raymond Isodore, with mosaics made from broken pottery. It's an extraorinary example of art naif.

Maison de l'Archeologie,
16 rue Saint-Pierre,
28000 Chartres.
Tel. 02 37 30 99 38.
Opening hours, July-Sept, daily, 14h00-18h00, closed
Tues. Oct-May, Wed, Sun, 14h00-17h00 or by arr.
Entrance tariff: EUR1. 5 (reductions).
The museum was created in 1993 to house collections of materials produced by the numerous archaeological excavations in Chartres since 1976. A new exhibition is staged every year on local archaeology.

Musée des Beaux-Arts,
29 Cloitre Notre-Dame,
28000 Chartres.
Tel. 02 37 36 41 39.
Opening hours, May-Oct, daily, 10h00-12h00, 14h00-18h00, except Tues, Sun mornings. Closes at 17h00, Nov-Apr.
Entrance tariff: EUR2. 45 (reductions0.
The former bishop's palace, close to the cathedral, has rich collections of older and contemporary art and also, unusually, a collection of 17th and 18th century harsichords. The museum also has a selection of old Indian canoes from North America.

Musée Départemental de l'Ecole,
1 rue du 14 juillet,
28000 Chartres.
Tel. 02 37 30 07 69.
Opening hours, Mon-Fri, all year, 10h00-12h00, 14h00-18h00.
Closed weekends and public holidays.
Entrance tariff: EUR3. 50 (reductions).
For anyone with fond memories of school, this is the place to
indulge a little nostalgia. The museum has a very authentic
reproduction of a 19$^{th}$ century rural school, complete with
classroom desks and posters.

Musée des Sciences naturelles et de prehistoire,
5 bis, boulevard de la Courtille,
28000 Chartres.
Tel. 02 37 28 36 09.
Web: http: //www, ville-chartres.fr
Opening hours, Wed, Sun, all year, 14h00-17h00. In July, Aug,
daily, except Sat, until 18h00. School holidays, daily, except Sat,
until 18h00.
Entrance tariff: free.

River Eure,
28000 Chartres.
Near the cathedral and town centre, you can relax on a three km
stretch of the River Eure, in a pedalo or in a canoe. It costs just
over EUR7. 50 to hire a pedalo for 30 minutes in the Parc des
Bords de l'Eure, at the foot of the Pont de la Courtille.

Walks around the old town,
28000 Chartres.
The old town of Chartres covers 60 hectares between the
cathedral, in the upper town, and the banks of the River Eure in
the lower town. Many of the streets date from the Middle Ages; in
the rue des Ecuyers, the houses are half-timbered. Very close to
the cathedral, on the place de la Poissonnerie, the Maison du
Saumon, its facade covered in wooden sculptures, is one of the
finest in Chartres. You can also walk down the five Tertres or
passages that link the upper and lower levels of the town.

CHATEAU LANDON,
80 km south of Paris.
Train: Gare de Lyon to Souppes sur Loing, then taxi.
Road: A6 from Paris.
Chateau Landon is a small, medieval town that's almost completely unspoiled. The place is so old that it dates back to a hill fort that was seized by Julius Caesar in 52BC. Many of its buildings dating from the Middle Ages are still lagrely intact today, so the place has a delightfully timeless air to it. Among the ancient buildings are the Abbaye de St-Séverin, the priory, the church of Notre-Dame with its 15th century 57 metre high bell tower and distinguished old houses, including the Hotel de la Monnaie. The ramparts are largely intact and you can have a pleasant walk along most of them, as well as climbing the steeply stepped alleyways that dart here and there in the old town. Stone from the quarries here was used to build Notre Dame in Paris.

CHATENAY-MALABRY,
15 km south of Paris.
Train: RER B (gare de Robinson).
Road: D906 from Paris.

Arboretum de la Vallée-aux-Loups,
46 rue Chateaubriand,
92290 Chatenay-Malabry.
Tel: 01 41 13 00 90 (01 43 50 42 48, weekends).
Web: www.hauts-de-seine.net
Opening hours, Mar 1-Nov 30, Wed, Sat, 14h00-17h00 (Mar, Oct, Nov), 14h00-18h00 (Apr-Sept).
Entrance tariff: free.
In the heart of this park, the arboretum, which is close to the Chateaubriand house and gardens, has remarkable collections of trees. A total of 500 different species of trees and shrubs are planted in its 13. 5 hectares. Some of the designed gardens here are very interesting to walk around, including the fruit gardens, a garden that has been landscaped in the English Romantic style and a striking autumn garden. Altogether, the arboretum is listed as one of the great garden sites of France. The whole park covers 56 hectares, has a country walking trail and from its higher points, remarkable views across the the Chateau de Sceaux (qv).

Centre de documentation sur les arbres et les jardins,
46-56 rue de Chateaubriand,
92290 Chatenay-Malabry.
Tel: 01 41 13 00 90.
Web: www. hauts-de-seine.net
Opening hours, by prior arr, Mon, Tues. Without booking, Wed and first Sat of each month, 11h30-17h30 (closes at 17h00, Oct-Mar). Closed July, Aug, Christmas.
Entrance tariff: free.
This centre is in the heart of the arboretum and it is a resource centre on the parks and gardens of the Hauts-de-Seine department. It has an excellent library of books and periodicals on the subject, as well as more than 6, 000 photographs of the natural heritage of the department.

Maison et parc de Chateaubriand,
87 rue Chateaubriand,
92290 Chatenay-Malabry.
Tel: 01 47 02 08 62.
Web: www. hauts-de-seine. net/maison-musee-Chateaubriand
Opening hours, Apr 1-Sept 30, daily, except Mon, 10h00-12h00, 14h00-18h00. Oct 1-Mar 31, daily, except Mon, 14h00-17h00.
Entrance tariff: EUR4. 5 (reductions).
Chateaubriand was the man of the great double life in the early 19th century, statesman and man of letters. The house where he lived between 1807 and 1818 has been meticulously restored, including absolutely authentic decor. There's a very special feeling about the house, where some of the greatest works in French literature were written. He was also responsible for planting the gardens, which he designed as a reflection of his native Brittany as well as his travels in America and the Mediterranean. The nomad in Chateaubriand was given full rein in his designs for the gardens, which are in immaculate condition.

CHATOU,
15 km west of Paris.
Train: RER A1 line to Chatou-Croissy.
Road: N13 from Nanterre.

Maison Levanneur,
Ile des Impressionistes,
78400 Chatou.
Tel: 01 39 52 45 35.
Opening hours, Wed-Sun, all year, 12h00-18h00.
Entrance tariff: free.
This centre for contemporary art on the island of impressionists is
housed in a building that was, in the early part of the 20th century,
the studio of André Derain and Maurice de Vlaminck. The centre
has four annual exhibitions, while it also stages various
programmes of artistic activity. It's also well worthwhile strolling
the rest of the island.

CHEPTAINVILLE,
45 km south of Paris.
Train: Gare de Lyon, Paris to Marolles en Hurepoix, then taxi.
Road, N20 from Paris, then D449 from La Ferté-Alais.

L'Ile aux Oiseaux,
Chemin d'Arpajon a Lardy,
91630 Cheptainville.
Tel: 01 64 56 15 81.
Web: www. ileauxoiseaux. fr
Opening hours, May 1-Sept 30, daily, 10h00-20h00, Mar 1-Apr 30
and Oct 1-Nov 30, closes at 18h30. Dec 1-Feb 28, daily, 10h00-
12h30, 14h00-18h00.
Entrance tariff: EUR6. 50 (reductions).
In this wilderness, with an abundance of flora and fauna and
many covered spaces, you can see many species of birds. Shop.

CHEVREUSE,
30 km south-west of Paris.
Train: Gare Montparnasse, Paris to St Rémy-les-Chevreuses,
then taxi.
Road: N118 from Paris.

Chateau de Breteuil,
Choisel,
78460 Chevreuse.
Tel: 01 30 52 05 02.
Opening hours, chateau, daily, all year, 10h00-17h30, grounds, daily, all year, 10h00-sunset.
Entrance tariff: free.
The chateau of the Marquis de Breteil has over 330 years of history within its elegant brick and stone walls and another feature that should appeal to visitors, young and old alike. Inside the chateau, there are 40 full-sized figures in wax of famous French historical figures, from Louis XVI to Marie-Antoinette and Marcel Proust, dressed in the costumes of their times.
A real life storyteller narrates the Perrault Tales and for many children, this is a magical experience that adults too will want to share in. Outside the chateau, you can explore the formal gardens, the very romantic parkland and the flower garden known as the Princes' Garden, complete with walking trails.


CLAMART,
8km south-west of Paris.
Train: Gare Montparnasse, Paris to Clamart, Métro: Corentin-Celton, then bus.
Road: D906 from Paris.

Centre d'arts plastiques contemporaines Albert Chanot,
33 rue Brissard,
92140 Clamart.
Tel: 01 47 36 05 89.
Opening hours, Mar-Oct, daily, except Mon, public holidays, 15h00-19h00. Nov-Feb, daily, except Mon, public holidays, 14h00-18h00.
Entrance tariff: free.
This is a wonderfully spacious and light arts centre, where regular exhibitions of contemporary art are staged, nine times a year. The centre itself is so interestingly designed that it adds much to visitors' appreciation of the art on show.

Fondation Arp,
21 rue des Chataigniers,
92140 Clamart.
Tel: 01 47 34 22 63.
Web: www. fondationarp. org
Opening hours, Mon, Sat, all year, 14h00-18h00.
Entrance tariff: EUR4. 57 (reductions).
Train: from Gare de Montparnasse, Paris. Metro: Corentin-Celton, then bus.

Designed by Sophie Taeuber in the sober style of the Bauhas, so fashionable in the 1920s, it was here that Jean Arp (1886-1966) lived and worked. Most of his sculptures were created here. In the centre, you can see many important examples of Arp's work, including bronze, stone and wood sculptures, as well as reliefs and collages, from all his periods, as well as works by Sophie Taeuber. You can actually touch all the work, to get to know them better, but you have to wear the special gloves provided.

CLICHY,
12 km north-west of Paris.
Métro: Mairie de Clichy.
Musee Clichy,
Boulevard de Général Leclerc,
92110 Clichy.
Tel: 01 47 15 33 07.
Opening hours, Tues, all year, 17h00-18h30, Wed, Sat, all year, 14h00-17h00.
Entrance tariff: free.

Clichy is renowned not just for its industrial history but its artistic connections too, all reflected in the elegant museum here. The most important of its manufacturing heritage was the crystal glass works that operated between 1842 and 1895 and whose output rivalled that of Baccarat and Saint-Louis. Many great names in French history had connections with Clichy, from Saint Vincent de Paul, who was the parish priest here between 1612 and 1625 to Gustave Eiffel, the man who created the Eiffel Tower. From the world of the arts, Debussy, Henry Miller and Verlaine all had associations with Clichy, as well as Louise Weber, otherwise known was "La Goulue", the famous star of the Moulin Rouge cabaret. All are chronicled here, although Henry Miller less than the other, probably because of his shocking notoriety during the 1930s.

COLOMBES,
15 km north-west of Paris.
Train: RER A1 line to Nanterre.
Road: D308 from Neuilly-sur-Seine.

Musée Municipal,
2 rue Gabriel Péri,
92700 Colombes.
Tel: 01 47 86 38 85.
Opening hours, Wed, Thurs, Fri, all year, 14h00-18h00, Sat, all year, 10h00-12h00, 14h00-18h00.
Entrance tariff: free
Train: Gare Saint-Lazare to Colombes.
This small but very compact and enticing museum captures well the spirit of the Paris suburbs as well as the history of Colombes itself. The many industries of Colombes are featured, including Guerlain, the perfumes company, and Hispano-Suiza, a noted aeronautics firm. You go also go back in history to explore the development of the 1924 Olympic stadium in Paris and the staging of the 1938 World Cup in football, also in Paris.

Parc Pierre Lagravère,
Rue Paul Bert,
92700 Colombes.
This is a lovely park, that once was a 25 hectare island in the River Seine, now incorporated into the banks of the river. You can have a delightful walk in the long stretches of the park, beside the river, using the five km of paths designed for walkers, joggers and runners. Plenty of sporting facilities are available, too, including a skating rink, an Olympic pool and tennis courts, while there's a children's play area and even a roundabout. Cafes in the park ensure that you won't go hungry!

COMPIÈGNE,
81 km north-east of Paris.
Train: Gare du Nord, Paris to Compiègne.
Road: E15 E19.

Chateau de Compiègne,
Tel: 03 44 38 47 02.
Opening hours, daily, all year, except Tues, 10h00-18h00. Nov 1-Feb 28, last admission to grand apartments is at 15h45. Closed Jan 1, May 1, Dec 25 and certain public holidays.
Entrance tariff: EUR4 (reductions).
The chateau is reconstruction dating from the mid-18th century, ordered by Louis XV and completed by Louis XVI, this chateau was then entirely restyled for Napoléon and you can see all kinds of imperial memorabilia. Napoléon III also had a great affection for this chateau and his legacy to the future was a central heating system that still works superbly today. The historic apartments are well worth seeing, as are the ballroom and the theatre. In the west wing, there's a car museum, open daily, that specialises in early transport, including the state coach of Napoléon and and 1899 Renault, one of the first from that firm. The stables close to the chateau today house the national stud farm, with about 55 stallions of all breeds. The stud is open daily to visitors, free of charge. The parkland outside is also worth exploring. It was redesigned on Napoleon's orders and one of its outstanding feature is the view from the chateau down the 4. 5 km long Allée des Beaux-Monts, inspired by the Schonbrunn estate in Germany. A tunnel of greenery, the Berceau de l'Impératrice, leads walkers into the depths of the forest.

Chateau de Pierrefonds,
60350 Pierrefonds.
Tel: 03 44 42 72 72.
Web: www. monum. fr
Opening hours, May 15-Sept 15, daily, 9h30-18h00. Sept 16-30 and Apr 1-May 14, Mon-Sat, 9h30-12h30, 14h00-a8h00. Oct 1-Mar 31, Mon-Sat, 9h30-12h30, 14h00-17h30. Sun, 9h30-178h30.
Entrance tariff: EUR6. 10(reductions).
This is an extraordinary castle, 8 km south-east of Compiègne. It's a fake, but nonetheless fascinating for that. Napoléon had bought the original castle ruins, which dated back to the 15th century, then Napoléon III had one tower restored for use as a hunting tower. In the end, the restoration project mushroomed and the whole castle was done up and extended, in a tremendously over-the-top pastiche of medieval and Renaissance style, designed by architect Viollet-le-Duc, to whom a permanent exhibition is devoted.

City Hall,
rue des Patissiers,
60200 Compiègne.
Opening hours, Mon-Sat, all year, 9h00-17h00.
Entrance tariff: free.
The Hotel de Ville is a late Gothic masterpiece, built between 1498 and 1530 and renovated at the end of the 19th century. At the top of the belfry, you can see one of the oldest city clocks in France; three figures strike the hours with their hammers.

Clairière de l'Armistice
Tel: 03 44 85 14 18
Opening hours, Feb 1-Oct 14, daily, 9h00-12h00, 14h00-18h00. Oct 15-Nov 31, daily, 10h00-12h00, 14h00-17h30. Dec 1-Jan 31, 14h0017h30. Closed Tues, Jan 1, Dec 25.
Entrance tariff: free.
In the forest, 4 km from Compiègne, you can inspect the Clairière de l'Armistice, a memorial to the place where the Germans surrendered to Maréchal Foch on Nov 11, 1918, thus ending the First World War. It was here too in the same place, that the French surrendered to the Germans in 1940. The clearing has a statue of Foch and a reconstruction of the railway carriage where the 1918 German surrender was signed. It has many interesting historical artefacts.

Église de Saint-Pierre-des-Minimes,
rue des Minimes,
60200 Compiègne.
This is the oldest church in town, dating back to the 12th century. Its architecture includes a fine Romanesque portal. The church interior is frequently used for art exhibitions and concerts.

Musée Antoine Vivenel,
2 rue d'Austerlitz,
60200 Compiègne.
Tel: 03 44 20 26 04
Web: http: //www.compiegne.fr
Opening hours, Mar 1-Oct 31, Tues-Sun, 9h00-12h00, 14h00-18h00. Nov 1-Feb
28, Tues-Sun, 9h00-12h00, 14h00-17h00. Closed Jan 1, May 1, July 14, Nov 1, Dec 25.

Entrance tariff: EUR2 (reductions).

Installed in the spectacular Songeons mansion, which was built in the 18th century, the museum has many notable archaeological finds, including a collection of painted vases from ancient Greece that's unique in France. Antoine Vivenel, who founded the museum in 1839, loved both prehistoric times and the Renaissance period, the latter illustrated by enamel work from Limoges and glasswork from Venice. The museum has many objets d'art, sculptures and tableaux from the 18th and 19th centuries.

Musée de la Figurine Historique,
28 place de l'Hotel de Ville,
60200 Compiègne.
Tel: 03 44 40 72 55
Web: http: //www.compiegne. fr
Opening hours, Mar 1-Oct 31, Tues-Sun, 9h00-12h00, 14h00-18h00. Nov 1-Feb 28, Tues-Sun, 9h00-12h00, 14h00-17h00. Closed Jan 1, May 1, July 14, Nov 1, Dec 25.
Entrance tariff: EUR2 (reductions)
This museum has an extraordinary collection of figurines, 100, 000 in all, depicting both civilian and military figures. They are placed in lifelike settings in dioramas and one of the most spectacular shows 12, 000 pieces, which depict the most celebrated battles of the First Empire.

Ramparts
In an area of green space called Les Remparts, you can see what's left of the city walls that were built between the 12th and 17th centuries.

Theatre Imperial de Compiègne,
3 rue Othenin,
60200 Compiègne.
Tel: 03 44 40 17 10.
This splendid theatre was designed in the classical style, with elaborate balconies and a magnificent domed roof. It was a long time coming-Napoléon III ordered its construction in 1871, but it wasn't officially inaugurated until 1991, 120 years later! However, the wait was worthwhile. The theatre has superb acoustics and sightlines and it's used for many performances throughout the year of ballet, drama, music and opera, even for film showings.

CONFLANS SAINTE-HONORINE,
20 km west of Paris.
Train: RER A3 line from Paris to Conflans-Fin d'Oise station. Train from St-Lazare, Paris.
Road: A15 from St-Ouen.
Conflans Sainte-Honorine is an attractive riverside town, where the river Seine and Oise meet. Since the mid-19th century, it's been an important river port and if you walk the length of the quays, you'll see many river boats tied up, for repairs or simply to refuel. The quayside cafés are convivial and atmospheric, with many of the river workers stopping off for refreshments. Close to the town centre, yo'll see the 12th century church of Saint-Maclou, with its shrine of Sainte-Honorine, the town's patron saint. The town also has the Tour Montjoie, dating from the 10th century and a remnant of the town's old fortifications, approached by small pedestrian streets. From the municipal park, there are extensive views of the River Seine.

Le Musée de la Batellerie (Barge Museum),
3 place Gévelot,
78700 Conflans-Sainte-Honorine
Tel: 01 34 90 39 50
Opening hours: Mon, Wed, thurs, Fri, 9h00-12h00; 13h30-18h00 (closed Tues mornings). Sat, Sun, 15h00-18h00 in summer, 14h00-17h00 in winter.
Entrance tariff: EUR4 (reductions).
This museum has the most extensive collection of material in France detailing the history of river navigation, with over 200 models and hundreds of objects, tableaux, engravings, documentation and tools that depict the life of the bargemen and women. The museum has five exhibition spaces, each devoted to a particular theme of waterborne life, including canal boats and canalized rivers. On the first floor, you'll see a presentation on the 53 different types of river boats that were in use before designs were made uniform.

Historic canal boats,
Port Saint-Nicolas.
Opening hours: Sat, Sun afternoons in summer.
Entrance tariff: EUR1. 50 (reductions).
In this quayside area of the town, you'll find two ancient river boats that have been well restored, Le Triton 25 and Le Jacques.

The latter boat is particularly interesting, built in 1904, the oldest steam powered river boat in France and a Monument Historique. This part of the port offers the chance for long riverside walks and meeting many of the retired mariners who live here.

Bateau chapelle (Boat chapel),
quai de la République,
78700 Conflans-Sainte-Honorine.
Opening hours: daily, all year, with daily religious service at 18h00.
Entrance tariff: free.
This river boat, named "Le Sers"), is 70 metres long and is painted white and blue but it has an unusual distinction. It's one of just six river boats in France that have been turned into chapels. In its days as a working barge, the boat could carry up to 1, 100 tonnes of merchandside, but since 1935, it's carrying heavenly souls. The interior has been fully converted into a chapel, complete with altar.

COULOMMIERS,
70 km east of Paris.
Train: Gare de l'Est, Paris to Coulommiers.
Road: N34 from Paris.

Medieval garden of the Commanderie des Templiers,
77120 Coulommiers,
Tel. 01 64 65 08 61.
Opening hours, May-Sept, Fri, Sat, sun, 14h00-18h00.
Entrance Tariff: EUR4 (reductions).
The great fort of the Commanderie des Templiers was built on the heights overlooking the town in the 12th century, then after the Order was dissolved in the early 13th century, the place became the Hopital de Saint-Jean de Jérusalem. During the Revolution, the buildings and land were sold off to local farm owners. Today, thanks to the work of a local association, over 4, 000 square metres of land have been planted with more than 250 varieties of medieval plants, making an astonishing garden that's well worth looking round.

Town centre
In the centre of Coulommiers, it's worth walking around to see the many historic buildings, including a medieval hall once used for

6

selling cheese. You can also take a barge trip along the Grand Morin river. The town's tourist office, tel. 01 64 03 88 09, organises walking tours of the town centre and the river trips.

COUPVRAY,
30km east of Paris.
Train: RER A line to Marne-la-Vallée-Chessy, then taxi.
Road: A4 from Paris.
Braille museum,
13 rue Louis Braille,
77700 Coupvray.
Tel. 01 60 04 82 80.
Opening hours, Apr-Sept, daily, except
Mon, 10h00-12h00, 14h00-18h00, Oct-Mar, daily, except Mon, 14h-17h00. Fri, by arr.
Entrance tariff: EUR4 (reductions).
Within easy reach of Disneyland Paris is the Braille museum, in the house where Louis Braille, inventor of the Braille system of reading for blind people, was born in 1809. His father was a harness maker and one day, when he was three years of age, young Louis was playing with his father's tools. One slipped into his eye; infection quickly spread to the other eye and Braille soon found himself sightless. Many books and artefacts from his life are on show in the museum. Apart from the museum, you can see the church where he was baptised, the local cemetery where he was originally buried (100 years after) and a commemorative monument.

COURANCES,
60 km south of Paris.
Train: Gare de Lyon, Paris to Boutigny sur Essonne, then taxi.
Road: A6 E15 from Paris.
Chateau Courances,
91490 Courances.
Opening hours, Apr-Oct, Sat, Sun, public holidays, daily, 14h00-18h00.
Entrance tariff: EUR5 (reductions).
No traces are left of the original chateau, which was built in 1550, but what you can see is the chateau that dates from the extensive renovations carried out during the 17th century. The interior has magnificent decor and furniture and particularly worth seeing are

the vestibule, entirely in marble, the so-called "Monkey Gallery" with its 16th century tapestries and the 200 metre long grand miroir. In the lakes in the gardens, you can see the magnificent jeu d'eaux performing on occasion.

COURBEVOIE,
15 km north-west of Paris.
Road: A14
Train: Gare St Lazare, Paris to Courbvoie.

Musée Roybet Fould,
178 boulevard Saint-Denis,
92400 Courbevoie.
Tel: 01 43 33 30 73.
Opening hours, daily, all year, except Tues, 10h30-18h00.
Entrance tariff: free.
Metro: Pont de Levallois, Bécon.
The museum dates back to 1951 and its setting is very unusual- the red pine pavilion built for Norway and Sweden for the Paris Universal Exhibition in 1878. Its collections show the development of artistic life in France in the second part of the 19th century and feature principally the works of Consuleo Fould and Ferdinand Roybet, as well as drawings, paintings and sculptures by many other artists of the period. This enchanting museum also has an interesting collection of toys, as well as many artefacts relating to local history, including posters and postcards.

COURSON,
35 km south-west of Paris.
Train: RER C line to Breuillet/Bruyéres-le-Chatel.
Road: A11 E50 from Paris.

Domaine de Courson,
91680 Courson.
Tel. 01 64 58 90 12.
Web: www.coursondom.com
Opening hours, park, Sun, public holidays, 10h00-18h00 (17h00 in winter), chateau, Sun, public holidays, Mar-Nov, 14h00-18h00.
Entrance tariff: EUR5 park-(reductions), EUR7. 50 chateau (reductions).

The park covers just overs 30 hectares and it has many rare trees and shrubs. It was created in the 19th and 20th centuries and has been restored immaculately. The chateau, which can also be seen, was built in the 17<sup>th</sup> century and it has been much restored since 1980.

CREPY EN VALOIS,
70 km north of Paris.
Train: Gare du Nord, Paris to Crepy en Valois.
Road: A1 to Senlis, then N324.

Abbaye Saint Arnoul,
place Saint-Simon,
60800 Crepy en Valois.
Tel. 03 44 94 25 73.
Opening hours, Apr-Dec, Sun, 14h00-18h00.
Entrance tariff: free.
The abbey dates back to 1006; some of the buildings have been restored, including the chapter house, the cloisters and the so-called warm room. You can also explore an extensive network of underground tunnels. The museum has many old tools and items of household equipment, as well as furniture, clothes and jewellery, from the 19th and earlier 20th centuries.

CROISSY-SUR-SEINE,
15 km west of Paris.
Train: RER A1 line to Chatou-Croissy.
Road: N13 or RN186 from Nanterre.

Maison Joséphine,
6 bis, Grande Rue,
78290 Croissy-sur-Seine.
Tel: 01 30 15 18 69.
Web: www.perso.wanadoo.fr/grenouillere
Opening hours, Tues, Thurs, Sun, all year, 14h00-18h00. Closed Dec 15-Jan 15.
Entrance tariff: EUR3. 20 (reductions).
During the latter part of the 19th century, the Grenouillère floating dance café in the River Seine at Croissy was a favourite leisure spot for Parisians, full of gaiety and fun. On Sunday afternoons, all the Paris of arts and letters came here. In many ways, the

Impressionist school of painting was born here. In the museum, with its substantial collections of artefacts, engravings, paintings and posters, you can drift back into the sublime atmosphere of this riverside town at the height of the Impressionist period. The museum has lots of interesting items, including gravure prints, tableaux and objets d'art. The Musée de la Grenouillere here, which is open Tues, Thurs and Sun all year, 14h00-18h00, also records local history.

DISNEYLAND RESORT PARIS,
77206 Marne-la-Vallée.
30 km east of Paris.
Train: RER A line to Marne-la-Vallée Chessy, TGV.
Road: A4 from Paris.
Tel. 01 60 30 60 23.
Web: www.disney.fr
Opening hours, summer, daily, 9h00-22h00, winter, 10h00-21h00.
Entrance tariff: EUR39 (one day ticket to theme park-reductions), EUR105 (3 day theme park Hopper ticket-reductions).
For children and adults alike, this is a marvellous play place, an enormous theme park made up of seven different villages, each with their own theme. If you're into cowboys and adventure, then the Adventureland village is just right for you. The most recent addition to Disneyland are the Walt Disney Studios, where you can see how films are made, including animation films, have a look at the costumes and all the special effects. There's such an enormous amount to do and see in the whole resort that you can quite happily spend a few days here, staying in one of the hotels here.

DOURDAN,
40 km south-west of Paris.
Train: RER C4 line.
Road: N20/D116 from Paris.
Dourdan is a most charming medieval town, among the most agreeable in the Ile de France. It is on the River Orge, a tributary of the River Seine and the town is surrounded by 1, 600 hectares of forests. The town itself has its original fortress, built in 1220 by Philippe Auguste, as well as the church of St-Germain, built between the 13th and 15th centuries and many fine old houses. The market was rebuilt in the 19th century. The town centre is full

of old streets, alleyways and steps, half-timbered houses and masses of flowers, a delight to stroll around. The two streets with the greatest abundance of ancient houses, dating back to the 14th century, are the Rue des Fossés du Ch6qtequ qnd the Rue de l'Abreuvoir. During June, the town stages a substantial medieval fair, complete with very authentic costumes for the townspeople taking part.

Chateau and museum,
place du Général de Gaulle,
91410 Dourdan.
Opening hours, Wed-Sun, including public holidays, 10h00-12h00, 14h00-18h00.
Closes Fri, 17h00. Closed Mon, Tues, Dec 25, Jan.
Entrance tariff: EUR3. 20 (reductions)
The fortified chateau is one of only a handful left well preserved in the Ile de France, the only 13th century castle in the region to have kept all its key structures. It's worth exploring the circular keep, with its three floors. It's a fine example of military architecture, complete with ribbed vaulting on the ceilings. Inside, you can still see the graffiti carved by prisoners. Alongside the keep is the municipal museum, which has all kinds of delightful and interesting items, from documents on the history of the town, to old furniture, old time jars and bottle once used by chemists in the 18th century and a fine collection of paintings with local themes. One fine painting, part of a substantial collection, was created between 1943 and 1945 by Robert Chailloux, is a most pleasing landscape of the town and also shows a farmer hard at work, with a horse-drawn cart.

Église de Saint-Germain l'Auxerrois,
91410 Dourdan.
This very fine church was built originally during the 12th and 13th centuries, but was partially destroyed during the 15th and 16th centuries. It was rebuilt and restored by Anne of Austria.

Old town centre
91410 Dourdan.
Much of the old medieval town that forms the heart of Dourdan has been well preserved, including the market hall, which was built in the 13th century and restored in 1836. The former Hotel

Dieu dates from the 18th century, while the Parterre, once a domestic residence, is now the hotel de ville, redolent with antiquity. A substantial portion of the ramparts can also be seen.

ECOUEN,
20 km north of Paris.
Train: Gare du Nord, Paris to Ecouen-Ezanville, then bus.
Road: N16 from St-Denis.

Musée National de la Renaissance,
Chateau d'Ecouen,
95440 Ecouen.
Tel: 01 34 38 38 50.
Opening hours, from Apr 15 to Sept 30, daily, except public holidays, 9h30-12h45, 14h00-17h45. Oct 1-Apr 14, daily, except public holidays, closes 17h15.
Entrance: EUR5 (reductions).
This chateau, an exceptional piece of 16th century architecture, created by Anne de Montmorency, is now the national museum of the Renaissance. Particularly outstanding are the painted fireplaces in the Fontainebleu style and the 75 metre long tapestry depicting the history of David and Bathsheba.

ELANCOURT,
25 km south-west of Paris.
Train: Gare Montparnasse, Paris to La Verrière, then bus.
Road: A13, A12 from Paris.

La France Miniature,
25 route du Mesnil,
78900 Elancourt.
Tel. 01 30 16 16 30.
Web: http: //www. franceminiature. com
Opening hours, Apr-Nov, daily, 10h00-18h00. July, Aug, until 19h00.
Entrance tariff: 13. 50 (reductions).
If you want to stroll round the whole of France in a couple of hours, this is the place to do it! The theme park with a difference has more than 160 models of well-known buildings and monuments from all over France, done in immaculate detail to 1/30th scale. Among them are the Eiffel Tower, the Stade de

France, the Chateau de Chambord, while there are even models of the luxury salons from the old "Normandy" liner and a model of a typical traditional neighbourhood grocery store. The models are always being joined by new ones, so there's always something new and exciting to see here. Restaurant, shop.

EMANCE,
60 km south-west of Paris.
Train: Gare Montparnasse, Paris to Gazeran, then taxi.
Road: N10 from Versailles to Rambouillet.

Réserve Zoologique du Parc du Chateau de Sauvage,
78125 Emance.
Tel. 01 34 94 00 94.
Opening hours, daily, all year, 9h00-19h00, in winter, until sunset.
Entrance tariff: EUR7. 50 (reductions).
All sorts of animals roam in the wild here, from antelopes to kangaroos and stags. The kangaroos that have been living in the wild in the forests around Rambouillet for the past 30 years and which you might see hopping around on your travels round this area, are descended from animals that escaped from here 30 years ago. The park also has a lake, with lots of pink flamingoes, and a tropicarium with many rare tropical birds.

ENGHIEN-LES-BAINS,
15 km N of Paris.
Train: Gare de Nord, Paris to Enghien-les-Bains.
Road: N14 from St-Denis.

Centre culturel François Villon,
4 rue Talma,
95880 Enghien-les-Bains.
Tel: 01 34 12 85 89.
This cultural centre in Enghien is a hive of artistic and community activity and frequent cultural events, concerts and exhibitions are staged here.

Centre des Arts,
18 rue de la Libération,
Enghien-les-Bains,
98550 Enghien-les-Bains.

Tel: 01 30 10 88 91.
This new cultural centre has a substantial gallery for exhibitions on cultural themes, which are held regularly, as well as an auditorium, where concerts are staged.

Galerie Hénot,
14 rue de Mora,
Enghien-les-Bains,
98550 Val de Oise.
Tel: 01 34 12 69 96.
This gallery puts on regular exhibitions of work by contemporary artists.

Lake,
98550 Enghien-les-Bains.
Enghien-les-Bains has a large lake, covering two sq km, dotted with islands. On one shoreline, the casino and restaurant attract people with loads of money to spend. You can hire boats on the lake for a pleasant afternoon's boating in shallow waters, that are up to five metres deep.

ERMENONVILLE,
60 km north-east of Paris.
Train: Gare du Nord, Paris to Ermenonville; RER B to Charles de Gaulle terminal 1, then shuttle bus.
Road: N2 to Ermenonville.

La Mer de Sable,
60950 Ermenonville.
Tel: 03 44 54 00 96.
Web: www. mer-de-sable. com
Opening hours, Mar-Sept, Mon-Fri, 10h30-18h30. Sat, Sun, closes at 19h00.
Entrance tariff: EUR15 (reductions).
This Wild West theme park is very popular with children and adults, a sea of sand in the heart of the forest. It was created in 1963, in the very heart of the forest, by Jean Richard, an actor, who had been inspired by countless classic adventure stories. Visitors can enjoy all kinds of live action shows as well as take part in activities that range from the gentle carousels to rides on the log fumes, which are very energetic and scary. You can also

take a quick trip around the world, sampling the Wild West, a Moroccan souk and Chinatown, complete with pagodas. The forest near here was the scene of one of the worst air crashes in French history, when a Turkish Airlines plane came down in 1974, killing all 346 people on board. A monument was subsequently built at La Baraque de Chaalis, in the southern part of the forest.

ÉTAMPES,
51 km south of Paris.
Train: RER C6 line to Étampes.
Road: N20 from Paris.
This little town, frequently called "Little Venice" because of all its rivers, has a feast of Renaissance houses, once the homes of merchants made rich by grain. It's one of the royal towns of the region and it's also noted for its plethora of churches, including the extraordinary fortified Eglise de Notre-Dame-du-Fort.

Base de Loisirs,
5 avenue Charles de Gaulle,
91150 Étampes.
Tel. 01 64 94 76 18.
Web: www.base-loisirs-etampes.net
Opening hours, Apr 1-May 30, daily, 8h00-20h00, June 1-Aug 31, daily, 8h00-22h00,
Sept 1-30, daily, 8h00-20h00, Oct 1-Mar 31, daily, 8h00-18h00.
Entrance tariff: from EUR1. 60.
This enormous leisure complex has something for everyone, from pedalos on the lake to surfing, pony rides to pétanque. It even has an open air theatre and cinema, where many entertainments are organised. Even the restored 19th century chateau is roped into the proceedings, for cultural and family events, such as weddings!

Musée Muncipal,
Town centre,
91150 Étampes.
Tel. 01 69 92 69 16.
Opening hours, Wed-Sun, all year, 14h00-17h00, closed Jan and public holidays.
Entrance tariff: EUR2 (reductions).
In the very heart of the medieval town centre, the municipal museum has all kinds of Gallo-Roman and medieval collections,

including artefacts unearthed during the excavations on the site of the Capetian palace in 1987. The museum also has lots of Renaissance objets d'art and paintings and sculptures from the 18th and 19th centuries.

Parc de Jeurre,
91150 Étampes.
Opening hours, daily, except Wed, Sat, public holidays. Guided tours at 10h00, 15h00.
Several important and interesting follies were built here during the 18th century, including a dairy, a cenataph and a temple of filial piety. They were saved from destruction in the late 19th century.

River walks,
91150 Étampes.
The town has some exceptionally agreeable riverside walks. Two small rivers, the Louette and the Chalouette, have been diverted and they merge at Les Portereaux sluice to form the main river in Étampes. You can walk easily along the river banks, which are made more picturesque with the small bridges and the old washhouses.

EVRY,
30 km south of Paris.
Train: Gare Montparnasse to Evry.
Road: N7 from Orly.

Cathedral,
1 clos de Cathédrale,
91000 Evry. Tel: 01 64 97 93 53
Opening hours: Mon-Sat, all year, 10h00-12h00, 14h00-18h00.
Sun, all year, 14h30-19h00.
Entrance tariff: free
Train: Gare de Lyon, Paris to Evry.
Road: A6 from Paris.
This remarkable cathedral, completed in 1995, was the first new cathedral to be built in France since the Second World War and designed to complement the new town of Evry. The cathedral is built in red brick, which gives a certain heaviness to the design, which gives the building the shape of a truncated cylinder.

FERRIÈRES-EN-BRIE,
25 km east of Paris.
Train: RER A line to Bussy-St-Georges.
Road: A4 E50 from Paris.

Chateau de Ferrières,
77164 Ferrières-en-Brie.
Tel: 01 64 66 34 97.
Web: http: //www.chateauferrieres.com
Opening hours, chateau, May-Sept, daily, 14h00-19h00, Oct-Apr, daily, 14h00-17h00.
Entrance tariff: EUR5 (reductions).
This is one of the most extraordinary chateau in the region, created by an equally extraordinary family, the Rothschilds, the great banking family. During the mid-19th century Second Empire, James de Rothschild decided to build this chateau and employed James Paxton, designer of the Crystal Palace in London, to create the chateau and its equally wonderful gardens. The mansion itself is a mixture of architectural styles, Italian Renaissance and Victorian. Entering the mansion, the vast hallway leads into the reception hall, which is astonishing in itself, often a venue for high society balls, and then you go up the huge staircase to the state rooms on the first floor. The decorative style of these rooms is highly ornate, a combination of Italian Renaissance and Rococo. The second floor is used as an exhibition space for contemporary art, the Museum of the Imagination. Six rooms are reserved for paintings, while one is devoted to sculptures. The English-style gardens covering the 135 hectares surrounding the chateau are equally impressive, a veritable arboretum, complete with statuary and water features.

FONTAINEBLEAU,
65 km south-west of Paris.
Train: Gare de St Lazare, Paris to Fontainebleau.
Road: A6 E15 from Paris.
The town of Fontainebleau, one of the great royal towns of France, owes its existence to François I, who was addicted to hunting in the great forests of this region. In order to accommodate the royal parties, the town was established and the great chateau was built. During the 19th century, the town expanded considerably. On the place de Gaulle, opposite the

main entrance to the chateau, you can see the many town houses that were built to accommodate visitors to the royal palace. Today, Fontainebleau offers a plethora of attractions for the visitor.

Forest of Fontainebleau,
77300 Fontainebleau.
The town is surrounded by forests extending over 25, 000 hectares. In the forest, more than 6, 500 species of animal live, from deer to wild boar. The forest has many pathways through it.

Musée Militaire,
88 rue Saint Honoré,
77300 Fontainebleau.
Tel: 01 60 74 64 89.
Web: http: //www.fontainebleau.fr/culture/musee-napo html
Opening hours, all year, Tues-Sat, 14h00-17h30. Closed Sun, Mon, public holidays.
Entrance tariff: EUR2. 50 (reductions).
This is the third largest military museum in France and it has impressive collections of costumes, equipment, uniforms and weapons dating back to Napoleonic times.

Musée National des Prisons,
1 rue du Sergent Perrier,
77300 Fontainebleau.
Tel: 01 60 74 99 99 (tourist office).
Web: www. justice. gouv. fr/musees
Opening hours: groups only, by arr with tourist office.
Entrance tariff: EUR8 (reductions).
This is a unique museum in France and Europe, telling what life was like in prisons from the 17th century to the present day. The prison itself dates from the 19th century and you can wander through the building, see the equipment and utensils in daily use and considerable documentation relating to prisoners. Among the correspondence on view are letters from such well-known previous detainees as Honoré Mirabeau, the 18th century statesman, Jean Genet and the Marquis de Sade, the latter two controversial writers in the 20th and 18th centuries respectively.
Opening hours, daily, all year, 14h00-17h00, except Sun, Mon, public holidays.

National Palace of Fontainebleau,
Tel: 01 60 71 50 60.
Web: www. musee-chateau-fontainebleau. fr/
Opening hours: June-Sept, daily, 9h30-18h00, closed Tues.
Oct-May, daily, closes at 17h00, closed Tues. Also closed Jan 1,
May 1, Dec 25.
Entrance tariff: EUR5 (reductions).
From François I yo Louis IV, the chateau was the family home to
the monarchs and each successive king extended the chateau.
The gardens, too, are well worth seeing, complete with canal and
carp lake. You can also admire the formal flowerbeds created by
the famous gardener, André Le Nôtre. From June to Sept, you
can go for a boat ride on the lakes and canal in the chateau
grounds and between Easter and All Saints' Day, you can also
take a one hour coach ride through the gardens of the chateau.

La Salle du Jeu de Paume,
Chateau of Fontainebleau.
Tel: 01 60 74 99 99 (tourist office).
Entrance fee: EUR8 (reductions).
Opening hours: groups only, by arr with the tourist office.
This is one of only three real tennis courts left in France today.
Tennis was one of the main sporting pursuits of the court and the
building reflects this interest in its grandeur.

FONTENAY-AUX-ROSES,
10 km south of Paris.
Métro: Porte d'Orléans.

Commisariat a l'Energie Atomique,
Route du Panorama,
92260 Fontenay-aux-Roses.
Tel: 0 810 555 222 or 01 46 54 88 60.
Web: www. cea. fr
Opening hours, Mon-Fri, all year, by arr.
Entrance tariff: free.
The first French nuclear reactor was started here in December,
1948 and today, the 13 hectare site is workplace to 1, 700
engineers, research scientists, scientists and technicians in the
French atomic energy establishment. Conducted tours are held of
the laboratories and plants and you can find all about radioactivity,

learn about the fuel cycle and how reactors work, control prototype robots and take a virtual reality tour. For anyone interested in science and in particular, atomic energy, this is fascinating stuff.

GENNEVILLIERS,
5 km north-west of Paris.
Train: RER C1 line to Gennevilliers.
Road: A86 from La Courneuve.

Le Port,
92230 Gennevilliers.
Tel: 01 40 58 28 76.
Web: www. ville-gennevilliers. fr/
Genevilliers is the leading inland port in France; it's on the River Seine, downstream from Paris, giving river connections to Rouen, Le Havre and the sea. It's a huge area, covering near 400 hectares and you can see the deep river channels, the barge traffic and all the road and rail links of this bustling industrial area. You can take a guided tour by bus around the whole port area and you can also visit some of the barges and ships tied up here. The bus tours are arranged four times a day, Mon-Fri, while the trips around barges and ships are arranged twice daily, at 9h30 and 12h00, Mon-Fri.

GERBEROY,
100 km north-west of Paris.
Road: A16 to Beauvais, then D133. No train.
Tel: 03 44 82 33 63 (Mairie).
Web: www. gerberoy. fr
This small medieval town, perfectly preserved and unspoiled, is one of the most attractive in the Ile de France. It has a long history; Philippe Auguste made Gerberoy a town in 1202. Its earlier history was stormy; between 1079 and 1437, the place was besieged no less than five times. Today, it's the very model of peace and tranquillity. Streets have 17th and 18th century houses, many of them half-timbered, while the streets themselves are cobbled. Off the main streets, lots of little laneways lead visitors on voyages of discovery. You can also inspect the ruins of

the old ramparts and an ancient fortress as well as see the 18th century town hall, which also serves as a market hall. The attractive church of Saint-Pierre was originally built in the 10th century and rebuilt in 1419. Interesting aspects include 15th century choir stalls. Guided tours of Gerberoy are available by arrangement with the Mairie.

Musée de Sidaner,
Hotel de Ville,
60380 Gerberoy.
Tel. 03 44 82 33 63.
Opening hours, Apr-Sept, daily, except Tues, 14h30-18h00.
Entrance tariff: free.
This museum, on the first floor of the town hall, is dedicated to the work of a painter called Henri de Sidaner, who had close connections with the townand it also details the history of Gerberoy.


GIVERNY,
75 km north of Paris.
Train: Gare Saint-Lazare to Vernon, then bus.
Road: A13 E5 from Paris.

Former Hotel Baudy rose garden,
Rue Claude Monet,
27620 Giverny.
Opening hours, Apr 1-Oct 31, daily, except Mon, 10h00-21h00.
Entrance tariff: free to patrons of the inn.
When the American artists arrived in Giverny shortly after Monet himself had settled here, they lived in what was the Hotel Baudy, now an inn. Inside, the dining room where they had their meals has been kept just as it was over a century ago, as has the studio where they worked. Outside, the rose garden has many ancient rose bushes on the slopes of the hill.

Monet's Garden,
Rue Claude Monet,
27620 Giverny.
Tel: 02 32 51 28 21.
Web: http: //fondation-monet.com
Opening hours, Apr 1-Nov 1, Tues-Sun, 10h00-18h00. Also Easter Mon, Whit Mon.
Entrance tariff: EUR5. 50 (house and garden-reductions).
Claude Monet spotted this house when he was passing through the district by train, on a line that has long since closed. He lived in this house from 1883 until he died in 1926 and the one hectare garden, which stretches down to the River Seine, is considered his greatest artistic masterpiece. Among its features are the water garden. He planted the garden so that each month, a different colour would predominate. The best months to visit are May and June, when the rhododendrons are in full flower around the lily pond and the wisteria entanges the Japanese bridge, but in fact, any month between spring and autumn, will be rewarding. Not only is the garden frequently photographed but it is one of the most popular visitor attractions in the Paris region. In the house itself, where Monet decorated the rooms in Japanese style, each room has its own very distinctive colour scheme. The house and gardens had fallen into a delapidated state before they were given the the Académie des Beaux Arts in 1966, which subsequently restored them to their original state.

Musée de l'Art Americaine,
Rue Claude Monet,
27620 Giverny.
Tel: 02 32 51 94 65.
Web: http: //www.maag.org
Opening hours, Mar21-Nov 30, Tues-Sun, 9h30-18h00. Also, Easter Mon, Whit Mon.
Entrance tariff: EUR5 (reductions).
This museum has displays of work from the Terra Foundation for the Arts; much of the display is changed annually, so that a wide diversity of periods in American art is on show. . The American Impressionist paintings on display, many of them painted in the locality by the commununity of American artists that formed here after Monet's arrival, form a useful addition to Monet's house and garden, which is just 100 metres away.

GUERMANTES,
26 km east of Paris.
Train: RER A4 to Torcy Marne la Vallée.
Road: A4 from Paris to Lagny, then A104.

Chateau de Guermantes,
77600 Guermantes.
Tel. 01 64 30 00 94.
Opening hours, Sat, Sun, public holidays, Mar-Oct, 14h00-18h00.
Entrance tariff: EUR5 (reductions).
The chateau was built at the beginning of the 17th century, in the style of Louis XIII and it's filled with a remarkable collection of furniture and objets d'art. One especial feature is the La Belle Inutile, a long, spacious gallery that epitomises the decorative art styles of the 18th century. The name of Guermantes is renowned because of Marcel Proust, who used it for the celebrated duchess in his novel, À la recherche du temps perdu. Outside, the English style gardens are equally impressive, with the windows of the chateau reflected in the still waters of the lake.

HERBLAY,
25 km north-west of Paris.
Train: Gare St-Lazare to Herblay.
Road: A15 from St-Denis.

Église St-Martin,
95220 Herblay.
Opening hours, daily, all year, 8h00-18h00.
Entrance tariff: free.
Inside the church, you can see the remarkable 16th century stained glass windows, which were made in Beauvaiss. Just outside the church, from the heights of the small graveyard, you can see in the distance, the Forest of St-Germain.

Riverside walks,
95220 Herblay.
Herblay is on the banks of the River Seine and in the vicinity of the town, there are attractive walks along the old quay and the riverside promenade.

HETOMESNIL,
110 km north of Paris.
Road: A16 from Paris to Beauvais, then D930. No train.

Museum of agricultural and rural life,
60320 Hetomesnil,
Tel. 03 44 46 32 20 (office du tourisme).
Opening hours, July, Aug, daily, except Tues, 14h00-18h00, Sept,
Sat, Sun, 14h00-18h00.
Entrance tariff: EUR5 (reductions).
This elaborate museum, set in a former agricultural college,
portrays the old agricultural and rural way of life in a series of
displays. The work of farmers and rural craftsmen is highlighted
along with many of the tools they once used.

ILE DE LA GRANDE JATTE,
92200 Neuilly-sur-Seine.
Métro: Pont de Levallois-Bécon.
The island is in the River Seine, between Neuilly-sur-Seine and
La Defènse and was once very industrialised. It's been much
restored now and it's an excellent place for a leafy riverside walk.
Much of the island is covered by a park, which is open daily, as
well as by a housing development designed in contemporary
style. The island is also noted for its agreeable, if expensive,
restaurants.

ILLIERS-COMBRAY,
115 km south-west of Paris.
Train: Gare Montparnasse, Paris to Illiers-Combray.
Road: A11-E50 from Chartres.
This small country town was idealised by Marcel Proust, the great
writer, who recreated the feelings and sensations of yesterday in
an idyllic format. He grew up here, living until he was 15 with his
aunt, Mme Amiot, who became La Tante Léonie in his works of
fiction. The house is the only real remaining link with Proust, apart
from his apartment in Paris (qv). Apart from the house, you can
also see many other sites in and around the village that have
connections with Proust-the local tourist office, 5 rue Henri-
Germond-has all the details, including guided tours. While you're
here, you can also enjoy the Petite Madeleine de Proust, the
small sponge cakes immortalised by the writer.

Boulangerie Patisserie Brossier,
12 rue de Beauce,
28120 Illiers-Combray,
Tel. 02 37 24 30 38.
Opening hours, Mon-Sat, all year, 8h00-18h00.
This bakery specialises in the cakes immortalised by Proust and you can sample some in the shop or take them away for a picnic as you wander around the town and recreate the immortal feelings of Proust.

Maison de Tante Léonie,
rue du Dr Proust,
28120 Illiers-Combray.
Tel. 02 37 24 30 97.
Web: http: //www.campac.online.fr
Opening hours, guided tours daily, except Mon.
Closed mid-Dec-mid-Jan, May 1, Nov 1 & 11.
Entrance fee: EUR5 (reductions).
Apart from Proust's former apartment in Paris (qv), the house of Aunt Léonie is the only real remaining link with Proust. The house itself, with its documents, family heirlooms and everyday objects, is much as it was in Proust's time and is now a museum. The local society of the friends of Marcel Proust and Combray, which owns the house, organises occasional temporary exhibitions.

ISSY-LES-MOULINEX,
8 km south-west of Paris.
Métro: Mairie d'Issy; RER C line, tram T2 to Issy-Val-de-Seine.

Maison de l'Environnement,
Parc de l'Ile Saint-Germain,
92130 Issy-les-Moulinex.
Tel: 01 55 95 80 70.
Web: www. hauts-de-seine. net/maisondelanature
Opening hours, Mon-Fri, all year, 9h00-12h30, 14h00-18h00, Sun, all year, 14h00-18h00. Closed in winter at 17h00.
Entrance tariff: EUR1. 50 (reductions).
This centre was set up in 1979 to provide education, information and training in a scientific approach to ecology and environmental matters. Exhibitions present the ecologies of three different milieux, town, garden and woodland. Over 10, 000 documents on the environment can be consulted. In the 1, 600 square metres of

gardens, you can use several different methods to explore them, including recreational and scientific approaches. The many plants in the gardens have been chosen so that they can be touched, smelled or merely observed.

Musée Français de la carte à jouer (Playing Card museum),
16 rue Auguste Gervais,
92130 Issy-les-Moulinex.
Tel: 01 46 42 33 76.
Web: www. issy.com/musee
Opening hours, Wed, Sat, Sun, all year, 10h00-19h00.
Entrance tariff: EUR3. 8 (reductions).
This is the only museum in France devoted to the history of playing cards. The original way in which the museum is laid out allows the visitor to trace this history on a time scale, from the 15th century to the present day; in the different cultures of East and West; through the decorative arts and the use of design; through manufacturing techniques and through the whole development of gambling. It's a fascinating story in a museum that is so intriguing in its own right for its very modern but very functional design. The museum also details the history of the town itself and its historic heritage, including the chateau of the Princes de Conti. The early days of aviation had their links with Issy and these too are detailed, as are the connections that such famous artists as Dubuffet, Matisse and Rodin, had with Issy. Altogether, it's a very well designed museum that will hold your interest for half a day. The museum deservedly won the European Prize for Museums in 1999.

JOINVILLE-LE-PONT,
11 km east of Paris.
Train: RER A2 line.
Road: A4 E50 from Paris.

Chez Gegene,
162 bis quai de Polongis,
Allée des Guinguettes,
94340 Joinville-le-Pont.
Tel. 01 48 83 29 43.
A guingette place in Joinville-le-Point, a town set on the banks of the River Marne and a favourite weekend place for Parisians where they continue to enjoy dancing and traditional music.

Le Petit Robinson,
164 quai de Polognis,
94340 Joinville-le-Pont.
Tel. 01 48 29 044 39.
Another favoured spot for enjoying guingette dancing and singing.

JOUY-EN-JOSAS,
15 km west of Paris.
Train: RER C line to Versailles-Chantiers-Juvisy.
Road: D907 from Boulogne-Billancourt.
This small town with just over 8, 000 inhabitants, in the shadow of
Versailles, offers numerous walks in the nearby forests and along
the banks of the River Bièvre. The Saint-Martin church dates from
the 13th century; it has a depiction of the Virgin Mary in
polychromatic wood, made in the 12$^{th}$ century.

Blum house,
4, rue Léon-Blum,
78350 Jouy-en-Josas.
Tel: 01 39 46 50 24.
Opening hours: Tues, Thurs, Sat, Sun afternoons, closed in
August and on public holidays.
Entrance tariff: EUR3 (reductions).
The house where veteran socialist leader Léon Blum lived with his
wife Jeanne, has been turned into a museum. He bought the
house in 1945 and lived here until his death in 1950. Many
documents detail his political career in the socialist movement in
France and you can also see the desk he worked at.

Musée de la Toile de Jouy (fabric museum),
54 rue Charles de Gaulle,
78350 Jouy-en-Josas.
Tel: 01 39 56 48 64.
Opening hours: daily.
Entrance tariff: EUR3. 80 (reductions).
This intriguing museum is dedicated to the ancient manufacture of
designs printed on cotton, for which the town was famous
between 1760 and 1843. The industry was founded by Christophe
Philippe Oberkampf and the museum has plenty on his life's work
and the early days of the industry. You can also inspect all the
different technical developments in the fabric printing processes.

Inside the museum, the exhibits are displayed on three levels, while outside, you can walk around the landscaped gardens.

LACHELLE,
85 km north-east of Paris.
Train: Gare du Nord, Paris to Compiegne.
Road: A1 E15 from Paris.

Chocolaterie de Lachelle,
41 rue de Monelieu,
60190 Lachelle.
Tel. 03 44 42 31 38.
Opening hours, Mon-Sat, all year, 9h00-17h00.
Entrance tariff: EUR2.50
In this delightfully tempting chocolate factory, you can see chocolate being made the old fashioned way and later, you can buy products in the factory shop. You can also relax in the tearoom, in front of the open fire in winter, and enjoy Lachelle Chocolat Chaud, a firm local favourite.

LA DEFÉNSE,
10 km west of Paris.
Métro: Grande Arche de la Défense.
Train: Gare St Lazare, Paris-La Défense, RER A line.
La Défense is a very modern sector to the west of Paris, with its main esplanade aligned with the Champs-Elysées. Most of the area is made up of ultra contemporary, glass fronted office blocks; in many cases, their design is stunning. Today, many leading French companies and multinational companies have their headquarters here, but the area is much more than just an office development.

Grande Arche,
92400 Courbevoie.
Tel: 01 49 07 27 57.
Opening hours: 9hr00 to 20hr00 daily, all year, closing one hour earlier in winter.
Entrance tariff: EUR5 (reductions).
The Grande Arche is a project that was favoured by former French President François Mitterand. Nearly 120 metres high, from the top, it offers exceptional views of Paris. From here, in a

straight line of sight, you can see right down the avenue de Charles de Gaulle (the main thoroughfare in Neuilly), down the Champs-Elysées and the Tuileries gardens to the Louvre. It's a stunning vista and this was exactly what Mitterand had planned. The scheme was a long time in the making; the first trees were planted as an extension of the Louvre as far back as 1640.

Le Musée de l'Automobile (Car Museum),
1, place du Dome, to the left of the Grande Arche.
94200 Courbevoie.
Tel: 01 36 67 0606.
Opening hours: 12hr00 to 19hr00 daily, all year, 21hr00 on Sats.
Entrance tariff: EUR10.
The Paris region seems awash with car and transport museums, but this one is exceptional and worth a visit to see a superb collection of over 100 vintage and veteran cars, each placed in a setting that details its history. The models on show range from a Ford Model T and a Talbot Bugatti to the long forgotten but once very popular, De Dion-Bouton K2, dubbed the "Populaire" or Popular car because it was just that. An important part of the space in the museum is given over to the Hauts-de-Seine region of the Ile de France, because this was where the French car industry started. Between 1880 and 1950, no fewer than 304 car makers and scores of coach builders worked in this area; today, the French car industry has just three main marques, Citroen, Peugeot and Renault, so this space is a fascinating glimpse into the past.

Le Dome Imax,
94200 Courbevouie.
Tel: 01 36 67 06 06.
This Imax cinema with the giant screen shows six films of different lengths on such subjects as the Grand Canyon and the Niagara Falls.

Tour,
Parvis de la Défense, foot of the Grande Arche.
94200 Courbevoie.
Tel: 01 42 62 24 00.
Opening hours, daily, Mar-Nov, 10h00-18h00.
Entrance tariff: EUR4. 60 (reductions).

You can take a 40 minute trip on the tourist train all round La Défense, to see the Grande Arche, all the other futuristic looking buildings, the church of Notre-Dame-de-Pentecote and the avant-garde works of public art by such renowned contemporary and near contemporary artists as Calder, César, Miro and Moretti.

LA FERTÉ-SUR-JOUARRE,
67 km east of Paris.
Train: Gare de l'Est, Paris to La Ferté-sur-Jouarre.
Road: A3 from Paris.

Abbaye de Jouarre,
6 rue Montmorin,
BP 30,
Jouarre,
77262 La Ferté-sur-Jouarre.
Tel. 01 60 22 06 11.
Web. www.abbayedejouarre.free.fr
Opening hours, daily, all year, 10h00-12h00, 14h30-17h30. Tower, Mon-Sat, 9h45-12h15, 14h30-17h15, Sun, 10h15-12h30, 14h30-18h00. Closed Tues.
Entrance tariff: EUR4. 50 (reductions). Tower, EUR4. 50 (reductions. Crypt, EUR4 (reductions).
The whole abbey of Jouarre is one of the most exquisite monastic settlements in the Ile de France, easily reached from La Ferté-sur-Jouarre, which is three km distant. The whole settlement was the idea originally of an Irish monk, Colomban (540-615), and it began with one abbey for men and another for women. After the Hundred Years War, the foundation had to be extensively rebuilt, work that was done especially in the 18th century. In the crypt, which can be visited by arrangement with the local tourist office, tel. 01 60 22 64 54, you can see the outstanding sacrophagi of the founders of the abbeys in the 7th century as well as an extraordinary beautiful tomb dedicated to a 13th century Irish princess, Saint Osanne. In the tower, you can see a detailed history of the abbey, with its life over the centuries; a 20 minute diaporama is included. On a religious note, one of the most moving events you can take part in is vespers, at 17h30 every day of the week and at 17h00 on Sundays. In the Briad museum here, you can see much on an entirely different subject-Brie cheese and the local cheese heritage.

LAGNY-SUR-MARNE,
25 km east of Paris.
Train: RER A4 line to Torcy and Chessy.
Road: A4 E50, D231 from Paris.

Musée Municipal Gatien Bonnet,
77400 Lagny sur Marne.
Tel. 01 64 30 42 52.
Opening hours, daily, all year, 14h00-18h00, closed Mon, Tues.
Entrance tariff: EUR4 (reductions).
Lagny is a delightful small town beside the River Marne, a place for commuters to Paris to live. You can also enjoy walks along the riverside promenades. The town also has a small but interesting museum that reflects the old way of life in the Marne valley that has been well and truly swept away by developments over the past three decades. The museum chronicles as far back as prehistoric times, before working through the Middle Ages. The museum, which details the now largely vanished rural culture in the area, as well as local artists, has been extensively restored.


LA-QUEUE-LES-YVELINES,
40 km south-west of Paris.
Train: Gare Montparnasse, Paris to La Queue-les-Yvelines.
Road: N12 from Versailles.

La Serre aux Papillons,
Jardin Poullain,
78940 La Queue-les-Yvelines.
Tel. 01 34 86 42 99.
Opening hours, Mar-Nov, daily, 9h30-12h00, 14h30-18h00.
Entrance tariff: 4. 50 (reductions).
This is an amazing collection of butterflies, more than 700 species altogether. Daily, between 10h00 and 15h00, you can see for yourself the butterflies being born, as they leave the chrysalis, an extraordinary sight. Most of the species come from equatorial jungles and here, you can also inspect a fine collection of rare plants and orchids.

LARCHANT,
80 km south-west of Paris.
Train: Gare de Montparnasse to Larchant.
Road: A6 E15 from Paris.

Basilica,
77140 Larchant.
Opening hours, daily, all year, daily, 10h00-18h00.
The basilica in this delightful village is dedicated to Saint Mathurin, a local healer and saint, who lived in the third century. This basilica became one of the main places of pilgrimage for the kings and queens of France. By the end of the 12th century, the basilica had become an enormous edifice, but much was destroyed in subsequent religious wars. Today, only the beautiful choir and the Virgin's chapel remain from the original basilica.

Dame Jehanne summit,
77140 Larchant.
Just outside the village, you can walk through the forest and climb to the summit of the Dame Jouanne rock formation; it's well worth the climb, as the view from the top is one of the best in this south-western part of the Ile de France.

LE BOURGET,
8 km north-east of Paris.
Train: RER B5 line to Le Bourget.
Road: N17 from Paris.

Musée de l'Air et de l'Espace,
Aeroport de Paris Le Bourget,
93352 Le Bourget Cedex.
Tel: 01 49 92 71 99.
Web: www.musee.air@mae.org
Opening hours, summer, daily, all year, 10h00-18h00, winter, daily, 10h00-17h00.
Entrance tariff: EUR7 (reductions).
Le Bourget was once the airport for Paris, very handily situated, just eight km from the city centre. With the growth in air traffic, Orly had to be expanded and the brand new airport at Roissy was opened in 1974. A third major airport for Paris is being planned. Le Bourget is no longer used for scheduled or charter traffic, but

business charters and private planes still use it and it remains famous for its airshows. It also has an exceptional museum of the air, which was created as long ago as 1919. With close to 200 planes, it shows the development of civilian and military aviation since then, while space travel is well documented. One of the highlights of the museum is the first prototype of Concorde, which has been joined by one of the Air France fleet of Concordes, which stopped flying in 2003.

LE RAINCY,
8km east of Paris.
Train: RER E2 line to Raincy-Villemomble.
Road: N3 from Paris.

Église Notre Dame du Raincy,
avenue de la Résistance,
93340 Le Raincy.
Tel. 01 43 81 14 98.
Opening hours, Mon-Sat, all year, 10h00-12h00, 14h00-18h00, Sun, all year, 10h00-12h00.
Entrance tariff: free.
This delightfully modern masterpiece was built in 1922-23 as a memorial to the dead of the First World War, when France lost 1. 4 million people. The architect was Auguste Perret and his most ingenious element in the church came with the windows-instead of stained glass, he used coloured blocks of glass, which create fantastic light patterns inside the church.

LEVALLOIS,
8 km west of Paris.
Train: RER C1 line to Periere Levallois.

Maison de la peche (fishing centre),
Ile de la Jatte,
22 allée Claude Monet,
92300 Levallois-Perret.
Tel: 01 47 57 17 32.
Web: http: //maisondelapeche.free.fr
Opening hours, Wed, all year, 10h00-13h00, 14h00-18h00. Sat, Sun, all year, 13h00-18h00.
Entrance tariff: EUR3 (reductions).

Métro: Becon, Pont de Levallois.

The freshwater world of the rivers and streams of France is captured in this ultra modern centre, complete with 18 freshwater aquaria. This contain all kinds of river species, including black bass, catfish, pike and roach. The museum also tells the story of angling, with a priceless collection of fishing rods and reels and other equipment. For any fisherman, this is a must see location.

L'HAY-LES-ROSES,
15 km south of Paris.
Métro: Villejuif-Louis Aragon, then bus.

Val-de-Marne rose garden,
rue Watel,
94240 L'Hay-les-Roses.
Tel: 01 47 40 04 04.
Opening hours, mid-May-mid-Sept, daily, 10h00-20h00.
Entrance tariff: EUR5 (reductions).
This is the oldest rose garden in Europe and it's an amazing sight, even for non-gardeners, with some 3, 300 varieties of rose to be seen. The sight of these roses and their intoxicating perfumes, make this a memorable visit.

L'ISLE ADAM,
30 km north of Paris.
Train: Gare St-Lazare to L'Isle Adam.
Road: N184 from St-Ouen.

Centre d'Art Jacques-Henri Lartigue,
31 Grande Rue,
95290 L'Isle Adam.
Tel. 01 34 08 02 72.
Opening hours, daily, all year, 14h30-18h00, except Tues.
Entrance tariff: EUR3 (reductions).
This restored 17th century house is dedicated to the work of Jacques-Henri Lartigue, one of the most renowned photographers of the 20th century. He was also a prolific painter and he and his wife Florette, who were friendly with the then Mayor of L'Isle Adam, donated 331 paintings to the town, covering his entire career. These paintings and a selection of unpublished photographs can be seen in the centre. Lartigue died in 1986.

La Plage,
1 avenue du Général de Gaulle,
95290 L'Isle Adam.
Tel. 01 34 69 01 68.
Opening hours, May-Aug, daily, 9h00-18h00,
Entrance tariff: EUR5 (reductions).
Described as the largest inland, riverside plage or beach in France, it was created in 1895 and covers three hectares. All kinds of sport can be played, including swimming, tennis and mini-golf, while you can take pedalos on the adjacent River Oise. Restaurant.

Musée d'Art et d'Histoire,
46 grande rue,
95290 L'Isle d'Adam.
Tel. 01 34 69 45 44.
Opening hours, daily, all year, except Tues, 14h-18h.
Entrance tariff: EUR3 (reductions).
In the late 19th century, L'Isle Adam was a centre of artistic creativity, with many painters living and working in the vicinity. The town has a very attractive setting, on the banks of the River Oise, with the great forest of the same name directly across the river. Today, that artistic heritage is commemorated in the town museum, established in 1950. Its collection is impressive, including 200 paintings, 470 designs and 1, 400 old photographs, as well as 3, 000 documents, covering the 16th to the 20th centuries, in its archives.

Pavilion Chinois,
rue de Beaumont,
95290 L'Isle Adam.
Strangely out of place in the wooded surroundings of L'Isle Adam, this nevertheless authentic Chinese pavilion was built in the 18th century, complete with very elaborate padoga-like roof structures. You can walk around the exterior.

LUZARCHES,
45 km north of Paris.
Train: Gare du Nord, Paris to Chantilly, then taxi.
Road: A1 from Paris.
It's worth stopping off in this very ancient village, which was the

birthplace of Robert de Luzarches, the 13th century architect of Amiens cathedral. The church in the village dates back to the 9th century; building continued until the 16th century.

MAGNY-LES-HAMEAUX,
30 km south-east of Paris.
Train: Gare Nontparnasse, Paris to Versailles, then taxi.
Road: RD938 from Versailles.
This is an important historical site in the Ile de France and you can see the ruins of the abbey, inspect the church that remains, as well as two museums. The abbey was founded as a monastery in 1204 and was upgraded to a monastery 10 years later. A famous school was created hre in 1641 and among its pupils was Racine. The Jansensists, a strong 17th century religious movement in France, free thinkers with a strong attachment to arts and science, developed here. Louis XIV had the abbey destroyed in 1710, the year after the remaining 300 adherents of Jansenism had been expelled.

Musée National des Granges de Port-Royal,
78114 Magny-les-Hameaux.
Tel. 39 30 72 72.
Web: http: //www,site.voila.fr/port royal
Opening hours, daily, Mar-Oct, 10h30-18h30, closed Tues. Jan-Mar, Sat, Sun, 10h30-18h30.
Entrance tariff: EUR3 (reductions).
The museum, set in the building that once housed the school here, explains in detail the history of the nearby abbey as well how the Jansenist movement came to be founded and what it meant. The well-known pupils of the school, including Racine, are recalled. Café.

Musée des Ruines de Port-Royal,
78114 Magny-les-Hameaux.
Opening hours, summer, Mon, Wed, Thurs, 14h00-18h00, Sat, Sun, 11h00-12h00, 14h00-18h00.
Winter, Mon, Wed, Thurs, Fri, 14h00-17h00, Sat, Sun, 11h00-12h00, 14h00-17h00.
Entrance tariff: EUR3 (reductions).
This museum, closed to the church belonging to the abbey (which still stands), as well as the ancient pigeon house, details the

history of the abbey until its destruction in the early 18th century. Close by, it's worth seeing the small church of St German and the surrounding graveyard, where many of the religious from the abbey are buried. Guided tours of the church are organised on Sat, 9h00-18h00.

MAINCY,
55 km south-east of Paris.
Train: Gare de Lyon, Paris to Melun, then taxi (6 km).
Road: A5 E54 from Paris.

Vaux-les-Vicomtes,
77950 Maincy.
Tel. 01 64 14 41 90.
Web: www. vaux-les-vicomtes. com
Opening hours, Mar-Nov, daily, 10h00-18h00.
Entrance tariff: EUR12 (reductions).
This great chateau, one of the finest in the Ile de France, was built in the mid-17th century by Nicolas Fouquet, the king's surintedant des finances or finance minister. He started building the chateau in 1653 and employed the finest talent of the day to design the house and garden. In August, 1661, he put on an incredibly lavish entertainment for the king, Louis XIV, the Sun King, who was so outraged by the extravagance of his minister that Fouquet spent the rest of his life in prison, after a trial that was patently rigged. However, the great chateau did inspire Louis XIV to build Versailles. Today, you can stroll around the interior of the great house, where some of the rooms, like the Grand Salon, were never completely finished. During the summer, on certain nights, the chateau and the gardens are lit up with a multitude of candles. Also during the summer, the spectacular fountains in the gardens put on incredible performances on occasion. In the demesne, you can also visit the Musée des Equipages et Jardins, which has the same opening hours as the chateau. The museum has one of the largest collections in Europe of horse-drawn carriages and their equipment.

MAISONS-ALFORT,
10 km south-east of Paris.
Train: Gare d'Austerlitz, Paris to Alfort Alfortville.
Road: N19/N6 from Paris.

Musée Fragonard d'Alfort,
École Nationale Vétérinaire d'Alford,
7 avenue Charles de Gaulle,
94704 Maisons-Alfort.
Tel: 01 43 96 71 72.
Opening hours: Mon-Fri, all year, 14h00-18h00, Sat, Sun, all year,
10h00-17h00.
Entrance tariff: EUR5 (reductions).
If you fancy being scared witless, come to this museum on a dark
winter's afternoon. The exhibits will give you the creeps in the half
light. The man who built up most of the collections here, in the
18th century, was Honoré Fragonard, who was related to the
painter and the founder of the perfume empire. But this man's
specialisation was the preservation of skinned corpses, of animals
and people. He made about 700 examples and around 20 of them
can be seen in the museum, including a 200 year old horse,
complete with jockey and neither with skin on them. The museum
is quite small, but it also contains a fine collection of
abnormalities, like monsters with two heads and Siamese twins in
various shapes. It's all very eerie, but if you've a taste for horror
films, this is the place to see some real horror.

MAISONS-LAFITTE,
22 km west of Paris.
Train: RER A3 line to Maisons-Lafitte.
Road: D308 from St Germain-en-Laye.

Chateau and horse racing museum,
78600 Maisons-Lafitte.
Opening hours: daily, all year, except Tues. From Apr 1-Oct 15,
10h00-12h30, 14h00-18h00. From Oct 16-March 31, 10h00-
12h30, 14h00-17h00.
Closed on Jan 1, May 1, Nov 1 and 11, Dec 25.
Entrance tariff: EUR6. 10 (reductions). Includes chateau and
museum. The great chateau here dates from the 18th century and
it's open for visitors. You can also visit the horse racing museum
here. The first horse races were held at Maisons-Lafitte, which is
close to the River Seine, back in 1833. A training centre was also
established, to rival Newmarket in England. In the late 19th
century, the great hippodrome was developed. Today, Maison-
Lafitte is still one of the most important horse racing and training

centres in Europe and even though activity has been reduced, there are still around 1, 600 horses in training here. The museum has all kinds of documentation and archival materia, models and a good selection of paintings and sculptures in the museum.

MANTES-LES-JOLIES,
50 km north-west of Paris.
Train: Gare St Lazare, Paris to Mantes-la-Jolie.
Road: A13 E5 from Paris.
The town, an important port town on the River Seine, was devastated during the Second World War and substantially rebuilt after the war. Despite the ravages of war, much of the historic town centre, around the Collegiate Church of Notre-Dame, which dates from the 12th and 13th centuries, remained intact. You can also enjoy quayside walks and stroll along the wooded islands in the centre of the river.

Hotel Dieu Musée
Tel: 01 30 97 91 40.
Web: www.ville-mantes-la-jolie.com/musee
Opening hours, Mon-Fri, all year, 12h00-18h00, Sat, Sun, all year, 12h00-19h00. Closed Tues.
Entrance tariff: EUR4. 57 (reductions).
The building that houses the municipal museum was originally constructed in the 14th century and rebuilt in the 16th century. It had numerous uses over the years, including as an orphanage and a theatre. The building was used as a cinema until 1962, when it was acquired by the municipality and turned into the town museum, which houses the Maximilien-Luce collections of paintings and over 600 piece of French and European ceramics. It has a permanent exhibition on the medieval town and stages frequent temporary exhibitions.

MARLY-LE-ROI,
24 km west of Paris.
Train: Gare Saint-Lazare, Paris to Marly-le-Roi.
Road: N13 from Neuilly-sur-Seine.

Chateau de Monte-Cristo,
78560 Le Port-Marly.
Tel. 01 30 61 61 35.

Opening hours, Apr 1-Nov 1, Tues-Fri, 10h00-12h30, 14h00-18h00, Sat, Sun, 10h00-18h00. Nov 2-Mar 31, Sun, 14h00-17h00.
Entrance tariff: EUR5 (reductions).
This Renaissance style chateau, surrounded by gardens in the English style, was very much the creation of Alexander Dumas and his fantasies. He built this home in 1844 after the success of The Three Musketeers and the Count of Monte Cristo. The salon is decorated in the Moorish style. You can also see the small neo-Gothic pavilion, the Chateau d'If, to which he often retired to work.

Musée Promenade de Marly-le-Roi Louveciennes.
78430 Louveciennes.
Tel: 01 39 69 06 26.
Opening hours, Wed-Sun, all year, 14h00-18h00.
Entrance fee: EUR3 (reductions).
The museum has a wonderful collection of paintings, engravings and models, which take you right back to the time of Louis XIV. One of the rooms in the museum explains the workings of the famous Machine de Marly, which supplied water to the ponds in Marly and Versailles. The originals of the sculptures in the grounds can be seen in the museum, testament to the splendours of that royal age. Look out for the renowned statues of the Marly horses that rear up over the water trough in the park. The royal park is open daily.

Old Marly,
You can wander through this rural village, with its narrow streets and colourful frontages. Down by the River Seine, you can see 30 reproductions of works by Impresssionist painters; these are on enamel plaques and are designed to allow visitors to follow in their footsteps.

MARNES-LES-COQUETTES,
15 km west of Paris.
Train: Gare Saint-Lazare, Paris, to Vaucresson, then bus.
Road: D7/D907 from Neuilly-sur-Seine.

Haras de Jardy,
Boulevard de Jardy,
92430 Marnes-les-Coquette.
Tel: 01 47 01 11 14.

Web: www.haras-de-jardy.com
Opening hours, open daily, all year.
Entrance tariff: free.
This sporting facility covers 76 hectares of parkland, on the edge of the forest of Fausses-Reposes and it's very reminiscent of the English style. The park has admirable facilities, open to all, for tennis, golf and horse riding.

Musée des Applications de la Recherche,
3 boulevard Raymond Poincaré,
92430 Marnes-la-Coquette.
Tel: 01 47 01 15 97.
Web: www.pasteur. fr
Opening hours, daily, except Sat, Sun, public holidays, 14h00-17h30. Closed Aug.
Entrance tariff: EUR4 (reductions).
This museum is housed in the mansion where Louis Pasteur, the great scientist died in 1895, has a useful and interesting selection of exhibits that tell the story of the great battle fought against infectious diseases by the scientists at the Institut Pasteur. Photographs, documents and artefacts are among the items used to tell this fascinating tale, but it's not just a story of combating diseases that have been known about for decades. The museum also details present day research into such present day scourges as AIDS, allergies and hepatitis. Perhaps the most fascinating aspect of the museum is details given on the future prospects for combating these modern day diseases.

MEAUX,
53 km east of Paris.
Train: Gare de l'Est, Paris to Meaux.
Road: N3 from Paris.
Meaux is a substantial town of around 50, 000 people; it's full of historical character, set on the River Marne. Much of its architecture shows the development of Gothic styles. The ancient Episcopal Palace today houses the Bossuet Museum, with its fine collections of archaeology, paintings and sacred art, while the surrounding gardens are finely landscaped in the classical style. A more modern monument is the American Monument, commemorating the Battle of the Marne at the start of the First World War in 1914. It was created by Frederick MacMonnies, very

much in the style of ancient classical statuary. Walks can be enjoyed along the quays that skirt the river. The Gallo-Roman ramparts can also be explored, as can the Gothic cathedral of St-Etienne, built in the late 12th century. The town also has two culinary specialities to its name, Brie cheese and mustard, that are essential to understanding its character.

Musée Bossuet,
rue Boussuet,
77100 Meaux.
Tel: 01 64 34 84 45.
Web: www. ville-meaux. fr
Opening hours, Apr 1-Sept 30, daily, except Tues, 10h00-12h00, 14h00-18h00. Oct 1-Mar 31, daily, 10h00-12h00, 14h00-17h00, except Mon, Tues, Sun mornings.
Entrance: EUR2 (reductions).
The episcopal palace, built between the 12th and 17th centuries, offers a municipal collection of paintings, sculptures and archaeological artifacts that is considered unique in the Ile de France. The collection of paintings begins with sacred works from the 16th century and concludes with many examples from the late 19th century School of Barbizon (qv). The museum is named after the man who was the Archbishop of Meaux between 1682 and 1704. The earliest piece of sculpture on show was made in the 12th century. Beside the museum, you can see the very historic cathedral, the oldest parts of which date back to Gallo-Roman times. The Bossuet Garden, within what is known as the Episcopal City, was created during the 17th century. On regular dates between June and September, a Grand Historical show is staged here. Details: 01 64 33 02 26.

MÉDAN,
35 km west of Paris.
Train: Gare St-Lazare, Paris to Médan.
Road: A3 E15 from Paris.

Chateau de Médan,
78670 Médan.
Tel: 01 39 75 86 59.
Opening hours, daily, all year, 10h00-18h00. Groups only, by arr
Entrance tariff: EUR6. 50.

This delightful and tranquil little village has long artistic connections, going right back to the 16th century. In the late 19$^{th}$ century, the artist Paul Cézanne was attracted here and painted two of his masterpieces in the village, in both cases, views of the chateau. He also painted the hillside on the opposite side of the river, which is a good viewpoint for all the barge traffic on the River Seine. At the end of 2003, this hillside was under threat of controversial redevelopment.

At the beginning of the 20th century, the Belgian Nobel Prize winning writer Maurice Maeterlinck (1862-1949), who was very interested in entomology, bought the chateau and settled here for many years. After the Second World War, the chateau was abandoned, before eventually being taken over in 1966 by a newspaper called "Combat". In 1974, it uttered the famous phrase, "Silence, we're sinking". In 1977, the chateau was bought and during the following 10 years, its new owners fully restored it to the charming glories it had during the 16th century. Visitors are welcome to see the interior, but only by prior arrangement with the owners.

Maison d'Emile Zola,
78670 Médan.
Tel. 01 39 75 35 65.
Opening hours, Sat, Sun, public holidays, all year, 14h00-18h30.
Daily, all year, for groups, by arr.
Entrance tariff: EUR5 (reductions).
When the great late 19th century writer Emile Zola (1840-1902) finally won literary fame in 1878 and acquired a certain amount of money, he bought this house close to the banks of the River Seine. As his literary fame grew along with his bank account, he aded two towers to the house, had the grounds landscaped, built a guest lodge and created a farm with stables. The house itself remains exactly as it was in Zola's time, complete with stained glass in the windows, the mosaic stone floor in the billiards room, the linen room and above all, his study, with the fireplace bearing his motto, "Nulla dies sine linea" ("not a day without a line"). Zola had many discussions here with his many literary friends and the association that now runs the house has gone to great lengths to preserve and maintain the wonderful late 19$^{th}$ century literary atmosphere.

MELUN,
48 km south-east of Paris.
Train: Gare de Lyon, Paris to Melun.
Road: N6 A5A from Paris.
Melun is a substantial town of about 40, 000 inhabitants, with a wealth of history dating back to Roman times. It's also a riverside town, since it is set on the banks of the River Seine. In 52 BC, Melin was captured by the Romans. Much later, between 1420 and 1429, it was occupied by the English, only coming back under the authority of the King of France in 1435. After the revolution, the town substituted for its royal patronage by industrialising, although this was done without spoiling the historic town centre. Many people well-known in French life, such as Paul Cézanne, the artist and Louis Pasteur, the biologist, have had connections with the town.

Musée de la Gendarmerie,
8 rue Emile Leclerc,
77000 Melun.
Tel: 01 64 14 33 17.
Opening hours: by arr.
Entrance tariff: EUR3 (reductions).
This museum tells the story of the Maréchaussee (horse mounted constabulary) that in 1791 took the name of "Gendarmerie", which continues to the present day.

Musée Municipale,
4 quai de la Courtille,
77000 Melun.
Tel. 01 64 79 77 70.
Opening hours, Mon, Thurs, Fri, all year, 14h00-18h00, Wed, Sat, all year, 9h00-12h00, 14h00-18h00.
Entrance tariff: EUR4 (reductions).
The museum of the muncipality has archaeological artefacts from the Roman times in Melun as well as many artefacts from the Middle Ages. It also has a collection of paintings by French, Flemish and Italian artists. It's on the island in the centre of the River Seine and at the eastern end of the island, there's the prison, while at the western end, there are the more agreeable botanic gardens.

MÉRIEL,
25 km north of Paris.
Train: Gare du Nord, Paris to Mériel.
Road: N1 from Paris.

Musée Jean Gabin,
place Jean Gabin,
95630 Mériel.
Tel: 01 34 64 87 92.
Opening hours: Sats, Suns, 14h00-18h00.
Closed mid-Nov-mid-Mar.
Entrance tariff: EUR4.
Jean Gabin, the famous French film actor, spent his boyhood and teenage years in this small town, which today honours its favourite famous son with a musuem dedicated to his honour. All kinds of memorabilia, including costumes, photographs, posters and trophies, delineate the man and his career. On the first storey of the museum, you can see all the details of his, while on the second floor, you can explore aspects of a myth, including with the help of a 26 minute video presentation. The town's tourist office, next to the museum, has prepared walks of various durations around the town to show the locations most closely connected with the young Gabin.

Notre Dame du Val,
95630 Mériel.
Tel: 01 30 36 41 78.
Opening hours: Mar 1-Sept 3o, daily, for groups only, by arrangement.
Entrance tariff: EUR3 (reductions).
This magnificent abbey is the oldest Cisterican foundation in the region and it is still magnificently preserved. It was founded in 1125. Today, the abbey is used for all kinds of events, including concerts and exhibitions. The president of the Friends of the Abbey, 11 rue Pasteur, 95630 Mériel, will send you full details of the events in the abbey if you write with a stamped envelope or international reply coupon. Many cultural events are also staged in the Espace Rive Gauche, rue des Petits Prés.

MEUDON,
13 km south-west of Paris.
Train: RER C line to Meudon Val Fleury.
Road: D906 from Paris.

Foret domaniale de Meudon,
92190 Meudon.
Opening hours, open daily, all year.
Entrance tariff: free.
This great forest extends over nearly 1, 100 hectares and has over 7, 000 different species of animals. You can explore the forest using the short and long distance walking trails. A key attraction is the Pierre aux Moines, or the Monk's Stone, a prehistoric monument built around 10, 000 BC.

Musée d'Art et d'Histoire,
11 rue des Pierres,
92190 Meudon.
Tel: 01 46 23 87 13.
Opening hours, daily, all year, except Mon, Tues, 14h00-18h00.
Closed Aug, public holidays.
Entrance tariff: EUR2. 50 (reductions)
This elegant town house, dating from the 16th century, details the history and the art of Meudon. The work of local artists and tradespeople is commemorated, as is the work of the people who once worked in the great chateau. This was built in the 16th century, destroyed in 1803, rebuilt, then burned down in 1871. In the museum and on the terrace in front of it, you can see a collection of 19th and 20th century sculptures by such artists as Auguste Rodin and Jean Arp. The museum has frequent exhibitions of local art and history. You can also walk in the one hectare park. To complete your visit, have a look round the observatory here.

Musée Rodin,
Villa des Brillants,
10 avenue Auguste Rodin,
92190 Meudon.
Tel: 01 41 14 35 00.
Opening hours, May 1-Oct 26, Fri, Sat, Sun, 13h30-18h00.
Entrance tariff: EUR2 (reductions).

Métro: Mairie d'Issy, then bus.

In 1895, Rodin, the great sculptor, and his wife Rose Beuret, left Paris, where they had lived, and moved to Meudon. He delighted in his new house and estate and loved welcoming friends and distinguished visitors. After Rodin died in 1917, the French State acquired the villa and its estate and set up a museum there with his sketches and preliminary castings for many of his great works. Apart from the casts on display, thousands more are in storage here. The villa itself and Rodin's studio were restored to their original state, complete with many old photographs. Furniture, display cabinets full of antiques and paintings were all placed back in their original positions, so it's all very much as Rodin would have seen them. At the front of the villa is the tomb of Rodin and his wife, surmounted by his famous statue, The Thinker, on a white plinth.

MILLY-LA-FORET,
56 km south of Paris.
Train: Gare de Lyon, Paris to Lyon-Maisse (7 km); then taxi.
Road: A5 E16 from Paris.

Conservatoire nationals des plantes à parfum mèdicinales et aromatique,
91490 Milly-la-Foret.
Opening hours, May-Sept, Fri, 9h00-17h00, Sat, 14h00-21h00, Sun, 14h00-18h00.
Entrance tariff: free.
This conservatory cultivates some 1, 200 different plants that have particular applications in homeopathic medicine and during the open days, visitors are free to inspect them for themselves.

Église de Notre-Dame,
91490 Milly-la-Foret.
Opening hours, daily, all year, 10h00-18h00.
Entrance tariff: free.
The ancient church complements the 12th century Chapelle St-Blaise. The interior of the church is particularly interesting because of all the decorations done by Jean Cocteau (1889-1963), a very versatile artist and poet. He lived in the village for many years and died here on October 11, 1963, just hours after Edith Piaf died. Cocteau is buried in the Chapelle St-Blaise.

Le Cyclop sculpture,
91490 Milly-la-Foret.
The sculpture of the Cyclops is an astonishing piece of work, a mechanical monster that stands 23 metres high and weighs 300 tonnes. The metalwork took 25 years to create, the work of Jean Tinquely, who died in 1991; he was assisted by 15 internationally renowned sculptors.

Market hall,
91490 Milly-la-Foret.
The market hall in the centre of the village was built from wood in 1479, so it's one of the most historic building here. However, the village itself is far older, dating back to its foundation in 289 BC, which makes it one of the oldest settlements in the Ile de France, right on the western edges of the Foret de Fontainbleau.

MONTCEAUX LES PROVINS,
90 km south-east of Paris.
Train: Gare d'Austerlitz to Provins (20 km).
Road: N4 from Paris.

L'Étoile de Montceaux,
77151 Montceaux les Provins.
Tel. 01 64 01 26 12.
Web: www. letoiledemontceaux.com
It's a long way to come for an entertaining night out, but if you're in nearby Provins, it might be worth considering staying over the night. This nightclub stages lavish entertainment spectaculars every Friday and Saturday night that recall the past century of the music hall stars of Paris. It certainly promises a lively night!

MONTFORT-L'AMAURY,
48 km south-west of Paris.
Train: Gare de Montparnasse, Paris to Montfort-l'Amaury.
Road: N12 from Versailles.

Musée Maurice Ravel,
The Belvedere,
5 rue Maurice Ravel,
78490 Montfort-l'Amaury.
Tel: 01 34 86 00 89.

Opening hours, Wed, Thurs, Fri, all year, 14h30-18h00, by appt. Sat, Sun, all year, 10h00-16. 30 (from Apr-Oct, until 17h30). Entrance tariff: EUR6. 10 (reductions).
A short distance from the great forest of Rambouillet, is the house where the composer and musician Maurice Ravel (1875-1937) lived and worked. He came here for peace and tranquillity and found the serenity he sought in abundance. Visitors will soon sense why Ravel felt so at home here. You can walk through the sequence of small rooms and find his life and works brought to life most admirably. Ravel did the interior decor himself and he also designed the small garden. From the balcony of the house, you can admire the panoramic views, stretching to the forest of Rambouillet.

MONTMACHOUX,
80 km south-east of Paris.
Train: Gare de Lyon, Paris to Montereau Fault-Yonne.
Road: A6 from Paris to Montereau Fault-Yonne.

L'Autruche Rieuse (ostrich farm),
1 Grande Rue,
77940 Montmachoux.
Tel. 01 60 96 29 49.
Opening hours, Mar-Oct, Tues-Sun, public holidays, 14h30-19h00.
Entrance tariff: EUR3. 50 (reductions).
This is a farm with a difference, since it only raises ostriches. You can walk around the farm and admire the birds, although they are such delightful creatures that you may find it difficult to eat an ostrich steak afterwards.

MONTREUIL,
8 km east of Paris.
Métro: Porte de Montreuil.

La Boite d'Accordéon,
8 rue du Sergent Bobillot,
93100 Montreuil,
Tel. 01 48 58 633 97.
Opening hours, Mon, 14h00-18h00, Tues-Fri, 9h30-12h30, 14h00-18h30, Sat, by arr.

For anyone with a love of traditional French music, this is the place to come. Not only can you have a look at the workshops, where they restore many instruments, such as accordeons and concertinas, but the shop has a wide range of brand new instruments for sale.

Marché aux Puces de Montreuil,
93100 Montreuil.
Opening hours, Sat, Sun, Mon, 7h30-19h00.
This enormous market has an equally large variety of second-hand things to sell, everything from car parts to bits and pieces for household equipment, clothes too. You never know quite what you'll find here, but the rummaging will be fun.

MORET-SUR-LOING,
74 km south-east of Paris.
Train: Gare de Lyon, Paris to Moret-sur-Loing.
Road: N6 from Fontainebleau.
This delightful small town, set on the River Loing, has 1,400 metres of ancient walls, two fortified gateways and 20 towers. The many fortifications of the town, the narrow streets of the town and the river banks, provided much inspiration for the Impressionist painter Alfred Disley, who lived and worked in the town for over 20 years at the end of the late 19th century. During his lifetime, he was spectacularly unsuccessful and died in poverty. Now, he is one of the most highly regarded impressionist painters. There's a statue to Sisley on the square Samois at the entrance to the town.

Musée du Sucre d'Orge des Religieuses de Moret,
5 rue du Puits du Four.
Tel: 01 60 70 35 63.
Opening hours: by arr.
Entrance tariff: free.
For anyone with a sweet tooth, this little museum dedicated to the barley sugar once made by the nuns in Moret should appeal. A video presentation explains its history and you can also taste the confection.

MORIENVAL,
60 km north-east of Paris.
Road: N2, D332 from Paris. No train.

Abbaye de Morienval,
rue de la Poste,
60127 Morienval.
Tel: 03 44 88 61 14.
Opening hours, by arr with the Mairie or Mme Moreau, tel. 03 44 88 61 14.
Entrance tariff: free.
The abbey was founded by Benedictine nuns in the 9th century. The tower and the upper two storeys date from the 12th century and the abbey also has effigies dating back to the time of the Crusades.

NANTERRE,
13 km west of Paris.
Train: Gare St-Lazare to Nanterre, RER A1 line.
Road: RD23 from Paris.

Cathédrale Sainte-Geneviève,
rue de l'Église,
92000 Nanterre.
Opening hours, daily, all year, 8h0-18h00.
Entrance tariff: free
This ancient church was founded in the fourth century, but wasn't elevated to cathedral status until 1966. Among its historic points are the 14th century bell tower, the underground chapel and the crypt.

Ancient locations,
92000 Nanterre.
Nanterre, which is an important centre for the University of Paris, has several interesting historical locations. In the rue Raymond-Barbet, you can see what's left of the ancient abattoirs; until 1874, Nanterre was the principal supplier of charcuterie to Paris. In the avenue de la Liberté and the rue François-Hanriot, you can see ancient quarries that were transformed into mushroom farms in the 19th century, while between the rue François-Hanriot and the rue Noel-Pons, you can see the remains of the old Pont de la Folie. This is the last surviving relic of the railway line that was opened between Paris and St-Germain-en-Laye in 1837, one of the very first railway lines built in France.

NEMOURS,
75 km south of Paris.
Train: from Gare de Lyon, Paris to Nemours.
Road: A6 E15 from Paris.
Nemours is an ancient town that considers itself unspoiled and one of the last of the old-time towns, undefiled by development, in the Ile de France. It's a very agreeable place, with the old part of the town encircled by the River Loing and canals, riverside gardens and shady moats that are a haven for fishermen.

Chateau Musée,
rue Gautier Ier,
77140 Nemours.
Opening hours, Wed, Thurs, Fri, all year, 14h00-17h30, Sat, Mon, all year, 10h00-12h00, 14h00-17h30.
Entrance tariff: free.
The chateau itself is very historic, dating from the 12th century and containing a particularly well preserved oratory. The municipal museum, which is in the chateau, has many examples of porcelain made during the time of the Revolution, as well as examples of the work of Sanson the sculptor. Regular exhibitions are staged here.

Église de Saint-Jean Baptiste,
77140 Nemours.
This remarkable church, by the riverside, dates back to the 12th century, and is well worth seeing for its interiors and statuary, as well as its exterior.

La Chocolaterie Artisanale,
Z1 du Rocher Vert,
Route de Sens,
77140 Nemours.
Tel: 01 64 29 20 20.
Opening hours, Sat, all year, 15h00. Group tours only.
Entrance tariff: EUR3. 5 (reductions).
In this fascinating guided tour, done every Saturday afternoon, you can see how the famous chocolate confections of Nemours are made and packed, you can sample the wares and then buy them at reduced prices.

Les Spécialités au Coquelicot,
Z1 du Rocher Vert,
Route de Sens,
77140 Nemours.
Tel: 01 64 29 20 20.
Opening hours, Mon-Sat, all year, by arr. Minimum group, 15
Entrance tariff: EUR3
At the same factory where they make all those utterly delicious chocolates, they also make another speciality, unique to Nemours-sweets made from poppies and also the Liqueur de Coquelicot. You can see how they are made and then join in the tastings.

Musée de Préhistoire d'Ile de France,
Route de Sens,
77140 Nemours.
Tel: 01 64 78 54 80.
Opening hours, daily, all year, 10h00-12h00, 14h00-17h30, except Wed.
Entrance tariff: EUR3 (reductions).
This museum contains extensive displays of archaeological finds from the Essonne and Seine et Marne departments. Large scale recreations of archaeological "digs" show work in progress, while the 60 square metres recreation of the excavation at Pincevet also has an audio-visual performance, 20 minutes long, depicting the way of life of the last hunters of the Palaeolithic period. Four inside gardens at the museum bring to life the climate and vegetation of prehistoric periods.

Tuilerie de Bezanleu,
Treuzy-Levelay,
77140 Nemours.
Tel: 01 64 29 06 28.
Opening hours: by arr.
Entrance tariff: free.
This fascinating factory, long established, makes bricks and tiles by traditional methods and visitors are welcome, by prior arrangement, to inspect the production processes.

NOGENT-SUR-MARNE,
13 km east of Paris.
Train: RER A2 line to Nogent-sur-Marne.
Road: N34 from Paris.
It's a pleasant riverside town, easy to reach from Paris, with walks by the riverside, along the promenade garlanded with flowers. and through the pleasure port on the river. Among the many attractions of the town is the grand organ, now fully restored, in the Gaumont-Palace cinema.

Musée de Nogent-sur-Marne,
36 boulevard Galliéni,
94130 Nogent-sur-Marne.
Tel: 01 48 75 51 25.
Opening hours, daily, all year, except Mon, Fri, public holidays, 14h00-18h00, Sat, 10h00-12h00, 14h00-18h00.
Entrance tariff: free.
This small museum tells the story of the loops in the River Marne. Many documents and photographs tell what life was like in the old days, including rural life, earlier periods in the towns of the district and religious life. Nogent has always been a very popular place of riverside recreation for Parisians, relaxing in riverside cafes, strolling on the river bank or going for a river trip on a steamer. This riverside leisure, especially during the 19th century, is well documented in the museum. The museum also documents the life and work of two well-known artists with Nogent connections, Watteau, who often painted the old fairs in the town and Francis Poulenc, the 20th century avant garde composer, who lived here.

River Marne cruises,
Port de Nogent,
94140 Nogent-sur-Marne.
Tel. 01 48 71 02 98 (Adam Croisières).
Web: www.adam-croisières.com
From May 1 until Sept 30, you can enjoy a commentated cruise on the River Marne. Departures are on the hour, every hour, between 15h00 and 18h00, Sat, Sun and public holidays. The tariff is EUR8 (reductions). The same boat company does La Navette des Guingettes, cruises on the Rivers Seine and Marne which depart from the Pont Neuf and the Port de Bercy in Paris that include all kinds of traditional musical entertainment, dancing and dining, La Navette des Guinguettes.

ORLY AIRPORT,
14 km south of Paris.
94396 Orly Aérogare.
Tel. 01 49 75 15 15.
Web: www.adp.fr
Train: RER C2 line to Orly.
Road: N7 from Paris.
Orly is the second of the two commercial airports serving Paris. Its
two terminals have a reasonable number of bars, restaurants and
shops, while it also has an art gallery.

OZOIR-LES-FERRIÈRE,
25 km east of Paris.
Train: Gare de l'Est, Paris to Ozoir-la-Ferrière.
Road: N4 from Paris.

Parc Zoologique du Bois d'Attilly,
Route de Chevry,
77330 Ozoir-les-Ferrière.
Tel. 01 60 02 70 80.
Opening hours, daily, all year, 9h30-18h00 (winter, 17h00).
Entrance tariff: EUR8. 50 (reductions).
This magnificent zoo covers 16 hectares and is set in the middle
of a forest, complete with lakes and makes for an ideal day out. It
is home to 250 mammals and 400 birds. The animals range from
American bison to giraffes and Shetland ponies. You can see the
hippopotami in their lake and the chimpanzees in their special
enclosure. All the animal enclosures are well designed and the
zoo itself is well paid out. In addition, there's the maison de
oiseaux, full of bird species. Bar, cafe, tearoom.

PARC ASTÉRIX,
60128 Plailly.
30 km north of Paris.
Tel. 08 92 68 30 10.
Web: www.parcasterix.fr
Opening hours, Apr, daily, 10h00, 18h00, May, June, Mon-Fri,
10h00-18h00, Sat, Sun, 9h30-19h00, July, Aug, daily, 9h30-
19h00, Sept, Oct, Wed, Sat, Sun, 10h00-18h00.
Entrance tariff: EUR31 (reductions).
Train: Gare du Nord, Paris to Senlis, then bus/taxi or Gare du
Nord to Charles de Gaulle airport, then shuttle bus.

Road: A1 E15 from Paris.

This theme park with a difference, south of Senlis, features the adventures of Astérix, the cartoon character, and his adventures in Roman Gaul 2, 000 years ago. The highlights of the park include a Gallo-Roman village, a dolphin lake, a giant roller coaster and the Flight of Icarus. Shows, too, are staged, including a wide variety of stunts. The Transdemonium is billed as the first family ghost train. The site also has hotels, six restaurants and 40 other places to eat in what is seen as a very French equivalent of Disneyland Paris.

PÉRIGNY-SUR-YERRES,
20 km east of Paris.
Train: RER D2 line to Boussy-Saint-Antoine.
Road: N7 from Paris.

Fondation Dubuffet,
Villa Falbala,
Ruelle aux Chevaux,
94520 Périgny-sur-Yerres.
Tel: 01 47 34 12 63.
Web: www.dubuffetfondation.com
Opening hours, all year, daily, except public holidays, by arr only.
Entrance tariff: EUR8.

A visit to the Dubuffet Foundation is an exciting experience. Jean Dubuffet (1901-1985, who was from the northern port city of Le Havre, was an exciting modernist painter, who had a totally original "take" on what he saw in the world. He designed the Closerie Falbala himself-it's a monumental sculpture that is an incarnation of a walled garden, but all in white, with random lines of demarcation. The sculpture is large, covering an area of 1, 610 squaremetres and in the centre of it is the windowless Villa Falbala, also designed in the same style by Dubuffet. It houses the Cabinet logologique. It's now a listed Historical Monument. The visit concludes with a tour of paintings from the Dubuffet collection in an adjacent building. You can also see a collection of architectural models from Dubuffet's studios. More of his work can be seen at the Dubuffet Fondation's offices in Paris 75006.

PIERREFONDS,
75 km north-east of Paris.
Train: Gare du Nord, Paris, to Compiègne, then taxi.
Road: A1 E15 from Paris.

Chateau de Pierrefonds,
rue Viollet le Duc,
60350 Pierrefonds.
Tel. 03 44 42 72 72.
Web: http: //www.napoleon.org
   also http: //www.perso.wanadoo.fr/ot.pierrefonds
   also: www. monum. fr
Opening hours, mid-May-Sept, daily, 9h30-18h00, Oct-Mar, Mon-Sat, 9h30-12h30, 14h00-17h30, Sun, 9h30-17h30, Apr-mid-May, as for Oct-Mar, but Mon-Sat, closes 18h00, Sun, closes 18h00. Closed Jan 1, Nov 1 & 11, Dec 25.
Entrance tariff: EUR5. 5 (reductions).
This is a highly impressive fortified chateau, originally built in the 14th century. At the beginning of the 17th century, Louis XIII ordered it demolished and the ruins stood forlornly for the next two centuries. The site was bought by Napoléon in 1810 and then in the mid-19th century, Napoléon III ordered its restitution. The architect Viollet-le-Duc was chosen for the work. Today, you can take the tour through the reception rooms, salons and bedrooms, while the great hall is remarkable for its size-it's 50 metres long. The castle and its restoration continue to be controversial, but it's certainly worth seeing. The village itself is equally charming.

POISSY,
33 km north-west of Paris.
Train: RER A5 line to Poissy.
Road: D308 from Colombes.

La Collégiale Notre-Dame,
8, rue de l'Eglise,
78300 Poissy.
Opening hours, Mon-Sat, all year, 8h00-19h00, Sun, 8h00-18h00.
Entrance tariff: free.
Poissy's great 13th century church is one of the architectural masterpieces of the Ile de France, a perfect example of the transition from Roman to Gothic styles. Among the features well

worth inspecting are the choir, carved in 1150 and the beautiful contemplative statue of Isabelle of France, carved in 1300.

La Distillerie du Noyau de Poissy,
105 rue du Général de Gaulle,
78300 Poissy.
Tel: 01 39 65 20 59.
Opening hours, group visits, Wed, Sat, 15h00. To be arranged through the Poissy tourism office, tel. 01 30 74 60 65.
Entrance tariff: free.
Since the 18th century, Poissy has had a very special liqueur all its own, "Noyau de Poissy", distilled from the kernels of fruit and still used in cocktails and aperitifs. It's a deliciously perfumed drink and you can see exactly how it's made at the distillery as well as sampling the two different kinds of Noyau de Poissy that are distilled today.

La Villa Savoye,
82 rue de Villiers,
78300 Poissy.
Tel: 01 39 65 01 06.
Opening hours, Mar 1-Oct 31, daily, 10h00-18h00. Nov 1-Feb 28, daily, 10h00-12h00, 13h30-16h30.
Entrance tariff: free.
This is one of the master works of the great architect Le Corbusier, who designed this weekend villa for the Savoye family. It's a perfect illustration of the five points of modern architecture put forward by the Swiss architect. The villa was built betweeb 1928 and 1931 and the Savoye family lived here from 1932 until 1940. During the Second World War, German occupation troops badly damaged the building. In 1958, the town of Poissy acquired it, but took six hectares of land surrounding it to build a new school. It was handed over to the State in 1962 and declared an Historic Monument in 1965. Subsequent restoration, as recently as 1997, has restored the villa to its original glory and it's well worth seeing as a prime example of advanced modern architecture.

Le Parc du chateau de Villiers,
avenue du Bon Roi Saint-Louis.
78300 Poissy.
Opening hours, Apr 1-Sept 30, Mon-Fri, 17h30-20h00, Sat, Sun, public holidays, 9h00-20h00. Oct 1-Mar 31, Mon-Fri, 17h30-19h00, Sat, Sun, public holidays, 9h00-19h00.
Entrance tariff: EUR5 (reductions).
The parkland surrounding this chateau, which dates back to the 19<sup>th</sup> century, is open to visitors. Children will enjoy the mini farm, with a whole range of farm animals. The chateau itself, which is usually used for municipal events, can be inspected, including its library, with fine views over the park.

Musée d'Art et d'Histoire,
Enclos de l'Abbaye,
78300 Poissy.
Tel: 01 39 65 06 06.
Poissy's municipal museum, opened in 1980, has a wealth of material on historic Poissy, including its royal attachments; the tradition of its weekly livestock fairs; the great painters who lived here in the 19th century and the town's industrialisation during the 20th century. The museum has been moved to a new location, beside the museum of childhood games.

Musée du Jouet (Museum of Childhood Games),
1 enclos de l'Abbaye,
78300 Poissy.
Tel: 01 39 65 06 06.
Web: www. ville-poissy. fr
Opening hours: Tues-Sun, all year, 9h00-12h00, 14h00-17h30. Closed Mons and public holidays.
Entrance tariff: EUR3. 20 (reduction).
For anyone who's fascinated by childhood games, this is just the place to indulge a little nostalia. The museum has all sorts of childrens' playthings and games from the 14th century up to the mid-20th century and that includes everything from dolls and teddy bears to a magic lanterne. The museum also has model electric railways. Press certain buttons and some of the games will start working! Also in Poissy, you can see a reconstruction of the 13<sup>th</sup> century bridge, which was fortified in the 17th century; it was destroyed by Allied bombing during the Second World War,

but a faithful reconstruction opened in 1952. Poissy also has a major museum of Arts and History, but it is presently closed for reconstruction and isn't expected to reopen before 2007.

PONTOISE
35 km north-west of Paris.
Train: Gare du Nord or Gare St-Lazare, Paris to Cergy-Pontoise.
Road: N14/A15 from St-Ouen.

Musée Camille Pissarro,
17 rue de Chateau,
Tel: 01 30 38 02 40.
Web: www. ville-fr
Opening hours: Wed-Sun, 14h00-18h00, closed Mon, Tues and public holidays.
Entrance tariff: EUR 9.
In the old town of , just three km from the new town of Cergy , you can visit the museum dedicated to the great Impressionist painter, Camille Pissarro (1830-1903). The setting is magnificent, in the valley of the Oise, with the old town nearby. Pissarro worked here between 1866 and 1883 and the museum, which opened in 1980, has a collection of his works (one painting and innumerable engravings and designs ) and also works from some of the many lesser known artists who worked in this region, between   and L'Isle-Adam, during his lifetime. However, extensive reconstruction work has been ongoing at the museum, and it's unlikely to open until the autumn of 2004.

PORT-MARLY,
22km south-west of Paris.
Train from Gare St-Lazare, Paris, RER A line to Port-Marly.
Road: A14 from Paris.

Chateau de Monte-Cristo,
78560 Port-Marly.
Opening hours, Apr 1-Nov 1, Tues-Fri, 10h00-12h30, 14h00-18h00, Sat, Sun, 10hoo-18h00. Nov 2-Mar 31, Sun, 14h00-17h00.
Entrance tariff: free.
This chateau is where Alexandre Dumas, the creator of the Count of Monte Cristo, lived and worked. The interior of the house betrays his vivid imagination, with his choice of decor inspired by

the Arabian Nights. A walk through the house will really bring to life the imagination and the works of Dumas. In the grounds, you'll see a tiny neo-gothic lodge in the middle of a small lake; this was used by Dumas as his study, a complete retreat from the real world.


PROVINS,
89 km south-east of Paris.
Train: Gare d'Austerlitz, Gare de Lyon, Gare de l'Est, Paris to Provins.
Road: N19 E54.
Provins is a very interesting medieval town that's been well preserved. It has many buildings that provide strong historical interest. The town makes for a very interesting day out, but there's so much here that you could easily spend a couple of days exploring the place.

Caesar's Tower,
77160 Provins.
Opening hours, Jan-Apr, Nov, Dec, daily, 14h00-17h00. Apr-Oct, daily, 10h00-18h00.
Entrance tariff: EUR3. 40 (reductions).
This 12th century tower is one of the best preserved of Provins' medieval fortifications and you can explore all levels. During the 100 Years War in the 15th century, Provins was occupied by the English, who took over and strengthened the tower. During the 19th and 20th centuries, more restoration work was done. The most recent work has been repairing the damage done during the great tempest of December, 1999. Inside the tower, you can inpsect the model room, which has a cross-section model of the building, as well as the governor's office and the guard room. At a higher level, you can have a look at the bells and walk out onto the parapet, which gives outstanding views of the town and the ramparts.

Les Aigles des Remparts,
77160 Provins.
Tel. 01 64 60 17 90.
Opening hours, daily, end Mar-beginning Nov. Shows staged in afternoons and evenings.
Entrance tariff: EUR7. 70 (reductions).
This is a grand entertainment spectacle staged at the heart of Provins' ramparts and features eagles, after which the show is named, as well as wolves, horses and camels. It's designed to bring to life the medieval lifestyle of Provins. Another show, staged daily on the ramparts during the summer, shows how primitive but effective machines were used to assault the ramparts in medieval times.

Musée de Provins,
77160 Provins.
Opening hours, daily, all year, 14h00-18h00. July, Aug, until 19h00.
Entrance tariff: EUR3. 40 (reductions).
The town museum has many collections of items showing life in Provins when it was an important medieval industrial centre, going right up to recent times.

Tythe Barn,
77160 Provins.
Opening hours, daily, all year, 10h00-17h00. From Apr-Aug, until 18h00 daily.
Entrance tariff: EUR3. 40 (reductions).
The Grange aux Dimes, otherwise known as the Tythe Barn, gives a very good insight into the craft skills of Provins. You can see how cloth was woven and how the cloth merchants plied their trade. Parchment making was another speciality of Provins and you can also find out how the quarrymen organised their trade. Pottery, too, was an important craft in medieval Provins and you can see how it was made, together with many clay exhibits. In those far-off times, traders came to Provins from many other parts of Europe and you can see what the lifestyles were like of the Flemish and Dutch merchants who came to the great fairs in Provins to sell their wares. Two of the skills most in demand then were letter writing and money changing. The 13th century Tythe Barn gives an exceptionally interesting view of medieval life and comes complete with its own cellars-see below.

Underground,
77160 Provins.
Opening hours, guided tours daily, all year. Contact Provins tourist office,
tel. 01 64 60 26 26.
Entrance tariff: EUR3. 70 (reductions).
Provins had a vast network of quarries and cellars; the quarries originated with the extraction of a certain kind of fuller's earth that was used in the cloth making industry in medieval Provins. Much later, these underground places were used to store Champagne during the great Champagne fairs in the town and they were even used by local freemasons. In addition to all the underground quarries, Provins has several dozen cellars in the lower town and 100 in the upper town. Even the old hospital went underground; you can see a cellar made in the 12th century that was used as a ward underneath the town hospital.

RAMBOUILLET,
53 km south-west of Paris.
Train: Gare Montparnasse, Paris to Rambouillet.
Road: N10 from Versailles.

Le Chateau de Rambouillet,
78102 Rambouillet.
Tel: 01 34 83 00 25.
Web: www. monum.fr
Opening hours, Apr 1-Sept 30, daily, 10h00-11h30, 14h00-17h30. Oct 1-Mar 31, daily, 10h00-11h30, 14h00-14h30. Closed Tues and during presidential visits.
Entrance tariff: EUR5. 50 (reductions).
This wonderful chateau dates from the 14th century and over the years, it has had connections with many people famous in French history. It was acquired by Louis XVI as a royal residence in 1783. The 18th century apartments used by Marie-Antoinette are well worth seeing, as is the neo-Pompeii style from the Ist Empire. The garden is very French in its design and has canals and six islands in the lakes. Once a royal chateau, today, it is still used for grand occasions, when international heads of state are making official visits to France. When this happens, the chateau and grounds are closed to the public.

La Bergerie Nationale,
Parc du Chateau,
78102 Rambouillet.
Tel: 01 61 08 68 70.
Web: www. educagri. fr/bergerie. nationale
Opening hours, Wed-Sun, public holidays, all year, 14h00-17h00.
Daily during school holidays. Closed for Christmas and New Year.
Entrance tariff: EUR4 (reductions).
This is the national sheep farm, an intriguing institution that children and adults alike will find intensely interesting. The main buildings were constructed in 1786 and are classified as Historic Monuments. The large flock of Merino sheep here produce very fine wool, which is woven into high quality garments, which you can buy here. More than 1, 000 lambs are born here annually.

La Laiterie et la Chaumière aux coquillages,
Chateau de Rambouillet,
781020 Rambouillet.
Tel: 01 34 83 29 09.
Opening hours, Apr 1-Sept 30, daily, 10h00-12h00, 14h00-17h30.
Oct 1-Mar 31, daily, 10h00-12h00, 14h00-15h30.
Entrance tariff: EUR6 (reductions).
Towards the end of the 18th century, some members of the royal family, particularly Marie-Antoinette, wanted to return to an idealized nature. The shell cottage was built between 1779 and 1780 and is one of the most beautiful of its kind in Europe. The dairy was built for Louis XV1 to please Marie-Antoinette; it includes an incredible piece of sculpture, called "Almathée et la Nymphe".

L'Éspace Rambouillet,
Route de Clairefontaine,
78120 Rambouillet.
Tel: 01 34 83 05 00.
Web: www.onf.fr/espaceramb
Opening hours, Apr-Oct, daily, 9h00-18h00. Nov-Mar, Tues-Sun, 10h00-17h00. Closed from mid-Dec to mid-Jan.
Entrance tariff: EUR7. 80 (reductions).
In the heart of the great forests that surround Rambouillet, 250 hectares are given over to an area where animals can live in totally natural conditions. Among the animals you should see

roaming in the wild are roe deer, roe bucks, stags and wild boars as well as trained falcons.

Musée du Jeu de l'Oie-collection Dietsch,
Place du Roi de Rome,
781020 Rambouillet.
Tel: 01 30 88 73 73.
Opening hours, daily, all year, 14h00-18h00, closed Mon.
Entrance tariff: EUR2. 50 (reductions).
This new museum, which is in a restored wing of the Palais du Roi de Rome shows all kinds of games, diversions, means of education and propaganda, from the 17th century to the present day, 2, 500 pieces in all. The museum is described as a unique source of information on the history of society, including costumes, industry and science. The games room, with animated games, is designed to keep younger members of the family happy. You can also wander through the extensive gardens of the former palace; it has been restored according to its original plans and includes a romantic garden.

Musée Rambolitrain,
4, place Jeanne d'Arc,
78120 Rambouillet.
Tel: 01 34 83 15 93.
Web: www.ot-rambouillet. fr
Opening Hours, daily, all year, 10h00 to 12h00, 14h00 to 17h30.
Entrance tariff: EUR3. 50 (reductions).
This miniature railway museum, described as the most comprehensive of its kind in France, has more than 5, 000 pieces of railway equipment, everything from miniature locomotives to carriages and signals, as well as 400 metres of track, on which all the miniature trains run. The museum aims to tell the whole story of railways in France.

ROCQUENCOURT,
15 km south-west of Paris.
Train: RER C5 line to Versailles Rive Gauche, then bus.
Road: A13 E05 from Boulogne-Billancourt.

Arboretum de Chevreloup,
30 route de Versailles,
78150 Rocquencourt.
Tel: 01 39 55 53 80.
Opening hours, Apr 1-Nov 15, Sat, Sun, Mon, public holidays, 10h00-17h00. Groups can visit daily, all year, by arr.
Entrance tariff: EUR5 (reductions).
This arborertum, which was established in the 1920s on the northern part of the Versailles estate, covers 200 hectares and has over 2, 700 species and varieties of trees grouped according to the geographical area of origin, Asia, the Americas and Europe, as well as about 5, 000 species of tropical plants. During the guided tour, you will see many important species as well as many unusual varieties. One of the most striking sites is the avenue planted with blue cedars from the Atlas Mountains in Morocco that separates the area planted with conifers from that planted with deciduous trees. Cafe, restaurant.

ROY BOISSY,
100 km north-west of Paris.
Road: A16 to Beauvais, then D901 from Beauvais. No train.

Moulin (mill),
1 rue Fontaine,
60690 Roy Boissy.
Tel. 03 44 46 32 20/03 44 46 21 67.
Opening hours, Third Sun in June, Sept, 13h-19h00, second and fourth Sun in July, Aug, 13h00-19h00.
Entrance tariff: EUR3 (reductions).
The 18th century flour mill at Roy Boissy is a most delightful and interesting place, 20 km from Beauvais. The mill itself has been perfectly preserved, along with its mill pond and waterwheel and you can see all stages of flour production inside the mill. Outside, attractive gardens cover nearly 5, 000 square metres.

RUNGIS,
14 km south of Paris.
Train: RER C2 line to Pont de Rungis/Orly.
Road: A6 from Paris.

Rungis wholesale market,
94514 Rungis Cedex.
Tel. 01 41 80 80 81.
Web: http: //www.rungisinternational.com
Opening hours, Mon-Sat, all year. The fish market is open, Tues-Fri, 2h00-7h00.
The meat market is open Mon-Fri, 4h00-10h00. The fruit and vegetable market is open 5h00-10h00, Mon-Sat.
Entrance tariff: free.
Rungis is the largest wholesale market in the world for fish and other produce; the markets used to be at Les Halles in central Paris, until they were relocated close to Orly airport over 30 years ago. The scale of the enterprise is vast; around 12, 000 people work here. Plenty of hotels and restaurants service the markets at Rungis and you can make a visit, as part of a group. The minimum numbers are 15. Email first to:
service.visites@semmaris. fr

SAINT-ARNOULT,
110 km north-west of Paris.
Train: Gare du Nord, Paris to Beauvais, then taxi.
Road: A16 to Beauvais, then D133 through Gerberoy.

Ancien Prieuré,
11 rue Principale,
60220 Saint-Arnoult.
Tel. 03 44 46 07 34.
Opening hours, Aug, daily, 14h00-17h00, Sept, Sat, Sun, 14h00-17h00.
Entrance tariff: EUR4 (reductions).
This delightful 15th century building, once an old priory belonging to the former Abbey of Beaubec in Seine-Maritime, is still in excellent condition. It's a very attractive half-timbered building made with cob walls, its walls painted ochre.

SAINT-ARNOULT-EN-YVELINES,
20 km southwest of Paris.
Train: RER C4 line to Dourdan, then taxi.

Musée des Arts et Traditions Populaires,
Tel: 01 30 59 31 99.
Opening hours, Apr-Sept, first and third Sun of the month, 14h00-18h00.
Entrance tariff: EUR4 (reductions).
This museum gets away from the great classical setpieces and the contemporary objects of so many museums and concentrates on the ordinary day-to-day life. Lots of ordinary objects and artefacts used in country households from time immemorial right up to the present day are on display. Some are sure to evoke nostalgic memories.


SAINT-CLOUD,
13 km south-west of Paris.
Métro: Boulogne-Pont de Saint-Cloud, then bus.
Road: D986 from Boulogne-Billancourt.

Ferme de Piqueur,
Domaine National de St-Cloud,
92210 St-Cloud.
Tel. 01 46 02 24 53.
Opening hours, Sat, Sun, all year, school holidays and daily in Aug, 10h00-12h30, 13h30-17h30.
Entrance tariff: EUR2
This farm, part of the Parc du St-Cloud, is designed to educate and you can observe a good range of farm animals, including cows, pigs, as well as poultry and rabbits.

Hippodrome de St-Cloud,
92210 St-Cloud.
Tel. 01 44 30 75 00.
This is one of the best-known horse racing tracks in the Paris region. It's set on the heights overlooking Paris, so the views from the track are quite spectacular, as they are from the restaurants. St-Cloud is one of two noted horse racing venues to the west of Paris-the other is Longchamps in the Bois de Boulogne (qv).

Musée municipal de Saint-Cloud,
60 rue Gounod,
92210 St Cloud.
Tel: 01 46 022 67 18
Web: www. ville-saint-cloud.fr/temps libre/musee.htm
Opening hours: Wed, Sat, Sun, 14h00-18h00.
Entrance tariff: free.
This museum is comparatively new, having been opened in the
Jardin des Avelines as recently as 1988; it is designed to display
the historic patrimony of this district on the western fringes of
Paris. Between 1697 and 1766, Saint-Cloud was noted for its
porcelain production, the town was noted for entirely different
artistic endeavours, when composers such as Gounod and Ravel
stayed in Saint-Cloud. The museum depicts these themes and it
also has the Oulmont collection, paintings and drawings from the
18th century.


SAINT-CYR-L'ÉCOLE,
25 km southwest of Paris.
Train: RER C line or train from Gare Montparnasse, Paris, to St-
Cyr-l'Ecole.
Road: A13 E05/A12 from Paris.

Musée du Lycée Militaire,
2 avenue Jean-Jaurès,
78210 Saint-Cyr-l'Ecole.
Tel: 01 30 85 88 02.
Opening hours: by prior arr with Versailles Tourist Office, tel. 01
39 24 88 88.
The military academy here has a long and distinguished history,
dating back to 1800. The various stages of its history are well
documented in this museum, organised in what used to be the
archives building.

SAINT-CYR-SUR-MORIN,
70 km east of Paris.
Train: Gare de l'Est, Paris to La Ferté-sur-Jouarre.
Road: A3 from Paris.

Musée de Pays de Seine et Marne,
17 avenue de la Ferté sous Jouarre,
77750 Saint-Cyr-sur-Morin.
Tel. 01 60 24 46 00.
Opening hours, daily, all year, 10h00-12h00, 14h00-17h00.
Between May and Sept, closes Sat, Sun, 18h00. Closed Mon and
on Jan 1, May 1, Dec 25.
Entrance tariff: EUR4 (reductions).
This enchanting regional museum details the history of society in
the northern part of Seine et Marne, including the old traditional
rural and agricultural way of life. Saint-Cyr-sur-Morin is five km
south-west of La Ferté-sur-Jouarre. The old village ways of life
are chronicled and so too are many craft traditions, from
beekeeping to quarrying. Even winegrowing, which disappeared
from the area at the beginning of the 20th century, is included.
There's much, too, on the folklore of the area, as well as a writer
well-known in the locality, Pierre Mac Orlan (1882-1970), who
lived in Saint-Cyr-sur-Morin and wrote extensively about local
ways and customs. The museum is particularly poingnant
because in recent years, with the development of the new town of
Marne la Vallée and Disneyland Resort Paris, much of the area
has been extensively developed and urbanised.


SAINT-DENIS,
10 km west of Paris.
Métro: Saint-Denis-Porte de Paris.
Road: N14 from Paris.

Basilique St-Denis,
6 rue de Strasbourg,
93200 St-Denis.
Web: www. monum. fr
Opening hours, Apr-Sept, Mon-Sat, 10h00-19h00, Sun, 12h00-
19h00. Oct-Mar, Mon-Sat, 10h00-17h00, Sun, 12h00-17h00.
Closed Jan 1, May 1, Nov 1, Nov 11, Dec 25.
Entrance tariff: free to nave, royal tombs, EUR5. 50 (reductions).
The basilica, which was begun in the first half of the 12th century,
is where the Gothic style all began; the rose window in the west
front was the first of its kind. Apart from its architectural glories, all
but three of the French monarchs from 1000 up to the Revolution

were buried here and you can inspect their tombs and effigies for a EUR5 fee. One of the most interesting tombs is that of Clovis, the king who destroyed Roman Gaul in AD500 and turned it into France, with Paris for its capital. Ironically, St-Denis has long been one of the working class strongholds of Paris, with a Communist influence to match, but is is equally revered as being the last resting place of so many French monarchs.

Musée de l'Art et de l'Historie de Saint-Denis,
22 bis, rue Gabriel-Péri,
93200 Saint-Denis.
Tel: 01 42 43 05 10.
Opening hours, Mon-Wed-Fri, all year, 10h00-17h30 (20h00, Thurs), Sat, Sun, all year, 14h00-18h30. Closed Tues, some public holidays.
Entrance tariff: EUR4 (reductions).
This museum has deservedly won many awards for its originality of conception and its displays. It's set in a former 18th century Carmelite convent and its displays describe vividly such events as the siege of Paris in 1870 and the Commune the following year. The museum also has many artefacts, including documents and paintings, that relate to Paul Élouard (1895-1952), the renowned poet with strong Communist leanings, who was born in Saint-Denis. The art collection is very wide ranging, from Daumier lithographs to Picasso designs. In ways, the most striking part of the museum is on the first floor, where the nuns' cells, bleak and austere, from the 18th century, have been carefully preserved just as they were.

Stade de France,
rue Francis de Pressensé, 93200 Saint-Denis.
Tel: 01 55 93 00 00.
Web: http: //www. stadefrance. fr/
Opening hours, daily, all year, 10h00-18h00, except during matches.
Entrance tariff: free.
This highly impressive 80, 000 seater stadium was built for the 1998 World Cup and in addition to football, it is also used as a large scale concert arena. It's well worth seeing just for its modernist, modular architecture.

## SAINTE-GENEVIÈVE-DES-BOIS,
25 km south of Paris.
Train: RER C4/C6 line to Sainte-Geneviève-des-Bois.
Road: A6 from Paris.

Russian cemetery,
Tel. 01 60 15 11 40.
Opening hours, Mar-Sept, daily, 8h00-19h00, Oct-Feb, 8h00-17h00.
Entrance tariff: free.
Russian emigrés living in Paris in the mid-1920s had this cemetery built and subsequently many well-known names from the extensive Russian community were buried here. Many of the great Russian names in French life during the 20th century are buried here, but probably the best-known is the Russian dancer, Rudolf Nureyev, considered the greatest male dancer of the 20th century. He defected in Paris in 1961 when he was on a tour to the city with a company from his homeland; he never returned. He died in Paris on January 6, 1993 and is buried here. You can also have a look at the small but ornate Russian Orthodox church within the cemetery; the church was built in 1938/39 and has a unique blue cupola, which evokes the blue of the sky.

## SAINT-GERMAIN-EN-LAYE.
21 km south-west of Paris.
Train: RER A line to St-Germain-en-Laye.
Road: N13 from Nanterre.

Maison Claude Debussy,
Tel: 01 34 51 05 12,
Opening hours: 14h00-18h00, daily, except Suns, Mons, public holidays, Mar-Oct. Closes at 17h30, Nov-Feb.
Entrance tariff: free.
This magnificent mansion was built in the 17th and 18th centuries and it's the primary exhibition space in France devoted to one of the country's greatest composers, Claude Debussy (1862-1918), who was the creator of musical impressionism. Nearby, in the Parc du Chateau and the Jardin Anglais, you can enjoy many walks, while from the terrace, you can enjoy an absolutely magnificent panorama of the western parts of Paris.

Musée des Antiquités Nationales,
Chateau St-Germain-en-Laye,
78100 Saint-Germain-en-Laye.
Tel: 01 39 10 13 00.
Opening hours: daily, all year, 9h00-17h15, except Tues.
Entrance tariff: free.
This magnificent collection of archaeological works from all over
the world, shows the evolution of man since his first appearance,
and the tools he used. The historical presentation includes Roman
France and the time of the Emperor Charlemagne.

Musée de la Fondation du Maréchal LeClerc,
place Royale.
78100 Saint-Germain-en-Laye.
This museum commemorates the life of this great French general,
from birth to death and all the armies he commanded in between.
Realignment work on the courtyard of the Quartier Gramont,
where the museum is situated, should be completed by now,
allowing access to the museum once again.

SAINT-GERMER DE FLY,
100 km north-west of Paris.
Road: A16 to Beauvais, then N31. No train.
Abbaye Benedictine,
60850 Saint-Germer de Fly,
Tel. 03 44 82 64 74 (Office de Tourisme du Pays de Bray Oise),
Opening hours, daily, all year, 10h00-12h00, 14h00-17h30 (Apr 1-
Sept 30, 18h00).
Entrance tariff: free.
One of the oldest religious foundations in the Ile de France, the
abbey was founded in 661. The chapel in the abbey is an exact
replica of the Sainte Chapelle, close to Notre Dame cathedral in
Paris.

SAINT JEAN-DE-BEAUREGARD,
28 kms south of Paris.
Train: Gare Montparnasse, Paris to Versailles, then taxi.
Road: A10 from Paris.

Domaine de St-Jean-de-Beauregard,
91940 Saint-Jean-de-Beauregard.
Tel. 01 60 12 00 01.
Web: www. domainesaintjeanbeauregard
Opening hours, Mar-Nov, Sun, public holidays, 14h00-18h00.
Daily, groups by arr.
Entrance tariff: EUR7. 40 (reductions).
The chateau of St-Jean-de-Beauregard, with its parkland and other attractions, is listed as an Historic Monument, bearing witness to the lifestyle of the 17th century. You can see the dovecote with its 4, 500 pigeon holes and the 17th century vegetable garden, with rare vegetables and masses of flowers. There's also a conservation room for grapes and fruits. Plant shows are held twice yearly, in April and November, while traditional craft shows take place in September.

SAINT-MESME,
20 km south-west of Paris.
Train: RER C4 line to Dourdan, then taxi.
Road: A4 E50 from Paris.

Musée du Costume Militaire,
1, rue Legaigneur,
78730 Saint-Mesme.
Tel: 01 30 59 42 71.
Opening hours: daily, by prior arr.
Entrance tariff: EUR4 (reductions).
The museum is housed in an almost unique building, a 15th century manor house of a type rarely to be seen in the Ile de France region nowadays. The octagonal tower, spiral staircase, half-timbered construction and French-style ceilings are all interesting. The collection is just as interesting as the house: 80 life sized models in French, British, German and American uniforms, covering the period from 1870 to the present day.

SAINT-OUEN,
8 km north of Paris.
Métro: Porte de Clignancourt, Porte de Saint-Ouen.

Le Parisien newspaper,
69/73 boulevard Victor Hugo,
93585 Saint-Ouen Cedex.
Tel. 0 825 003 0020.
Le Parisien, a popular Parisian tabloid, operates from ultra-modern premises in Saint-Ouen and groups (minimum 15) can see how the editorial content is put together, then how the newspaper is produced on state of the art printing presses.

Marché aux Puces (antiques fair),
Tel. 01 42 58 00 00.
Opening hours, Sat, Sun, Mon, all year, 7h00-19h00.
The Marché aux Puces, at Saint-Ouen on the western outskirts of the city, is the most famous market for antiques in Paris. There's a veritable maze of alley ways and stalls and you can browse for hours. Each dealer's stand is different from the next and with a magic atmosphere to this antiques village each weekend. These days, the market is devoted mainly to good quality antiques, largely furniture, but it also has lots of trendy modern stuff, from traffic lights to petrol pumps.

Within the whole complex, there are 12 official markets, each with their own specialities. Each day, between 2, 500 and 3, 000 stall holders present their wares. Antica, Biron, Cambo and Malassis all sell seriously expensive antique furniture. The oldest market, the Marché Vernaison, has the widest selection of old and new furniture and decorative items. The Marché des Rosiers has mostly 20th century decorative pieces, while Malik is mostly clothes, including some very posh cast-offs from the fashion houses. Two other markets, Jules-Vallès and Lécuyer-Vallès are in ways the most fun, because they are the cheapest and most likely to produce the unexpected bargain. But the whole area of the Marché aux Puces is so vast that you could spend entire days, if not weekends, perusing the stalls and more than likely find some venerable bargains.

SENLIS,
52 km north of Paris.
Train: Gare du Nord to Senlis.
Road: A1 from Paris.

Ancien chateau royal,
place du Parvis Notre-Dame,
Tel. 03 44 32 00 81.
Opening hours, Mon-Fri, 10h00-12h00, 14h00-18h00, Sat, sun, public holidays, 11h00-13h00, 14h00-18h00.
Entrance tariff: EUR1 (reductions).
There's not much left to see as you walk around the ruins of the ancient chateau of Senlis and the even older remains of the wall that was built in Roman times. However, the ruins will give a sense of the long history of the place.

Cathédrale de Notre-Dame,
Opening hours, daily, all year, 8h00-18h00.
Entrance tariff: free
The cathedral in the centre of this historic town, whose history dates back more than 2, 000 years, is a masterpiece of Gothic creation. Building began in 1155 and it was consecrated in 1191. The interior is worth seeing for its many tombs and carvings, while the west door, surrounded by a stone relief showing the coronation of the virgin, is equally spectacular.

Musée de l'Art,
place Norte-Dame,
60300 Senlis.
Tel. 03 44 53 00 80 extn 1247
Opening hours, daily, all year, 10h00-12h00, 14h00-18h00. Closed Tues, also Wed am. From Nov to Mar, closes at 17h00.
Entrance tariff: EUR4 (reductions). This entrance tariff covers all four museums in Senlis. This museum, in an ancient episcopal palace, has substantial archaeological collections, from Roman, Merovingienne and medieval times. It has also picture galleries with many paintings done between the 17th and 20th centuries, as well as a collection of 20th century naif paintings.

Musée de l'Hotel de Vermandois,
place du Pravis Notre-Dame,
60300 Senlis.
Tel. 03 44 53 00 80 extn 1219.
Opening hours, as above.
Entrance tariff: as above.
The museum is based in a 12th century mansion and after extensive restoration, it will show in detail the history of the cathedral and of the town itself. For the moment, two short audio-visual presentations outline this history.

Musée des Spahis,
Chateau Royal,
60300 Senlis.
Tel. 03 44 53 00 80 extn 1315.
Opening hours, as above.
Entrance tariff: as above.
The museum commemorates a now little known facet of French military life. Between 1800 and 1814 and from 1830 until 1964, this cavalry regiment was recruited from people living in the French North African colonies, including Algeria. The men of this cavalry regiment, riding their horses with their burnous (headwear) flapping in the breeze, once made familiar illustrations to France's colonial history and those connections are recalled here.

Musée Venerie,
Chateau Royal,
60300 Senlis.
Tel. 03 44 53 00 80 extn 1315.
Opening hours, as above.
Entrance tariff: as above.
This museum is in the same chateau as the Spahis museum, but its subject matter couldn't be more different; it depicts the progress of hunting, from the 15th century up to the present day. That historical progression is portrayed through paintings, designs, engravings and a host of ancient trophies and objets d'art inspired by hunting. Before you start your visit, an audio-visual presentation outlines the history that's about to be unveiled.

Town centre streets,
60300 Senlis.

The centre of Senlis, adjacent to the cathedral, has many ancient streets and passageways that date back to medieval times and have been little changed since. It's one of the best places in the Ile de France to see what a medieval streetscape looked like, with half-timbered houses, ancient walls, garlanded with wild flowers in springtime. In the south of the town centre, the Bellevue Ramparts overlook La Nonette river.

SENS,
110 km south of Paris.
Train: Gare Montparnasse, Paris to Sens.
Road: A5-E54 from Paris.

Cathédrale,
89100 Sens.
Opening hours, daily, all year, 8h00-18h00.
Entrance tariff: free.

The cathedral of St-Etienne is the oldest of the Gothic cathedrals in France, built in the 12th century. Particularly worth seeing are the stained glass windows, made between the 12th and 16th centuries; one of their features is a tribute to Thomas a Becket, the English churchman who was murdered in Canterbury cathedral in 1170.

Musée de Sens,
place de la Cathédrale,
89100 Sens.
Tel. 03 86 64 15 27/03 86 64 46 22.
Opening hours, June-Sept, daily, 10h00-12h00, 14h00-18h00, Oct-May, Mon, Thurs, Fri,
14h00-18h00, Wed, Sat, Sun, 10h00-12h00, 14h00-18h00.
Entrance tariff: free.

The museum is in two buildings adjacent to the cathedral. One of the building is the 12th century Palais Synodal, while the other is the former archbishops' palace. The museum, which extends over five floors, has rich collections of prehistoric, Roman and medieval material from the Sens region. One interesting feature is the liturgical robes worn by Thomas a Becket in the 12th century, when he was in exile in Sens, before returning home to England.

Old town centre,
89100 Sens.
The old town centre in Sens, on the eastern bank of the River
Yonne, has many many medieval buildings. The whole old town
district is encircled by a ring of tree-lined boulevards. Also worth
seeing in this part of Sens are the wooden and iron "halles",
dating from the 18th century, where markets are held every week.

SERRIS,
30 km east of Paris.
Train: RER A line to Montéverain-Val d'Europe.
Road: A4 E50 from Paris.
La Valle Village,
3 cours de la Garonne,
777000 Serris.
Tel: 01 60 42 35 00.
Web: www. lavalleevillage.com
Opening hours, daily, summer, 10h00-20h00 (19h00 in winter).
This shopping centre, just a few minutes from Disneyland Paris
has many shops selling top brands in fashions, homeware and
luxury items, but at considerably reduced prices. The minimum
reduction is 33 per cent and the cuts go up to 60 per cent. The
centre also has 10 restaurants, so you can have a great shopping
day out here.

Sea Life Center,
Val d'Europe,
14 cours Danube,
777000 Serris.
Tel. 01 60 42 33 66.
Web: www. sealife. fr
Opening hours, Mon-Fri, all year, 10h00-17h30, Sat, Sun, all year,
10h00-19h30.
Entrance tariff: EUR11 (reductions).
This modernistic aquarium has over 300 species of fish and you
can see them in the panoramic tunnel, which gives total 360
degree vision. Among the interesting features of the aquarium,
you can follow the course of the Seine from its source to the sea,
while you can also observe the aquatic life of the Brittany coast
and the Atlantic Ocean as far as the Antilles.

SÈVRES,
12 km south-west of Paris.
Métro: Pont de Sèvres.
Road: N10 from Boulogne-Billancourt
Musée National de la Céramique,
place de la Manufacture,
92310 Sèvres.
Tel. 01 41 14 04 20.
Opening hours, Mon, Wed-Sun, all year, 10h00-17h00.
Closed Tues.
Entrance tariff: EUR4 (reductions).

This marvellous ceramics museum began as a private firm in Vincennes in 1738; 18 years later, it was moved to its present location and soon afterwards, was taken over by the State. The museum has an incredible array of Rococo style pieces from the 18th century, as well as many later examples of its work. There is much more than just ceramics from Sèvres on show here; the museum has many other styles on show, including Delftware and Meissen. Shop, showroom.

SOUPPES-SUR-LOING,
90 km south of Paris.
Train: Gare de Lyon, Paris to Nemours, then bus.
Road: A6 E15 from Paris.

Le Parc Animalier de l'Emprunt,
77440 Souppes-sur-Loing.
Tel. 01 64 29 76 55.
Opening hours, May-Sept, daily, 10h00-19h00. Oct-Apr, daily, 13h30-17h30.
Entrance tariff: EUR5 (reductions).

This vast animal park includes six hectares of woods and a sizeable lake, where the animals roam freely. The species here range from rabbits and goats to ponies and there's also a mini-farm. Fish, too, are well stocked.

THÉMÉRICOURT,
60 km south-west of Paris.
Road: A15/N14 from Paris (no train).

Regional Nature Park of the Vexin Français,
Visitor Centre and museum,
Chateau de Théméricourt,
95450 Théméricourt.
Tel: 01 34 66 15 10.
Opening hours, daily, all year. Mon-Fri, 9h00-12h30, 14h00-18h00. Sat, Sun, public holidays, 10h00-18h00.
Entrance tariff: EUR4 (reductions). A EUR8 pass, valid for one day, gives access to all museums.
The visitor centre and museum will give a sound introduction to the vastness of this regional park, which covers 66, 000 hectares in 94 communes in the Departments of Val-d'Oise and Yvelines. It also extends far into Normandy. The museum gives good insights into the old way of life and popular culuture of the Vexin.

Three other museums in the park are also worth seeing. The Musée de Moisson at Sacy, in the southernmost part of the parc, near Théméricourt, has many agricultural implements. The region has long been known as the bread basket of Paris, because of the amount of wheat cultivated. At Commeny, also near Théméricourt, you can visit the Maison du Pain and discover the history of bread baking. At St-Clair-sur-Epte, in the far north-west of the park, there's the interestingly named Musee de la Pomme et des Fruits Oubliés. Many varieties of apples and pears are planted here and you can investigate many fruits that have otherwise been confined to history. This museum also has a collection of cider making equipment.

The sloping landscapes of the Seine valley are very beautiful and unspoiled. You can explore the park on its eight cycle trails or along the more than 500 km of signposted footpaths, or indeed on horseback, following trails of one to five days duration. In the area between Vétheuil and La Roche-Guyon, you can inspect some of the 470 species of plants, including 14 protected species. You may also see lots of flights of migrating birds, a spectacular sight. River tourism is also represented in the park and there's an information point dedicated to it at the Port d'Illon in Saint-Martin-la-Garenne.

THOIRY,
40 km south-west of Paris.
Train: Gare St-Lazare, Paris to Dreux.
Road: From Paris, A13 E 5, then N12 towards Dreux.

Parc Zooloogique de Thoiry,
BP9,
78770 Thoiry-en-Yvelines,
Tel: 01 34 87 40 67.
Web: http: //www.thoiry.tm.fr
Opening hours, daily, all year, 11h00-18h00. July, Aug, 10h00-18h00. Nature reserve, 10h00-17h30.
Entrance tariff: EUR25 (chateau, gardens, zoo, nature reserve; reductions).
Thoiry makes a full day out, but you'll need a car to make the most of the zoo and nature reserve. The Chateau de Colombier has a full audio-visual presentation on the history of the families who've lived there, while the gardens are a delight. One of the highlights is the Ile Mystérieuse, which is approached by small bridges. On the island, with its gigantic foliage, children can enjoy toboganning and other attractions. The zoological gardens have a tourist train. In the zoo and nature reserve, you can see many animal species from Africa and the Americas, over 800 animals in all. Shop, "L'Eléphant Gourmand" restaurant.

THOMERY,
60 km south of Paris.
Train: Gare de Lyon to Avon-Fontainebleu.
Road: A5 from Paris.

Chateau de By,
77810 Thomery.
Opening hours, Wed, Sat, all year, by arr by mairie, tel. 01 64 70 51 65.
Entrance tariff: free.
This 15th century chateau was the home in the late 19th century to Rosa Bonheur (1822-1899), the celebrated painter of animals. In her time, she was as well known as Picasso was in the 20th century. You can see her studio preserved as it was in her time, complete with paintings, studies, designs and tableaux. Bonheur lived in the chateau for many years; she kept a pet African lion,

which had the run of the gardens and kept local people awake with its roaring. After her death, the chateau fell into disrepair, but in recent years, it has been renovated.

Town walks,
Thomery is an attractive small town beside the River Seine, 5 km from the better-known Fontainbleu. In Thomery, you can walk through the town centre, admiring the medieval buildings, including the 12th century Gothic church. This was a bustling river port in medieval times and you can walk along the quiet riverside quays. Thomery is surrounded by the Forest of Fontainbleu, ideal for walks.

TRIEL-SUR-SEINE,
30 km north-west of Paris.
Train: Gare St-Lazare to Triel.
Road: D55 from Poissy.

Le Parc aux Étoiles,
2 rue de la Chapelle,
78510 Triel.
Tel: 01 39 74 75 10.
Web: http: //www.parcauxetoles.fr.st
Opening hours, Wed, all year, 15h30-17h00, Sun, all year, 15h00-17h00.
Entrance tariff: EUR5. 50 (reductions).
This observatory gives an excellent introduction to the stars, not only through observation, but through the many lectures and courses that it runs.

TROYES,
171 km south-east of Paris.
Train from Paris Gare de Lyon to Troyes.
Road: N19 from Provins.

Abbaye Saint Loup,
1 rue Chrestien de Troyes,
10000 Troyes.
Tel: 03 25 76 21 68.
Opening hours: daily, 10h00-12h00, 14h00-18h00, except Tues and public holidays. June-Sept, daily, 10h00-13h00, 14h00-18h00, except Tues and public holidays.
Entrance fee: EUR5 (reductions).
This abbey has no less than three museums. The regional archaeological museum has a collection of items from the ancient caves of the Abbey of Saint Loup, 5th century jewellery and a magnificent Gallo-Roman statue of Apollo. The fine arts museum has paintings from the Dutch and Flemish schools, betweeen the 14th and 19th centuries, as well as medieval and 19th century sculptures. The natural history museum will particularly appeal to children, with its birds, fossils, insects and mammals besides meteorites.

Apothicairerie de l'Hotel Dieu le Comte (chemists' museum),
Quais des Comtes de Champagne,
10000 Troyes.
Tel: 03 25 80 98 97.
Opening hours: Mon, Wed, Sat, Sun, 10h00-12h00, 14h00-18h00. June-Sept, daily, 10h00-13h00, 14h00-18h00, except Tues and public holidays.
Entrance tariff: EUR2.
This charming evocation of ancient medicine dates from the 18th century and is in an old hospital. You can see 330 wooden boxes full of potions, as well as porcelain pots and other rare tools of the trade. The actual setting is as fascinating as the collection itself.

Centre Culturel Marguerite Bourgeoys,
38 rue de Clémenceau,
10000 Troyes.
Tel: 03 25 73 37 30.
Web: www.cnd.m.com
Opening hours: Tues-Sat, all year, 10h00-18h00, Sun, 14h00-18h00. July, Aug, Tues-Sat, open 12h00-18h00.
Entrance tariff: free.
Marguerite Bourgeoys was an important figure in the life of Troyes in the 17th century and she also founded the Congregation of

Notre Dame in Montreal. This centre captures well her life and her life-work. Also in Troyes, you can visit the cathedral and nine churches built between the 13<sup>th</sup> and 19th centuries.

La chapelle St-Luc,
10000 Troyes.
Opening hours: Mar 16-Oct 31, Wed, Sat, 14h00-19h00, Suns, public holidays, 9h00-19h00. Nov 1-Mar 15, Wed, Sat, 14h00-16h30, Suns, public holidays, 9h00-16h30.
Entrance tariff: free.
This park, with its lakes, extends to 6. 5 hectares and includes many exotic species of flowers, a teaching farm, places where you can explore science in nature and an insectarium.

Musée de l'Art Moderne,
place Saint-Pierre,
10000 Troyes.
Tel: 03 25 76 26 80.
Opening hours: 11h00-18h00 daily, except Mons, public holidays, all year.
Entrance tariff: free on Wed and first Sun of each month.
This collection of modern art is considered one of the finest in Europe. It's housed within the ancient episcopal palace right in the heart of Troyes and has a magnificent collection that includes paintings, designs, sculptures and glassworks. Many of France's leading artists from the late 19th century onwards, including Braque, Matisse and Rodin are represented, but it's not just European art that is so well represented. The museum also has plenty of African art.

Musée de l'Outil (tool museum),
7, rue de la Trinité,
10000 Troyes.
Tel: 03 25 73 28 26.
Web: www. maison-de-l-outil. com
Opening hours: daily, all year, 10h00-18h00, except Mon, 13h00-18h00.
Entrance tariff: free.
The tool museum in Troyes not only has a magnificent collection of tools, around 15, 000 altogether, but it is set in an absolutely magnificent building constructed around 1550 for a rich merchant

family. After the Revolution, the house was used for many different purposes, even as the offices of a local newspaper. In 1966, it was taken over by the town of Troyes and renovated, and opened as a tool museum in 1974. Today, visitors can see this extraordinary collection of tools, used by all types of workmen and their apprentices, displayed in close to 2, 000 square metres of exhibition space. Anyone who is really dedicated can also explore the archives, with their 25, 000 volumes of books. But in addition to all the tools, the house is also well worth seeing for its own architectural interest.

Quays.
You can enjoy magnificent walks along the quays in Troyes. The city is set on the River Seine, but traversing the city centre, there's a basin and you'll enjoy the walks along the quays, which will also give good sightings of the magnificent medieval architecture of central Troyes.


VAL D'EUROPE SHOPPING CENTRE,
77700 Serris (adjacent to Disneyland).
Train: RER A4 to Val de l'Europe.
Road: A4 E 50 from Paris.
Tel: 01 60 42 39 39.
This vast shopping centre is highly impressive, its design inspired by the late 19th century architecture of Paris. The shopping village has countless shops, while there's also an extensive catering and leisure area.

VALMONDIS,
40 km north-west of Paris.
Train: Gare du Nord to Valmondis.
Road: N184 from St-Ouen to Mériel.


Musée des Tramways à vapeur et chemins de fer secondaires,
Cour de la gare des Marchandises,
65760 Valmondis.
Tel. 01 34 73 04 40.
Opening hours, Apr-early Nov, Sat, Sun, public holidays, 14h30-18h00. Closed Sat, July, Aug.
Entrance tariff: EUR5 (reductions).

This museum will appeal to all railway enthusiasts and many more visitors besides. It depicts the old steam-driven tramways of France and also the country's secondary railway lines, with a marvellous collection of old engines and carriages. Altogether, it has a dozen old locos and three times that number of coaches and goods wagons. Besides inspecting all this old railway equipment, you can also go for short trips on a steam hauled train.

VERDERONNE,
75 km north of Paris.
Train: Gare du Nord, Paris to Creil.
Road: N16 from Paris.

Jardin d'Agrément de Verderonne,
9 rue du Chateau.
Tel. 03 44 73 10 67.
Opening hours, May-Sept, Sat, Sun, 14h00-19h00.
Entrance tariff: EUR5 (reductions).
This most delightful garden surrounds 18th century buildings and it's superbly laid out, with a greenhouse, a pond and lots of old roses as well as water flowers. The combination is a pleasure to the eye.

VERNEUIL-EN-HALATTE,
65 km north of Paris.
Train: Gare du Nord, Paris to Creil.
Road: N16 to Creil, then D120.

Graffiti Museum,
Allée Jules Ferry,
60550 Verneuil-en-Halatte.
Tel. 03 44 24 54 81.
Web: www. memoiresmurs. com
Opening hours, daily, except Tues and public holidays, 14h00-18h00.
Entrance tariff: 4. 60 (reductions).
This is a museum with a difference, devoted to graffiti, from ancient times right up to the present day and claimed to be the only one of its kind in Europe. Photographs, drawings and mouldings depict all the graffiti, which range from the amusing to the wildly funny, shocking, sacreligious or scurrilous by turn.

VERSAILLES,
21 km south-west of Paris.
Train: RER C5 line to Versailles.
Road: A3 E5 from Boulogne-Billancourt.
Versailles is the ultimate royal town, with an incredible palace that's known the world over. But the palace and its gardens are only a part of what's to be seen in Versailles.

Academy of Equestrian Arts,
La Grande et la Petite Ecurie,
avenue Rockefeller,
78000 Versailles.
Tel: 01 39 02 07 14.
Opening hours, Tues-Fri, all year, 9h00-13h00, Sat, Sun, all year, 11h00-14h00.
Coach museum: Sat, Sun, Apr-Oct, 9h00-18h30.
Entrance tariff: EUR7 (reductions).
Monumental stables were built for Louis XIV in the late 17th century. The Grand Stables were designed to house the riding horses used by the king and the princes of the court; today, the Academy of Equestrian Arts has revived these horse riding skills. Daily, you can see horse men and women at work. The Lesser Stables were used for lesser horses and for the carriages. The coach museum houses an excellent selection of royal coaches. It's only open on Sat, Sun, all year.

Antiques.
Versailles is the best place for antiques in the Ile de France, apart from Paris itself and its outskirts. In Versailles, the trade is suitably upmarket and is conducted from shops rather than stalls. The best area is La Geole, an historic quarter, in Le Bailliage, the Passage de la Geole annd the Village des Antiquaires. Altogether, you'll find around 40 antique shops in Versailles, specialising in everything from old clocks and dolls to porcelain.

Boat trips. One of the most relaxing ways of seeing Versailles is by taking a trip on a barge along the Grand Canal, complete with classical musical entertainment. Details from the tourist office, tel. 01 39 24 88 88.

Cathédrale Saint-Louis,
place St-Louis,
78000 Versailles.
This magnificent church was built between 1743 and 1754 by
Mansart de Sagonne and elevated to cathedral status in 1802.
Not alone is the interior a masterpiece of 18th century design, but
the building houses the famous Clicquot organ, with 3, 636 pipes.
Frequent recitals are given.

Église Notre-Dame,
35 rue de la paroisse,
78000 Versailles.
This church, built in 1684, was the parish church for the palace. all
the births, marriages and deaths in the royal family were recorded
in its registers.

Gardens of the Royal Palace,
78000 Versailles.
Opening hours, open daily, all year, except in bad weather, from
7h00 in summer and 8h00 in winter, until sunset.
Entrance tariff: EUR3 (over 18). Free to under 18s.
The gardens of the royal palace are vast, covering 900 hectares,
of which 80 are made up of the Petit Parc; you could spend the
day walking round just some of the most prominent sites. Thse
include the Grand et Petit Canal and the Pièce d'Eau des Suisses,
the two magnificent water features of the estate. Many of the trees
were blown down during the hurricanes at the end of 1999 and
the start of 2000, but gradually, the magnificence of the gardens is
being restored.

Helicopter ride.
The most spectacular way to see Versailles is from the air, so that
you can see the whole panorama of the palace, the gardens and
the towns. Helicopters aren't allowed to fly over the Versailles
domaine, but you can get near enough. Details from: Héliport de
Paris, tel. 01 45 54 04 44.

Hotel des Affaires Etrangères et de la Marine,
5 rue de l'Indépendance Américaine,
78000 Versailles.
Tel: 01 39 07 13 20.

Opening hours, Tues, Thurs, all year, 14h00-19h00 (18h00 in July, Aug). Fri, all year, 14h00-18h00. Wed, Sat, all year, 10h00-18h00. Closed first two weeks Aug.

Entrance tariff: free.

The building dates back to 1761 and it was used by the royal Ministry of Foreign Affairs for the rest of the 18th century. Today, the Ministry of Foreign Affairs is in the seventh arrondissment of Paris, on the quai d'Orsay. Much of the French input into the revolution that won independence for the US was prepared in this building. Today, the building houses the municipal library, but it has lost none of its architectural magnificence. The next door building, Number 3, was built as the Ministry of War in 1759.

Jeu de Paume,
rue de Fontenary,
78000 Versailles.
Tel: 01 30 85 77 88.
Opening hours, Sat, Sun, all year, 12h00-17h00.
Entrance tariff: free.

This royal tennis court, built for the court and the people of Versailles, is one of the few such courts left in existence. It was built about 1686 in classical style and it has another claim to fame-it was here, on June 20, 1789, that the deputies of the third estate met, one of the events that precipitated the start of the French Revolution.

Marché Notre-Dame
rue de la Paroisse/rue du Maréchal Foch,
78000 Versailles.
Opening hours, Tues, Fri, Sun, 7h30-14h00.

The town market has been in this square since it was created in 1671. The present covered market dates from 1841 and regular weekly markets are held here, with an enormous variety of food, flowers and other items.

Mass in the Royal Chapel.
Mass is held in the Royal Chapel in the Palace once a month. For dates and times, tel: 01 30 83 78 00.

Musée Lambinet,
54 boulevard de la Reine,
78000 Versailles.
Tel: 01 39 50 30 32.
Opening hours, Tues, Fri, all year, 14h00-17h00, Wed, Thurs, all year, 13h00-18h00, Sat, Sun, all year, 14h00-18h00.
Entrance tariff: EUR5 (reductions).
This 18th century mansion, set in delightful gardens, evokes perfectly the spirit of the Age of Enlightenment in the century it was built, as well as relating much of the history of Versailles through its collections. The original wood panelling and furniture heighten the sense of historical perspective. As well as many artefacts from the revolutionary era, the museum also has religious items from the Middle Ages.

Musée Les Grandes Heures du Parlement,
Palace of Versailles,
78000 Versailles.
Tel: 01 39 25 70 70.
Opening hours, daily, all year, except Sun, Mon, 9h00-17h30.
Entrance tariff: EUR3 (reductions).
Built in 1875 in the south wing of the palace, meetings of the Congress of the French parliament were held here to debate constitutional issues. Today, this is a museum of parliamentary history.

Osmothèque, 36 rue du Parc de Clagny,
78000 Versailles.
Tel: 01 39 55 46 99.
Opening hours: Wed and first Sat of every month, 14h15-17h00, third Sat of every month, 10h00-12h30.
Entrance tariff: free.
This is a perfume maker's paradise, where over 1, 200 perfumes have been brought together and preserved for posterity. Some of the scents are very historic, like the early 20th century creations of Coty and the eau de Cologne used by Napolean when he was in exile on St Helena.

Palace of Versailles,
78000 Versailles.
Tel. 01 30 83 76 20.
Web: http: //www.chateauversailles.fr
Opening hours, Apr-Oct, Tues-Sun, 9h00-18h30, Nov-Mar, Tues,
closed one hourearlier.
Entrance tariff: EUR7. 50 (reductions).
After Louis XIV saw the splendours of Vaux-le-Vicomte (qv), he
decided to go one better by changing a simple hunting lodge into
a vast palace. Voltaire described Versailles as being a
masterpiece of bad taste and magnificence. By 1682, Louis XIV
was ready to move in and after that, rarely went to Paris. During
the 18th century, many additions were made to the palace itself
and to the town of Versailles as it expanded. The palace itself is
vast, able to accommodate the 20, 000 people who made up the
royal court and its entourage. After the fall of the monarchy in
1792, most of the furniture was taken out. After the 1830
revolution, Louis-Philippe saved the palace from destruction.
Today, a vast programme of restoration is going on, costing
around EUR400 million. The vast Hall of Mirrors has already been
completed. In the palace, you can see such splendours as the 73
metre long Hall of Mirrors, where the negotiations between victors
and vanquished took place after the First World War. There are a
vast number of other great rooms and salons, including the
queen's bedchamber, where she gave birth in full view of her
courtiers, so that there was no doubt as to the new child's
authenticity. For an extra EUR4, you can also take a guided tour
of the king's bedchamber.

Petit Trianon and Grand Trianon,
Potager du Roi,
10 rue du Maréchal Joffre,
78000 Versailles.
Tel: 01 39 24 62 62.
Opening hours, Tues-Sun, Apr-Oct, 12h00-18h30, Nov-Mar, until
17h00.
Entrance tariff: EUR4. 5 (reductions).
The Grand Trianon is a palace in the grounds, in the northern part
of the park, built for Mme de Maintenon, the mistress of Louis XIV.
The smaller, neo-classical Petit Trianon was built for Mme de
Pompadour, mistress of Louis XV, but she died before it was
completed.

Royal kitchen gardens.
Opening hours: as gardens.
The king's kitchen garden was created in 1678 to satisfy the needs of the kitchens in the Palace. The old sections of the kitchen garden, with their hollow sections, has been carefully preserved, along with the small Balbi landscaped garden, created in the 18th century. Today, the kitchen garden has a working as well as an historical purpose; it houses the national horticultural school. For anyone with even a passing interest in gardening, this is a must place to visit.

Theatre Montansier,
13 rue des Réservoirs,
78000 Versailles.
Tel. 01 39 24 05 06.
One of the finest theatres in France, it was the brainchild of Louis XVI and Marie-Antoinette. Its interior is a triumph of neo-classical decor, in blue, and in recent years, it has restored to its former glory. Tours of the theatre can be arranged with the Versailles tourist office, tel. 01 39 24 88 88.

VILLENEUVE-LA-GARENNE,
8 km north-west of Paris.
Train: Métro to Porte de Clignancourt.

Cirque de Paris,
115 boulevard Charles de Gaulle,
92390 Villeneuve-la-Garenne.
Tel. 01 47 99 40 40.
Opening hours, Oct-June, Wed, Sun, 10h00-17h00. Circus performance, 15h00.
Entrance tariff: EUR41 (reductions).
For anyone who's fascinated by circuses, and not just children, this is the place to come. You can see for yourself how some of the best circus tricks, such as juggling or tightrope walking, are done. You can go backstage and even have lunch with the stars before seeing the show. The circus theme continues in the adjacent museum, while you and your children can also enjoy a puppet show or go for a ride on a merrygoround.

Parc des Chanteraines,
46 avenue Georges Pompidou,
92390 Villeneuve-La-Garenne.
Opening hours, daily, summer, 7h30-21h00, winter, 8h00-17h00.
Entrance tariff: free.
This park, which extends over 70 hectares, is quite enticing, with its grassy lawns, valleys and groves of trees. Particularly interesting is the reconstruction of a 19th century Normandy farm, complete with kitchen garden, fruit orchards and animal enclosure, with cattle, chicken, goats and sheep. The park and its lakes are also home to many water sports, aimed at 12 to 18 year olds. You can also see the park in a very relaxed way by taking the tourist train that wends its way through the park on a 5. 5 km circuit.

VINCENNES,
10 km south-east of Paris.
Train: Métro to Chateau de Vincennes, Porte-Dorée; RER A4 line to Vincennes.
Road: A4 E 50 from Paris.

Bois de Vincennes,
94300 Vincennes.
This vast park on the south-eastern outskirts of Paris covers 995 hectares and it has a considerable variety of attractionns, including a chateau, a horse racing track and a zoo. The famous Baron Haussmann, who regenerated central Paris in the mid-19th century, was largely responsible for its creation. The park itself has splendid lakes, four in all, including the Lac Daumesnil, which has boats for hire. Close by is a Buddhist centre with a Tibetan temple. For exercise, the park has 17. 5 km of cycling tracks, while for entertainment, the Theatre de la Cartoucherie serves up all kinds of musical entertainments and spectacles.

For anyone interested in bird watching, the park has an extensive bird reserve, while the 5 ha farm has all kinds of animals and shows ancient methods of cultivation. It's open on weekends and public holidays, 13h00-18h30, while in July and Aug, it's open from Tues to Sun, with the same times.

Chateau de Vincennes,
Avenue de Paris,
94300 Vincennes.
Tel. 01 48 08 31 20.
Web: www. monum.fr
Opening hours, May-Aug, daily, 10h00-12h00, 13h00-18h00, Sept-Apr, closes at 17h00.
Entrance tariff: EUR4 (reductions).
The chateau has considerable heritage behind it, as it was a royal residence between the 12th and 18th centuries. Subsequently, it had a very varied career and at one stage was even a porcelain factory. Restoration began under Napoleon III in the mid-19th century and it hasn't finished yet! Today, the donjon is closed, but you can see the rest of the chateau, including the marvellous stained glass in the 16th century Saint-Chapelle. The Pavilions des Rois et de la Reine have lots of historical material relating to the French armed services.

Hippodrome de Vincennes,
94300 Vincennes.
Tel. 01 49 77 17 17.
This horse racing track with a difference is a popular venue; the races are harness racing, rather than straightforward horse racing. Vincennes is one of the leading trotting tracks in the world and it's just as exciting to watch as conventional horse racing. In sporting parlance, it's hot to trot. The Parisian newspapers, including the sports papers, have full details of meetings here.

Parc Floral,
94300 Vincennes.
Opening hours, summer, daily, 9h30-20h00, winter, 9h30-dusk.
Entrance tariff: EUR2.
This floral park, in the north of the Bois de Vincennes, is one of the best public gardens in Paris. The Jardin des Quatres Saisons has a vast array of flowers and plants, with something always in bloom. In the floral park itself, you can see all sorts of species, from cacti to bonsai trees. For anyone interested in gardening, this is a must place to visit in Paris.

Zoo,
53 avenue St-Maurice,
75012 Paris.
Tel. 01 44 75 20 10.
Opening hours, Mon-Sat, summer, 9h-18h00, Sun, public holidays, until 18h30. In winter, Mon-Sat, closes at 17h00, Sun, public holidays, 17h30.
Entrance tariff: EUR8 (reductions).
The zoo is part of the Bois de Vincennes, but its main entrance is in the 12th. Opened in 1934, it covers 14. 5 hectares and has around 1, 200 animals, 60 species in all. These vary from Asian elephants to white rhinoceros and hippos. The three belvederes on the Grand Rocher, which stands 65 metres high, have been restored and from here, there are marvellous views. Children will enjoy the farm that has been especially designed for them.

VITRY-SUR-SEINE
10 km south-east of Paris
RER C line to Vitry sur Seine

Musée de l'Art Contemporain du Val du Marne,
place de la Liberation,
94400 Vitry-sur-Seine Cedex.
tel. 01 43 91 64 20
www.macval.fr
Opening hours, all year, Tues, 12h00-21h00, Wed-Sun, 12h00-17h00
Entrance tariff: EUR4
Vast new setting, opened at the end of 2005, showing contemporary art from 1950 to the present. Artists whose work is on show include Dubuffet, Miro and Picasso. Out of the entire collection of about 1, 000 works, it's planned to show 150 a year. Also documentation centre, cinema, restaurant.

Printed in the United Kingdom
by Lightning Source UK Ltd.
112161UKS00001B/63